TRAVEL WISE

CHINESE

by
Wu, Shu-hsiung
Ulrich Hoss

Edited by
John S. Montanaro
Kathleen Luft

BARRON'S

Photo Sources
U. Hoss, Tübingen: page 15; IfA, Stuttgart: page 193; Mairs Geo-
graphischer Verlag, Ostfildern: pages 80/81; all others: B. Heusel,
Berlin

All inquiries should be addressed to:
Barron's Educational Series, Inc.
250 Wireless Boulevard
Hauppauge, NY 11788
http://www.barronseduc.com

Library of Congress Catalog Card No. 98-7810

International Standard Book No. 0-7641-7098-8 (package)
                      0-7641-0373-3 (book)

Library of Congress Cataloging-in-Publication Data

Wu, Sha-hsiung.
  [Reisewörterbuch Chinesisch. English]
  Travelwise Chinese / by Sha-hsiung Wu, Ulrich Hoss ; English
version translated by John Montanaro and Kathleen Luft, edited by
John S. Montanaro.
     p. cm.
  ISBN 0-7641-0373-3. — ISBN 0-7641-7098-8 (bk. / cassette)
  1. Chinese language—Conversation and phrasebooks—English.
I. Hoss, Ulrich.
PL1125.E6W7813 1998
495.1'83421—dc21   98-7810
                                                                CIP

Printed in Hong Kong
9 8 7 6 5 4 3 2 1

Contents

Preface

Barron's *TravelWise Chinese* is a guide to both comprehension and conversation in Chinese. By using it you will not only acquire a series of useful words and phrases, but, more importantly, you will learn how to understand and be understood.

The most commonly heard expressions are provided for everyday situations you will encounter during your travels. These are structured as dialogues, so that you not only learn what to say but will also understand the corresponding responses.

TravelWise Chinese is divided into eleven topical units that accompany you through every phase of your travel: your arrival, checking into a hotel, seeing the sights, and even meeting with business associates.

With the help of phrases and word lists, as well as the additional glossary provided at the end of the book, you can readily adapt the sample sentences to your own individual real-life situations.

The following Pronunciation Guide and Short Grammar toward the back of the book will help familiarize you with the sounds and constructions of the Chinese language. The *pinyin* system of transliteration, which is standard in international usage, has been used throughout the book. Pictures and helpful tips will give you valuable information and acquaint you with features of Chinese culture and the beauties of China's landscape.

Barron's *TravelWise Chinese* can be used wherever Mandarin is spoken, as well as in Taiwan and, to a limited extent, in Hong Kong and Singapore.

Pronunciation

Many of the sounds of Chinese are close enough to English sounds as to present no real difficulty for English speakers. Others are less similar and will require some practice. Finally, still others do not exist at all in English and will need considerable practice.

Initials (beginning-of-word sounds)

f, l, m, n, s, y, and **w**	are roughly the same as English
b, d, and **g**	are similar to English but are not voiced (the vocal cords do not vibrate when they are produced)
p, t, and **k**	similar to English but much more heavily aspirated (when produced they are accompanied by a strong puff of breath)
h	like the *h* in German "Ba*ch*," and so much rougher than English *h*.
j	similar to initial sound of English word "*g*esture"
q	similar to English initial sound of word "*ch*eap" or "*j*eep"
x	between English initial sounds "*sh*ip" and "*s*ip" or "*s*ee" and *sh* of "*sh*e"
z	like the *ts* in "i*t's*," without any breath; another example: the *ds* of "ca*ds*"
c	like the *ts* in "i*ts*," but with strong puff of breath
zh	like the *j* in "*j*ewel" without puff of breath
ch	like *zh* above, but with strong puff of breath
sh	similar to English *sh* of "*sh*rub" or *sh* of "*sh*oe"
r	as in English *r* of "*r*ead" or "*r*un"

8

Finals (word-ending sounds)

a	as in "f*a*ther" with mouth wide open
o	as in "m*o*re" or "w*o*rn"
e	as in "h*e*r"; after **y** like the **e** in "y*e*t"
i	as in "mach*i*ne" (when **i** occurs alone it is written **yi**)
u	as in "r*u*le" or "s*u*per" (in isolation **u** is written **wu**)
ü	like German **ü** (in isolation **ü** is written **yu**)
er	Like American English *"err"*

When two or more finals follow each other, as in **ai,** they preserve their original sound values, except that with **_ian,_** **an** is pronounced more like **_en,_** in **_zhi, chi, shi, ri,_** the letter *i* presents the *ir* in American English "s*ir*."

Regional Differences in Standard Chinese

In northern China, particularly in the regions around Beijing (Peking), an **r**-like consonant is added to many words. In southern China it is omitted or replaced by a different consonant:

zhe*r*	=	**zhe**
dian*r*	=	**dian**
na*r*	=	**nali**

Word Formation

A portion of the vocabulary of standard Chinese consists of one-syllable words, with a concept being expressed by a single syllable or, in writing, by a single character.

lu	road, street	**xiang**	to think	**zhong**	heavy
shan	mountain	**fei**	to fly	**gao**	high, tall

The majority of the words in Chinese today, however, are multi-syllabic, in which two or more syllables, with their own independent meaning, are joined to form a word. Here are some examples:

qiche	steam+vehicle = car
huoche	fire+vehicle = locomotive, train
huochezhan	fire+vehicle+station = train station
dianshi	electricity+see = television
diannao	electricity+brain = computer
dianhua	electricity+speak = telephone
dianhuajian	electricity+speak+room = phone booth
fadianzhan	generate+electricity+station = power station
zhishengfeiji	straight+rise+fly+machine = helicopter

To make the individual components of the words clear and thus make learning easier, the individual syllables of words are written separately in Chapters 1–3 of this book: **qi che** = car. In Chapters 4–11, words appear in the standard form with no separations: **qiche** = car.

The Four Tones

In Chinese, there are four different tones. That means that a syllable, **ma,** for example, can be pronounced with four different pitches. Since the meaning of a word changes with the tone, it is important to pronounce the syllable with the correct pitch. In the first tone, **ma** means "mama, mother," while **ma** in the second tone means "hemp, flax." In the third tone, **ma** means "horse," and in the fourth, **ma** is "to curse, to scold." The four tones are always indicated by four different marks. They are as follows:

first tone (high-level pitch)	¯
second tone (rising pitch)	´
third tone (low dipping/rising pitch)	ˇ
fourth tone (high-falling pitch)	`

There are, however, a few syllables that remain unstressed—that is, that have no tone. Following standard practice, they are unmarked in this work.

The diagram below indicates the pitch levels at which the four tones are spoken:

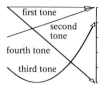

5 top of speaker's voice range

4 high mid-range

3 mid-range

2 low mid-range

1 bottom of speaker's voice range

If you visualize the range of the human voice on a scale of 1 (lowest pitch level) to 5 (highest pitch level), the syllable **ma** in the first tone is spoken with a high-level pitch, starting near the top of the speaker's voice range (5) and continuing on that level until the end. In the second tone, **ma** is spoken with a rising pitch, starting at mid-range (3) and rising rapidly to the top of the range (5). In the third tone, the speaker starts below mid-range (2), dips to the lowest pitch (1), then rises above mid-range (4). In the fourth tone, the speaker starts near the top of the range (5) and falls very rapidly to the bottom of the range (1).

There is one exception: When two third tones occur together, the first third tone is pronounced like a second tone, to make pronunciation easier:

ní hǎo   Hello! How do you do?

In a complete sentence, this produces a melody of rising and falling pitches:

xiàn zài jí diǎn zhōng?   What time is it now?

The end of the sentence stays at the pitch level of the last syllable.

The Chinese Writing System

The rudiments of Chinese writing are to be found in decorations on neolithic ceramic vessels of the Yang Shao culture, which predates the first dynasty (Xia Dynasty, about 2200–1750 B.C.). The first true characters that have been preserved, however, are oracle inscriptions of fortune tellers found on the larger bones of cattle and the flat portions of tortoise shells from the Shang Dynasty (1750–1100 B.C.). The vocabulary recorded in these inscriptions already includes some 3,000 pictographs and ideographs, of which about 1,000 can now be deciphered. A vocabulary of about 3,000 characters is also found on decorative bronze art of the late Shang Dynasty and early Chou period (1100–256 B.C.).

The subsequent development of Chinese writing was closely linked with the use of various writing materials. At first, a stylus and strips of bamboo were used. They were replaced with the brush (about 300 B.C.) and paper (roughly 100 A.D.), which have contributed appreciably to the distinctive style of Chinese characters.

Chinese characters can be subdivided into approximately four categories:

1. Characters Which Represent Pictures of Things

| rén | 人 | man | rì | 日 | sun |
| mù | 木 | tree | yuè | 月 | moon |

These characters, however, represent only a tiny portion of the total vocabulary.

2. Characters with Symbolic Content

yí	一	one
èr	二	two
sān	三	three
shàng	上	above
xià	下	below
běn	本	tree trunk

This category includes both abstract concepts (for example, "above" and "below") and concrete concepts (for example, "tree trunk").

3. Characters with Meaning Derived from Symbolic Combinations

xiū   休   **person + tree = rest**

In this category, two or more characters are combined to produce a new character, the individual components relating to each other and yielding a new meaning. In the above example: put a person in the shade of a tree and you get the concept of "rest/take a break."

4. Characters Composed of Both Sound and Meaning Components

lún	轮	wheel	Links the meaning "cart" (on left) with the sound-provider, **lun** (on right).
fān	翻	turn over	Links the meaning element for "feather" (on right) with the sound-provider, **fan** (on left).
huā	花	flower	Links the meaning element for "plant" (on top) with the sound-provider, **hua** (on bottom).
tāng	汤	soup	Links the meaning element for "liquid" with **tang**, the sound-giver.
yuán	园	garden	Combines the meaning element, "enclosure" (which encloses the entire character), with the sound-indicator, **yuan** (in the center).
wèn	问	ask	Links the meaning indicator for "mouth" (within the character) with the sound-provider, **men.** In this case, the sound-indicator is not entirely reliable.

Over 80 percent of the characters fall into this category. Here two characters are joined, as in category three above, but with one providing the sound element (giving some indication of pronunciation) and the other supplying the meaning element. The sound component uses an existing character whose sound is identical or similar to the target word, while the meaning component puts the word into a context of meaning, usually quite wide and general.

Thus, for example, the meaning component of a word that has to do with language is the character for words.

Nevertheless, for the great majority of the characters, the meaning and pronunciation cannot be readily discerned, because the sound may have changed over time (see last example) and the meaning component can give only a rough notion of a character's sense. Therefore, the meaning and the pronunciation of each character have to be learned afresh every time.

So-called meaning-classifiers (also known as "radicals") were introduced to organize the extensive stock of characters, estimated to number 50,000 to 60,000. The classifiers are character components that provide a clue to the meaning of a character. For example, all characters that have something to do with water, liquid, or flowing are to be found under the classifier for "water." (See character for "soup" above.) Only by organizing the characters according to such classifiers and according to the respective number of writing-strokes involved is it possible to list the characters in a dictionary and locate them, again with the help of the classifiers. The number of classifiers employed, however, ranges between 214 and 230. In order to read fluently, a person must have learned at least 3,000 individual characters and their many, many associated compounds (combinations of two or more characters which form words).

The characteristic appearance of Chinese characters is traceable to the former custom of writing with brush and ink.

The value the Chinese assign to their writing system is obvious from the fact that calligraphy is considered one of the major forms of art in China, and that fine examples of calligraphy bring prices just as high as fine paintings.

The term "Chinese character" is rendered in Chinese as "Han zi," literally, "the characters of the Han." "Han" is the term the Chinese apply to themselves as a people.

Abbreviations

adj	adjective
adv	adverb
Buddhi.	Buddhist
chines.	Chinese
f	feminine
f.s.	to, for someone [indirect object]
m	masculine
med.	medical
n	noun
o.s.	oneself
pers prn	personal pronoun
pl	plural
poss prn	possessive pronoun
prp	preposition
s.o.	someone [direct object]
s.t.	something

1 **The Essentials**
重要词汇

Frequently Used Expressions	常说常听的

cháng shuō, cháng tīng de

Yes/Correct.	duì.
No/Incorrect.	bú duì.
Yes/True.	shì.
No/Not so.	bú shì.
Yes/Okay.	hǎo.
No/Not okay.	bù hǎo.
Yes/I want it.	yào.
No/I don't want it.	bú yào.

*There are four different affirmations and negations in Chinese: A question as to whether something is "right/not right" is most often answered with **duì/bu duì**; questions involving "to be/not to be," with **shì/bu shì**; questions of "consenting/refusing," with **hǎo/bu hǎo**; and questions of "wanting/not wanting," with **yào/bu yào**.*

Please/After you.	qǐng.
Thanks.	xiè xie.
You're welcome.	bú xiè!
Please say it again.	qǐng zài shuō yí biàn?
Excuse me, what did you say?	duì bù qǐ, nǐ shuō shén me?
No problem!/Of course!	méi wèntí! dāng rán!
Fine!/That's fine!	hǎo!
Okay!	hǎo!
Okay. You may. No problem!	hǎo, ké yǐ, méi wèntí!
Excuse me!/Sorry!	duì bù qǐ!
Please wait a moment.	děng yí xià.
Enough!	gòu le!
Help!	jiù mìng a!
Attention!/Look out!	zhù yì!

Be careful!	xiǎo xīn!
Who?	shéi?
What?	shén me?
What …?	shén me …?
When?	shén me shí hou?
Where?	nǎ li? /nǎr?
Where is/are …?	… zài nǎ li?
Where are you from?	cóng nǎ li lái de?
Where are you going?	qù nǎ li?
Why?	wèi shén me?
What are you doing?	zuò shén me?
How ...?/How can I ...?	zěn me …?
How many?/How much?	duō shǎo?
For how long (in time)?	duō jiǔ?
How long (in length)?	duō cháng?
Is there any …?	yǒu …?
I'd like some …	wǒ yào …

Numbers/Measures/Weights

shù zì/chǐ cùn/zhòng liàng

0	○	líng
1	一	yī
2	二	èr
3	三	sān
4	四	sì
5	五	wǔ
6	六	liù
7	七	qī
8	八	bā

9	九	jiǔ
10	十	shí
11		shí yī
12		shí èr
13		shí sān
14		shí sì
15		shí wǔ
16		shí liù
17		shí qī
18		shí bā
19		shí jiǔ
20		èr shí
21		èr shí yī
22		èr shí èr
23		èr shí sān
24		èr shí sì
25		èr shí wǔ
26		èr shí liù
27		èr shí qī
28		èr shí bā
29		èr shí jiǔ
30		sān shí
31		sān shí yī
32		sān shí èr
40		sì shí
44		sì shí sì
50		wǔ shí
60		liù shí
70		qī shí

80		bā shí
90		jiǔ shí
99		jiǔ shí jiǔ
100	一 百	yì bǎi
101		yì bǎi líng yī
110		yì bǎi yī shí
111		yì bǎi yī shí yī
200		liǎng bǎi

The number "two" used with measure words or counters is **liǎng,** not **èr.**

340		sān bǎi sì shí
1,000	一 千	yì qiān
2,000		liǎng qiān
3,400		sān qiān sì bǎi
10,000	一 万	yí wàn
50,000		wǔ wàn
54,000		wǔ wàn sì qiān
54,300		wǔ wàn sì qiān sān bǎi
100,000		shí wàn
1,000,000		yì bǎi wàn
10,000,000		yì qiān wàn
100,000,000	一 亿	yí yì

The Chinese divide larger amounts not into units of thousands, but into units of ten thousands (see Numerals under A Short Grammar).

first	dì ī
second	dì èr
third	dì sān

fourth	dì sì
fifth	dì wǔ
sixth	dì liù
seventh	dì qī
eighth	dì bā
ninth	dì jiǔ
tenth	dì shí
1/2	èr fēn zhī yī
1/3	sān fēn zhī yī
1/4	sì fēn zhī yī
3/4	sì fēn zhī sān
1/10	shí fēn zhī yī
1/100	bǎi fēn zhī yī
3.5	sān dián wǔ
3.5%	bǎi fēn zhī sān dián wǔ
27 ˚C	èr shí qī dù
–5 ˚C	líng hsià wǔ dù
1998 (year)	yī jiǔ jiǔ bā
61986 (tel.)	liù yī jiǔ bā liù
millimeter	háo mǐ
centimeter	gōng fēn
meter	gōng chǐ, mǐ
kilometer	gōng lǐ
mile	lǐ
nautical/mile	hái lǐ
square meter	píng fāng gōng chǐ, píng fāng mǐ
square kilometer	píng fāng gōng lǐ
acre	gōng mǔ
hectare	gōng qǐng

liter	gōng shēng
gram	gōng kè
100 grams	yì bǎi gōng kè
1/2 kilogram	jīn
kilogram	gōng jīn
dozen	yì dǎ

Expressions of Time 时刻

shí kè

Telling Time	zhong dian/xiao shí
What time is it?	xiàn zài jí diǎn?
May I ask what time it is?	qǐng wèn, xiàn zài jí diǎn?
Now it's (just around) …	xiàn zài (gāng hǎo/dà gài) …
three o'clock.	sān diǎn.
five after three.	sān diǎn (gùo) wǔ fēn.
ten after three.	sān diǎn shí fēn.
3:15.	sān diǎn yí kè.
half past three.	sān diǎn bàn.
3:45.	chà yí kè sì diǎn.
five minutes before four.	chà wǔ fēn sì diǎn.
one o'clock.	yì diǎn.
twelve noon.	zhōng wǔ shí èr diǎn.
midnight.	bàn yè.
Is this watch (clock) correct?	zhè biǎo (zhōng) zhǔn ma?
It's five minutes fast/slow.	kuài/màn wǔ fēn (zhōng).
It's too late/too early.	tài wǎn le/zǎo le.
At what time?	jí diǎn?
When?	shén me shí hou?
At one o'clock.	yì diǎn.

At two o'clock.	liǎng diǎn.
Around four o'clock.	sì diǎn zuǒ yòu.
An hour from now/ After an hour.	yí ge zhōng diǎn (tóu) yǐ hòu.
After two hours.	liǎng ge zhōng tóu yǐ hòu.
Before nine A.M.	zǎo shàng jiǔ diǎn yǐ qián.
After eight in the evening.	wǎn shàng bā diǎn yǐ hòu.
Between three and four o'clock.	sān dào sì diǎn.
How long?	duō jiǔ?
Two hours.	liǎng ge zhōng tóu.
From ten to eleven o'clock.	cóng shí diǎn dào shí yī diǎn.
Until five o'clock.	dào wǔ diǎn.
Until what time?	dào jí diǎn?
What time does it begin?/Since when?	cóng shén me shí hou (kāi shǐ)?
(It starts) at 8 A.M./ Since 8 A.M.	cóng zǎo shàng bā diǎn (qǐ).
For half an hour.	bàn ge zhōng tóu le.
For eight days.	bā tiān le.

Other Expressions of Time
qí tā de shí kè

in the evening	wǎn shàng
every half hour	měi bàn xiǎo shí
every two days	měi liǎng tiān
on Sunday	xīng qī rì/tiān
on the weekend	zhōu mò
soon	bù jiǔ
immediately	mǎ shàng
this week	zhè xīng qī
around noon	zhōng wǔ (zuǒ yòu)
yesterday	zuó tiān

today	jīn tiān
this morning/evening	jīn tiān zǎo shàng/wǎn shàng
in 14 days	shí sì tiān hòu
within one week	yí ge xīng qī nèi
every day/daily	měi tiān
now/nowadays/ presently/	xiàn zài
just now	gāng gāng
last Monday	shàng xīng qī yī
sometimes	yǒu shí hou
at noon	zhōng wǔ
tomorrow	míng tiān
tomorrow morning/ evening	míng tiān zǎo shàng/wǎn shàng
in the (early) morning/ before noon	zǎo shàng, shàng wǔ
in the afternoon	xià wǔ
next year	míng nián
at night	wǎn shàng
every hour	měi xiǎo shí
every day/daily	měi tiān
in the daytime	bái tiān
day after tomorrow	hòu tiān
at this time	zài zhè duàn shí jiān
from time to time/ sometimes	yǒu shí
ten minutes ago	shí fēn qián
day before yesterday	qián tiān
in the morning/before noon	shàng wǔ

Days of the Week 星期 xīng qī

Monday	xīng qī yī
Tuesday	xīng qī èr
Wednesday	xīng qī sān

Thursday	xīng qī sì
Friday	xīng qī wǔ
Saturday	xīng qī liù
Sunday	xīng qī rì/tiān

Months of the Year 月 yuè fèn

January	yí yuè
February	èr yuè
March	sān yuè
April	sì yuè
May	wǔ yuè
June	liù yuè
July	qī yuè
August	bā yuè
September	jiǔ yuè
October	shí yuè
November	shí yi yuè
December	shí èr yuè

Seasons 季节 jì jié

spring	chūn tiān
summer	xià tiān
fall	qiū tiān
winter	dōng tiān

Western Holidays jié rì

New Year's Day	xīn nián/yuán dàn
Easter	fù huó jié
Christmas	shèng dàn jié

Official Chinese Holidays

zhōng guó jié rì

New Year's Day, January 1	yuán dàn
Spring Festival/Chinese New Year, February	chūn jié
International Working Women's Day, March 8	fù nǚ jié
International Labor Day, May 1	láo dòng jié
Anniversary of Founding of Communist Party, July 1	jiàn dǎng jié
Anniversary of Founding of PLA (Chinese army), August 1	jiàn jūn rì
National Day, October 1	jiàn guó rì

Traditional Holidays (Chinese "old"/ lunar calendar)

mín jiān jié rì

Lantern Festival/mid-February to mid-March	huā dēng jié/yuán xiāo jié
Tomb Sweep Day/ Worship Ancestors Day/ April 4–6	qīng míng jié
Dragon Boat Festival/ early–mid-May	duān wǔ jié
Mid-autumn Festival/ late September–early October	zhōng qiū jié

The Date

rì jì

What's today's date?	jīn tiān jǐ hào?
What day of the week is it?	jīn tiān xīng jī jǐ?
Today is Wednesday, May 1.	jīn tiān wǔ yuè yí hào, xīng qī sān.

Weather   天气

tiān qì

Because China is so huge, there are tropical and relatively colder zones, much like the United States. Nevertheless, most of China lies in the temperate zone. Generally speaking, it is warm and humid in southeastern and central China, while the northern and northeastern parts of the country are relatively dry and much colder. To imagine the difference between the extreme north and the extreme south, think of Boston in the winter and Miami in the summer.

How's the weather today?	jīn tiān de tiān qì zěn me yàng?
The weather's fine/not too good/variable.	tiān qì hěn hǎo/bú tài hǎo/huì biàn.
The weather won't get worse/better.	tiān qì bú huì biàn huài/hǎo.
The weather will get hotter/colder.	tiān qì huì biàn rè/lěng.

Karst landscape, Giulin in Southern China.

It might rain/snow.	huì xià yǔ/xuě.
The weather's cold/hot/muggy.	tiān qì lěng/rè/mēn le.

There's a big storm on the way.	bào fēng yǔ yào lái le.
There might be a storm (today).	huì yǒu fēng yǔ.
It's foggy/windy.	yǒu wù/fēng.
It's cloudy/overcast.	yǒu yún/yīn tiān.
It's a clear day.	qíng tiān.
The sky is clear.	wàn lǐ wú yún.
What's the temperature today?	jīn tiān (qì wēn) jǐ dù?
It's 20 degrees Centrigrade.	xiàn zài èr shí dù.
What are the road conditions in ...?	dào ... de lù kuàng zěn me yàng?
The roads are slippery.	lù shàng hěn huá.
Visibility is very poor.	néng jiàn dù hěn chà.

Word List: Weather

air/atmosphere	kōng qì
air pressure	qì yā
barometer	qì yā jì
bright/sunny	qíng lǎng
changeable	duō biàn
climate	qì hòu
cloud	yún
cold	lěng
damp	shī
dry	gān zào
dusk	huáng hūn
earthquake	dì zhèn
ebb tide	tuì cháo
flood	shuǐ zāi
floods/rising tides	zhǎng cháo
fog	wù
foggy	yǒu wù
frost	jié shuāng
hail	bīng báo
heat	yán rè
high pressure	gāo qì yā
hot	rè
ice	bīng

ice forming	jié bīng
lightning	shǎn diàn
low pressure	dī qì yā
overcast/cloudy	yīn tiān/yǒu yún
rain	yǔ
rain/rainy	xià yǔ
rainy season	yǔ jì
sandstorm	fēng shā
snow	xuě
sultry	mēn rè
sun	tài yáng
sunny	qíng tiān
sunrise/daybreak	rì chū
sunset/sundown	rì luò
temperature	qì wēn
thermometer	wēn dù qì
thunder	dǎ léi
typhoon	tái fēng
velocity	fēng lì
warm	nuǎn huo
weather forecast	tiān qì yù bào
wind	fēng

Word List: Colors

beige	mǐ sè
black	hēi sè
blue	lán sè
brown	zōng sè
colored	cǎi sè de
dark ...	shēn ...
golden	jīn sè
gray	huī sè
green	lǜ sè
light ...	qiǎn ...
multi-colored	duō zhǒng yán sè de
pink	fěn hóng sè
purple	zǐ sè
red	hóng sè
silver	yín sè
single-colored	dān sè de
tangerine/reddish orange	júhóng sè
turquoise	qīng sè
white	bái sè
yellow	huáng sè

2 **Making Contact**
社交活动

Saying Hello/Introductions/Getting Acquainted

dǎ zhāo hū/jiè shào/xiāng shì

Good morning!	zǎo!/zǎo ān!
Good day!/Hello!/Hi!	ní hǎo!
Good evening!	wǎn ān!
Hello!	wèi! hā lóu!
How do you do!	ní hǎo!

*Normally, people don't shake hands in China when they meet—except possibly at business gatherings, where international social conventions are customary. It is enough to say **nǐ hǎo** and make eye contact or nod slightly. Chinese who know each other well also greet each other by saying "Have you already eaten?" **(chī guo fàn ma?)** or "Where are you going?" **(nǐ shàng nǎr qù?).** Ordinarily, however, this is inappropriate for foreigners. The traditional Chinese form of greeting—bowing with hands clasped together and held at chest height—is no longer in use today.*

Please/Excuse me, what's your (last) name?	qǐng wèn, nín guì xìng?
What's your name?	nǐ jiào shén me?
My family name is … and my first name is …	wǒ xìng … wǒ jiào …

*China differs from the Western world in that the family name **(xìng)** comes first, followed by the first name **(míngzi): Lǐ Dàzhōng.***
*Since the family plays a very important role in China, great value is placed on the family name. Consequently, it always is mentioned first when introductions are being made. On closer acquaintance, people address each other either by their entire name (family name plus first name) or by their first name if they know one another quite well; otherwise, only the family name is used with the form of address or title: Mr. Li **(Lǐ xiān sheng)** or Ms. Wang **(Wáng nǚ shì)** or Teacher Zhang **(Zhāng lǎoshī).***

Let me introduce you:	ràng wǒ jiè shào yí xià,
This is …	zhè shì …
Mrs. Wang.	Wáng nǚ shì.
Miss Li.	Lǐ xiáo jiě.

Mr. Zhang.	Zhāng xiān shēng.

*As a form of address, **xiān sheng** is used in China for men who have earned public respect. It is also used for "Mr." when Chinese address foreigners. **nü shì**, used to address women, translates as "Ms." or "Miss." **xiáo jie** can be used to address younger women and is sometimes used in conjunction with the woman's maiden name. For a married woman, the address **tài tai** can also be used, in combination with the husband's last name. This term is less common in the People's Republic, where the term **fūrén** for "Mrs." is now more usual. Two other forms of address—**shī fu** (for people in the services sector) and **tóng zhì** (comrade or colleague)—have come into common use but **tóng zhì** is much less frequent nowadays. The discussion above is only a general guide. Forms of address, like many other things in China, are changing rapidly in the wake of economic liberalization, the opening to the West, and the tremendous influx of foreign tourists. Keep in mind that all these titles follow the surname: **Wáng xiànsheng, Wáng táitai, Wáng xiáojie, Wáng fūrén,** etc.*

my husband.	wǒ xiān shēng.
my wife.	wǒ tài tài.
my son.	wǒ ér zi.
my daughter.	wǒ nǚ ér.
my older brother.	wǒ gē ge.
my younger brother.	wǒ dì di.
my older sister.	wǒ jiě jie.
my younger sister.	wǒ mèi mei.

*In a Chinese family distinctions are made not only between brother and sister but also between older and younger sister (**jiějie** and **mèimei**) and between older and younger brother (**gēge** and **dìdi**).*

my friend.	wǒ péng you.
my colleague/fellow worker.	wǒ tóng shì.

*In the Chinese language, no distinction is made between masculine and feminine. Therefore, **tóng shì** can refer to either a male or a female colleague, and **péng you** to either a male or a female friend.*

I'm very pleased to meet you (polite).	hěn gāo xìng rèn shì nín.

| How do you do?/How are you? | nín/ní hǎo ma? |

*Chinese, unlike French or German, for example, does not draw a clear distinction between the familiar "you" and the polite "you." Normally, the familiar pronoun, **nǐ,** is used to address everyone. But in exceptional cases, when you would like to pay special honor to someone (for example, someone whom you admire or who holds a special position), you should employ the polite pronoun, **nín.***

How are you?/How have you been?	ní hǎo ma?
Thank you. And you?	xiè xie. nín/nǐ ne?
Where are you from?	nín/nǐ cóng nǎ li lái de?

The typical Chinese position for viewing: squatting.

| I'm from ...
 the United States/ America | wǒ cóng ... lái de.
 měi guó |
| How long have you been in ...? | nǐ dào ... duō jiǔ le? |

I've been in Beijing for …	wǒ dào Běi-jīng … le.
How long will you be staying?	nǐ hái dāi duō jiǔ?
Is this your first trip to Shanghai?	nǐ dì yī cì dào Shàng-hǎi ma?
Do you like China?	nǐ xǐ huān Zhōng-guó ma?
Yes, I do (like China).	wǒ hén xǐ huān.
Did you come alone or with a tour group?	nǐ yí ge rén/gēn lǚ xíng tuán lái de ma?
Neither, I've come with my family/friends.	bú shì, wǒ gēn jiā rén/péng you yì qǐ lái de.

Traveling Alone/Making a Date

dān dú lǚ xíng/yuē huì

Are you waiting for someone?	ní děng rén ma?
What do you want to do tomorrow?	míng tiān ní xiǎng zuò shén me?
Do you have any free time tomorrow?	nǐ míng tiān yǒu kòng ma?
Let's go together, okay?	wǒ men yì qǐ qù, hǎo ma?
Let's go out together this evening, okay?	wǒ men jīn tiān wǎn shàng yì qǐ chū qù, hǎo ma?
May I invite you to eat?	wǒ qíng nǐ chī fàn, hǎo ma?
When shall we meet?	shén me shí hou jiàn miàn?

I'll pick you up, okay?	wǒ jiē nǐ, hǎo ma?
Where shall we meet?	zài nǎ li jiàn miàn?
Let's meet at nine …	wǒ men jiú diǎn … jiàn miàn.
at the entrance to the movie theater.	zài diàn yǐng yuàn mén kǒu
at … square.	zài … guáng chǎng
in the coffee shop.	zài kā fēi guǎn lǐ miàn
Are you married?	nǐ jié hūn le ma?
Do you have a boyfriend/girlfriend?	nǐ yǒu nán/nǚ péng you ma?
I'll take you home, okay?	wǒ sòng nǐ huí jiā, hǎo ma?
I'll take you to …	wǒ sòng nǐ dào …
When can we meet again?	wǒ men shén me shí hou zài jiàn ne?
I hope we can meet again soon.	xī wàng wǒ men néng hěn kuài zài jiàn miàn.
Thanks for your hospitality.	xiè xie nǐ de zhāo dài.
Please leave me alone!	bú yaò chán zhe wǒ!
Go away!	zǒu kāi!
Beat it!	gǔn kāi!
Enough already!	gòu le!

A Visit 拜访

bài fǎng

In general, Chinese are very hospitable and very receptive to foreigners. Consequently, you may frequently find yourself invited to the homes of Chinese families. For the host or hostess, you should take either a little gift from your own country or fruit, sweets, or pastry. Show some restraint in expressing political opinions.

May I ask, does Mr./ Mrs./Miss Wang live here?	qǐng wèn, Wáng xiān shēng/nǚ shì/ xiáo jiě zhù zhè lǐ ma?
He/She has moved.	tā bān zǒu le.
Do you know where he/ she moved to?	nǐ zhī dào tā bān dào nǎ li ma?
May I speak with Mr./ Mrs./Miss Wang?	wǒ ké yǐ gēn Wáng xiān shēng/nǚ shì/xiáo jiě shuō huà ma?
I'm looking for Mr./ Mrs./Miss Wang.	wǒ zhǎo Wáng xiān shēng/nǚ shì/ xiáo jiě.
He/She is not here.	tā bú zài.
When will he/she be back?	tā shén me shí hou huí lái?
Please tell him/her …	qǐng gào sù tā, …
I'll be back after a while.	wǒ děng yí xià zài lái.
Please come in!	qǐng jìn!
Please sit down/make yourself at home.	qǐng zuò.
Paul sends his regards to you.	Bǎo-luó wèn hòu nǐ.
What will you have to drink?	hē diǎn shén me?
Please have some tea.	qǐng hē chá.
Do you drink tea?	nǐ hē chá ma?

In China it is customary to offer a guest tea or cigarettes. The wide range of teas available and the various methods of preparation, as well as the Chinese tea ceremony, frequently provide host and guest with an abundance of conversational topics. To politely refuse a cigarette, say: **Duìbuqǐ wǒ bù huì chōu yān.**

Thank you, I'd like tea.	xiè xiè. wǒ hē chá.
This tea is very fragrant; what kind is it?	zhè chá hěn xiāng, shì shén me chá?
Do you smoke?	xī yān ma?
Have a cigarette!	xī gēn yān ba!
Thanks, but I don't smoke.	xiè xie, wǒ bù xī yān.
Won't you please stay for lunch/dinner!	qǐng liú xià lái chī wǔ/wǎn fàn ba!
Thanks! If it's no trouble.	xiè xie! rú guǒ bù má fán de huà.
Thanks all the same, but I've got to be going.	xiè xie, kě shì wǒ děi zǒu le.

Saying Good-bye 告别

gào bié

Good-bye!/So long!	zài jiàn!
See you some other day!	gǎi tiān jiàn!
See you tomorrow!	míng tiān jiàn!
Good night!	wǎn ān!
Hope everything goes well!	yí qiè shùn lì!
Hope you have fun!	zhù nǐ wán de yu kuài!
Bon voyage!/Have a good trip!	yí lù shùn fēng!
I will keep in touch/ get in touch with you.	wǒ hui gēn nǐ lián luò.
Please give my regards to ...	qǐng wèn hòu ...

Asking a Favor/ Expressing Thanks 请求/致谢

Qǐng qiú/zhì xiè

Fine, thank you/thanks.	hǎo, xiè xie.
No, thank you.	bú yào, xiè xie.
Excuse me?	duì bù qǐ?
Can you help me with something?	nǐ néng bāng wǒ ge máng ma?
I'm extremely grateful.	fēi cháng gǎn xiè.
You're welcome.	bú kè qì.
Terrific, thanks a lot.	tài hǎo le, xiè xie nǐ.
Thanks for your help!	xiè xie nǐ de bāng máng!
Not at all!/You're welcome!/Don't mention it!	bú kè qì/bù xiè!

Apologies/Regrets 道歉

dào qiàn

I'm so sorry!	duì bù qǐ!
I'd like to apologize.	wǒ gāi dào qiàn.
Excuse me.	duì bù qǐ.
No problem! Don't bother about it.	méi shì!
Too bad!	tài kě xí le!
Unfortunately this is impossible.	kě xí zhè shì bù kě néng de.
Perhaps another time.	yě xǔ xià huí ba.

Congratulations/Best Wishes 祝福

zhù fú

Congratulations to you!	gōng xǐ nǐ!
May everything go well for you!	zhù nǐ, yí qiè rú yì!
Happy birthday!	zhù nǐ shēng rì kuài lè!
I wish you success!	zhù nǐ chéng gōng!
I wish you the best of luck!	zhù nǐ hǎo yùn!
I hope you get well soon!	zhù nǐ zǎo rì kāng fù!

Language Difficulties

tīng bù dǒng

Excuse me, what did you say?	duì bù qǐ, nǐ shuō shén me?
I don't understand. Please say it again.	wǒ tīng bù dǒng, qǐng zài shuō yí cì.

Please speak a little slower/a little louder.	qǐng nǐ shuō màn yì diǎn./dà shēng yì diǎn.
I understand.	wǒ dǒng le.
Do you speak … Mandarin (the national language)?	nǐ huì shuō … pǔ tōng huà ma?

*The national language is the northern Chinese dialect with the pronunciation of the Beijing area regarded as standard. This variety of Chinese, now taught in all schools, is called Mandarin or **pǔ tōng huà.***

English?	yīng yǔ ma?
French?	fá yǔ ma?
German?	dé yǔ ma?
I can only speak a little …	wǒ zhǐ huì shuō yì diǎn …
What is the meaning of this?	zhè shì shén me yì si?
How do you say … in Mandarin?	… pǔ tōng huà zěn me shuō?
What does this word mean?	zhè ge zì shén me yì si?
How do you pronounce this word?	zhè ge zì zěn me niàn?
Please write it down!	qǐng xiě xià lái!
Please write it in pinyin!	qǐng nǐ pīn xià yīn!

Expressing Opinions

biǎo dá

I like it very much.	wǒ hěn xǐ huān.
I don't like it.	wǒ bú tài xǐ huān.
I'd prefer …	wǒ bǐ jiào xǐ huān …
The best/best one is …	zuì hǎo shì …
That's terrific!	nà tài hǎo le!

With pleasure!	lè yì fèng péi!
Wonderful!/Terrific!	hǎo jí le!
I'm not interested.	wǒ méi xìng qu.
I don't want to.	wǒ bú yào.
That/It won't do!	bù xíng!
It absolutely won't do!	jué dui bù xíng!
I still don't know.	wǒ hái bù zhī dào.
Perhaps/Maybe.	yě xǔ.
Probably/Quite likely.	dà gài.

Personal Information 生平

shēng píng

Age   nián jì

How old are you this year?	nǐ jīn nián duō dà?
I'm 39 this year.	wǒ jīn nián sān shr jiǔ suì.
When were you born?	nǐ shén me shí hou shēng de?
I was born on April 12, 1954.	wǒ yi jiǔ wǔ sì nián sì yue shí èr hào shēng de.

Professions/Education/Training   shí yè/jiào yù chéng dù

Where do you work?	nǐ zài nǎr gōng zuò?
I'm a worker.	wǒ shì gōng rén.
I'm an office worker/ a member of the staff.	wǒ shì zhí yuán.
I'm a civil servant.	wǒ shì gōng wù rén yuán.

I'm self-employed.	wǒ shì zì yóu yè zhě.
I'm retired.	wǒ tuèi xiū le.
I'm unemployed.	wǒ shī yè zhōng, méi gōng zuò.
I work in …	wǒ zài … gōng zuò.
I'm still in school.	wǒ hái zài shàng xué.
I attend high school.	wǒ shàng zhōng xué.
I'm a college student.	wǒ shì dà xué shēng.
Where do you go to college?	nǐ zài nǎr shàng dà xué?
What do you study?	nǐ xué shén me?
I study … in Beijing.	wǒ zài Běi-jīng xué …
What hobbies do you have?	nǐ yǒu shén me ài hào?

Word List: Professions/Education/Training

accountant	kuài jì, cái shuì rén yuán
actor	yǎn yuán
agent	dài lǐ shāng
agricultural technician	nóng yè jì shù rén yuán
archeology	káo gǔ xué
architect	jiàn zhú shī
architecture	jiàn zhú
art academy	yì shù xué yuàn
art history	yì shù shǐ
artist/painter	huà jiā, yì shù jiā
author	zuò jiā
auto mechanic	qì chē jī xiè shī
baker	miàn bāo shī fu
biologist	shēng wù xué jiā
biology	shēng wù
bookseller	shū shāng
bricklayer/mason	zhuān wǎ shī fu, ní wǎ gōng shī fu
business school	shāng yè xué xiào
butcher	ròu pù shī fu
carpenter/woodworker	mù gōng

cashier	chū nà yuán
chef	chú shī
chemistry	huà xué
civil servant	gōng wù yuán
college	dà xué
college student	dà xué shēng
college teacher	dà xué jiāo shī
comprehensive school	zòng hé xué xiào
computer engineer	diàn nǎo gōng chéng shī
computer programmer	diàn nǎo shè jì shī
computer studies	diàn nǎo xué
computer technician	diàn nǎo jì shù rén yuán
conservator	xiū fù yì shù pǐn rén yuán
course of study	xué kē
craftsman	shǒu gōng yè zhě
decorator	zhuāng huáng rén yuán
dental technician	yá jì shī
dentist	yá yī
designer	shè jì shī
director/chair(man)	zhǔ rèn
doctor	dài fu
draftsman	huì tú yuán
driving instructor	jià shǐ jiào liàn
druggist	yào jì shī
economics	jīng jì xué
economist	jīng jì xué jiā
editor/compiler	biān jí
electrician	diàn gōng shī fu
electronics	diàn zi xué
engineer	gōng chéng shī
English language and literature	yīng guó yuyán wén xué
environmental specialist	huán bǎo zhuān yuán
faculty member	jiào yù rén yuán
farmer	nóng fū
fisherman	yú fu
fitter/assembler	zhuāng pèi jì gōng
florist	huā diàn jì gōng
forest management worker	sēn lín guǎn lǐ rén yuán

gardener	yuán dīng
gatekeeper/watchman	mén fáng
general manager	zǒng jīng lǐ
geography	dì lǐ xué
geology	dì zhí xué
geriatric nurse	yǎng lǎo yuàn kān hù shì
glazer	bō lí chuāng pèi jì gōng
grade school	xiǎo xué
hairdresser/barber	lí fǎ shī
high school	zhōng xué
history	lì shǐ
housewife	jiā tíng fù nǚ
institute	xué yuàn
interpreter	kǒu yì rén yuán
janitor/concierge	fángwū gǔanlǐ yuán
jeweler	zhū bǎo shāng
journalist	jì zhě
judge	fǎ guān
junior high school	chū zhōng
laboratory technician	shì yàn shì jì shù rén yuán
law	fǎ lǜ
lawyer	lǜ shī

Women picking tea leaves in Hangzhou, a favorite tourist spot in eastern central China, not far from Shanghai.

lectures	jiǎng kè
librarian	tú shū guǎn yuán
literature/linguistics	wén xué/yǔ yán xué
machinist/mechanic	jī xiè shī fu
mailman	yóu dì yuán
massage therapist	àn mó shī
mathematics	shù xué
mechanical engineering	diàn jī
medicine	yī xué
merchant	shāng rén
metal worker	wǔ jīn gōng
meteorologist	jì hsiàng rén yuán
midwife	zhù chǎn shì
model	mó tè er
music	yīn yuè
musician	yīn yuè jiā
natural healer	zìrán liáofǎ dàifu
notary	gōng chèng shī
nurse	kān hù/ hù shì
office worker/ member of staff	zhí yuán
optician	yàn guāng shī
pastor	mù shī
pastry chef	gāo diǎn shī fu
pharmacist	yào fáng jì shī
pharmacology	yào jì xué
philosophy	zhé xué
photographer	shè yǐng shī
physical therapist	wù lǐ yī liáo rén yuán
physician	yī shēng
physician's assistant	yī shēng zhù shǒu
physicist	wù lǐ xué jiā
physics	wù lǐ xué
physiotherapist	wù lǐ zhì liáo jiā
pilot	fēi jī jià shǐ yuán
plasterer	fěn shuā shī fù
plumber/electrical fitter	ān zhuāng jì gōng
policeman/ policewoman	jǐng chá

political scientist	zhèng zhì xué jiā
postal official	yóu zhèng rén yuán
printer	yìn shuā jì gōng
professor	jiào shòu
psychologist/ psychotherapist	xīn lǐ xué jiā, xīn lǐ yī shēng
psychology	xīn lǐ xué
railroad worker	tiě lù yuán gōng
real estate broker	fáng dì chǎn jīng jì shāng
restaurant owner	fàn diàn diàn zhǔ
retiree	tui hsiū rén yuán
roofer	wū miàn gōng
sailor	hǎi yuán
salesclerk	shòu huò yuán
scholar	xué zhě
school	xué xiào
secretary	mì shū
security officer/ policeman	gōng ān rén yuán
senior high school	gāo zhōng
shoemaker	xié jiàng
social worker	shè huì gōng zuò rén yuán
sociology	shè huì xué
specialist	zhuān zhí rén yuán
steward	háng kōng fú wù yuán
student	xué shēng
studies	xué yè
tailor	cái féng shī
tax advisor	shuì wù gù wèn
taxi driver	chū zū chē sī jī
teacher	lǎo shī
technician/skilled worker	jì shù rén yuán, jì gōng
theater studies/theory	xì jù lǐ lùn
theology	shén xué
toolmaker	gōng jù shī fu
tour conductor	dǎo yóu
tour guide	zhǐ dǎo yuán
trainee	xué tú
translator	fān yì yuán
truck driver	kǎ chē sī jī

truck mechanic	kǎ chē jī xiè shī
universities/colleges	dà zhuān
university	dà xué
veterinarian	shòu yī
vocational school	zhí yè xué xiào
waiter	pǎo táng
watchmaker	zhōng biǎo shī fu
worker	gōng rén
writer	wén xué jiā

The state-owned China International Travel Service (CITS or, in Chinese, **Zhōngguó Gúojì Lǚxíngshè**) offers a wide range of services for foreign visitors. Mainly it concerns itself with organizing and making travel arrangements for group tours, but it also supplies interpreters and tour guides, arranges for travelers to be picked up and accompanied, and assists with the necessary travel and customs formalities. In addition, it is a good idea to have CITS handle room reservations, call taxis, and above all, reserve plane, ship, and train tickets for you, because lines at the various counters in question are very long, and foreigners often come off badly in the attempt to buy a ticket in the throng. Keep in mind, however, that if CITS makes the ticket purchases, the tickets will be tourist-priced (much more expensive than the price paid by native Chinese) and there will also be a service charge. CITS has been providing services for travelers since 1954, but now many travelers get around China by themselves, without dealing with CITS. In addition to CITS there is the China Travel Service (CTS), which is in competition with CITS and concentrates on the Western-tourist market. In the United States CTS has an overseas office in San Francisco (tel. (800) 332-2831) and Los Angeles (tel. (818) 288-8222).

The main office in China for CITS is:
China International Travel Service (CITS) Head Office
103 Fuxingmennei Avenue
Beijing, China 100800

Calling from the United States is a bit of a problem because there is a 12-hour time difference and quite a long telephone number. But, if you're adventurous, here's the number:
First dial 011 (to get an international line)
Then dial 86, the country code for China
Then dial 10, the city code for Beijing. (Other cities in China have different city codes that can be supplied by international operators.)
Finally, the local Beijing number: 601-1122.
To fax a message, use the codes above, and locally fax to 605-9512.

CTS has offices in the United States, where it is known as the China National Tourist Office. The New York branch is located at:
Lincoln Building, 60 E. 42nd Street, Suite 3126, New York, NY 10165
Tel: (212) 867-0271; Fax: (212) 599-2892

The Los Angeles branch is located at:
33 West Broadway, Suite 201, Glendale, CA 91204
Tel: (818) 545-7505; Fax: (818) 545-7506
See also Chapter 9 for more on telephoning.

Giving Directions   地点/方向

dì diǎn/fāng xiàng

left	zuǒ biān
right	yòu biān
straight	yì zhí
in front	qián biān
behind	hòu biān
beside/on the side/ next to	páng biān
opposite	duì miàn
here	zhè lǐ
there/over there	nà lǐ
near/nearby	jìn
far/far away	yuǎn
towards/in the direction of	wǎng
road/route	lù
intersection/crossroads	shí zì lù kǒu
curve	zhuǎn wān

Car/Motorcycle/Bicycle

qì chē/mó tuō chē/zì xíng chē

Information	wèn lù
May I ask, how does one get to ...?	qǐng wèn, ... zěn me zǒu?
Please point it out for me on the map.	qǐng zài dì tú shàng zhí géi wǒ kàn.

*Right-hand traffic is the rule in China, and the international road signs are used. Traffic is very chaotic, and the law of the strongest seems to predominate. For travel, high-quality maps of almost every Chinese city are readily available for sale in China, from bookstalls or street vendors, or from the Xinhua Bookstores, the major bookseller in China. You can also buy good maps at your hotel, but keep in mind that only tourist centers sell maps in English. Look for maps in English at hotel gift shops, Friendship Stores, and some foreign language bookstores. Perhaps the best solution is to purchase the **Lonely Planet Travel Survival Kit: China,** which is full of maps and is easily the best guidebook available.*

The Badaling section of the Great Wall, near Beijing

How far is it?	duō yuǎn?
By car it will take …	kāi chē yào …
Excuse me, does this road go to …?	qǐng wèn, zhè tiáo lù dào … ma?
How do I get to the highway that goes to …?	wó zěn me kāi dào wǎng … de gāo sù gōng lù?

A toll is charged on Chinese superhighways. The amount varies, depending on the distance traveled and on the province. Speed limits are indicated at appropriate points.

Go straight ahead …	yì zhí wǎng qián dào …
And then/ …	rán hòu …
at the light	zài hóng lǜ dēng de dì fāng
at the next traffic corner	zài xià yí ge lù kǒu
turn left/right.	zuǒ/yòu zhuǎn.
Follow the road signs.	gēn zhe lù biāo zǒu.

Please write it out in pinyin, okay?	qǐng bǎ tā xiě chéng pīn yīn, hǎo ma?	
Please write it down for me. Help me write a note.	qǐng bāng wǒ xiě ge tiáo zi.	
You've gone the wrong way.	ní zǒu cuò le.	
Drive back to ...	nǐ kāi hui dào ...	

注意	zhùyì	Watch Out/Careful/Caution
危险	wēixiǎn	Danger
高速公路	gāosù gōnglù	Superhighway
出口	chūkǒu	Exit/Off Ramp
入口	rùkǒu	Entrance/On Ramp
单行道	dānxīng dào	One-Way Road
前有修路	qián you xīulù	Construction Ahead
绕道行驶	rǎo dào xíngshǐ	Detour
施工中	shīgōng zhōng	Under Construction

At the Gas Station   jiā yóu zhàn

Gas stations in China, which once seemed to be well concealed, now are easily visible, quite numerous, and up to Western standards. There is no self-service, however; customers are served by an attendant.

Where is the nearest gas station?	zuì jìn de jiā yóu zhàn zài nǎr?

I want ... liters	wǒ yào jiā ... gōng shēng de
of regular.	pǔ tōng qì yóu.
of super/premium.	gāo jí qì yóu.
of diesel.	chái yóu.
of mixed (gasoline-benzol mixture).	hùn hé qì yóu.
of unleaded with ... octane.	... xīn wán de wú jiān qì yóu.
200 yuan of premium/super.	liǎng bǎi kuài de gāo jí qì yóu.
Fill it up.	jiā mǎn.
Please check the oil/tires.	jiǎn chá yí xià yóu liàng/lún tāi.
Please check the coolant level.	qǐng ni jiǎn chá yi xià lěng què shǔi.
Please change the oil.	qǐng ni huàn xià lùn huá yóu.
I'd like a car wash.	wǒ yào xǐ chē.
I'd like a road map of the area.	wǒ yào yì zhāng fù jìn de gōng lù tú.

*The Temple of Heaven,
Hall of Annual Prayers,
Beijing*

Where's a bathroom?	năr yŏu cè suŏ?

Parking · **tíng chē**

Is there a parking lot nearby?	fù jìn yŏu tíng chē de dì fāng ma?
May I park the car here?	wŏ ké yĭ bă chē tíng zài zhè lĭ ma?
Can you change this hundred yuan bill into tens?	nĭ néng bă zhè zhāng yì băi kuài huàn chéng shí kuài de ma?
Is the parking lot guarded?	tíng chē chăng yŏu rén kàn shŏu ma?
Full/No spaces left.	tíng măn le.
How long may I park?	wŏ ké yĭ tíng duō jiŭ?
How is the parking fee calculated?	tíng chē fèi zĕn me suàn?
By the hour?	mĕi xiăo shí?
Daily?	mĕi tiān?
Is the parking lot open all day (long)?	tíng chē chăng zhĕng tiān kāi zhe ma?

停车场	tíngchēchăng	Parking Lot
禁止停车	jīnzhĭ tíngchē	No Parking

Car Trouble · **gù zhàng**

My car has broken down/has a flat tire.	wŏ de chē huài le/bào tāi le.
Can you help me make a phone call to the (repair) garage?	nĭ néng bāng wŏ dă diàn huà gĕi xiū chē chăng ma?
My license plate number is …	wŏ de chē hào shì …

Can you loan me some gas?	nǐ néng jiè gěi wǒ yì xiē qì yóu ma?
Can you help me change a tire?	wǒ yào huàn lún tāi, nǐ néng bāng wǒ ma?
Can you tow my car to the (repair) garage/gas station?	nǐ néng bǎ wǒ de chē tuō dào xiū chē chǎng/jiā yóu zhàn ma?
Can you take me to the (repair) garage/gas station?	nǐ néng dài wǒ dào xiū chē chǎng/jiā yóu zhàn ma?

At the Auto Repair Shop

zài xiū chē chǎng

Is there a garage nearby?	fù jìn nǎr yǒu xiū chē chǎng?
My car won't start.	wǒ de chē fā bú dòng.
I don't know why.	wǒ bù zhī dào wèi shén me.
The motor appears to have a problem.	mó tuō hǎo xiàng yǒu wèn tí.
The brakes won't work.	zhà chē shī líng.
… is/are broken.	… huài le.
The car is leaking oil.	chē lòu yóu le.
Please check it out/ take a look.	qǐng jiǎn chá yí xià?
Please change the spark plugs.	qǐng huàn xià diǎn huǒ sāi.
Do you have original parts?	ní yǒu yuán zhuāng líng jiàn ma?
Just do the necessary repairs.	zhǐ zuò bì yào de xiū lǐ, jiù hǎo le.
When will it be fixed/ ready?	shén me shí hòu xiū hǎo?
Approximately how much will it cost?	dà gài duō shǎo qián?

A Traffic Accident	**chē huò**

There's been a traffic accident.
fā shēng chē huò le.

Please hurry and call ...
   an ambulance.
   the police.
   the traffic police.
   the fire engine/
   department.
   a doctor.

qǐng mǎ shàng jiào ...
   jiù hù chē.
   jǐng chá.
   jiāo tōng jǐng chá.
   jiù huǒ chē.

   yī shēng.

Please care for the injured.
zhào gù yí xià shòu shāng de.

Do you have a first-aid kit?
ní yǒu jí jiù bāo ma?

It's my/your fault.
shì wǒ/nǐ de cuò.

You ...
   did not yield the right of way.
   turned into the wrong lane.
   turned without a turn signal.

nǐ ...
   méi zūn shǒu gǎn dào xiān hsíng.

   zhuǎn wān luè xiàn le.

   méi dǎ zhǐ shì dēng, jiù zhuǎn wān.

You ...
   drove too fast.
   drove too close.
   ran a red light.

nǐ ...
   kāi tài kuài.
   kāi tài jìn.
   chuǎng hóng dēng.

I was only driving ... kilometers per hour.
wǒ cái kāi shí sù ... gōng lǐ.

Should we call the police or resolve it ourselves?
zhǎo jǐng chá lái, hái shì wǒ men zì jǐ jiě jué?

The damages will be paid by my insurance company.
sǔn huài yóu wǒ de báo xiǎn gōng sī péi cháng.

I'll give you my address, license number, and insurance number.
wó gěi nín wǒ de dì zhǐ hé chē huò báo xiǎn hào mǎ.

Please write down your name, address, and insurance number.	qǐng bǎ nín de xìng míng dì zhǐ he chē huò báo xiǎn hào mǎ xiě xià lái.
Can you help me and be a witness?	nǐ néng bāng wǒ zuò zhèng rén ma?
Thanks for your help.	xiè xiè nǐ de bāng máng.

Car/Motorcycle/ Bicycle Rental	**chū zū chē/mó tuō chē/zì xíng chē**

Touring China by car or motorcycle is basically impossible at this time unless you go with an accompanied large group, can get permits, and are willing to pay high fees. Some good news is that Beijing and Shanghai now have drive-away car rental, but you can only drive within city limits and the cost is quite high.

Where can I rent a car?	nǎ li ké yǐ zū chē.
I'd like to rent ... for two days/one week.	wó xiǎng zū ... liǎng tiān/yí ge xīng qī.
a jeep	yí liàng jí pǔ chē
a motorcycle	yí liàng mó tuō chē
a small/light motorcycle	xiǎo xíng mó tuō chē
a moped	qīng xíng mó tuō chē
a bike	zì xíng chē
How much is it per day/week?	měi tiān/xīng qī duō shǎo qián?
How much is it per kilometer?	měi gōng lǐ duō shǎo qián?
How much is the deposit?	yā jīn duō shǎo?
I would like this one/that one.	wǒ yào zhè/nà liàng.
Does this vehicle have comprehensive insurance?	zhè chē yǒu quán é bǎo xiǎn ma?

Do you want additional insurance?	yào zài é wài báo xiǎn ma?
Show me your driver's license!	wǒ kàn yí xià nǐ de jià shǐ zhí zhào!
May I drive off immediately?	ké yǐ mǎ shàng kāi zǒu ma?
May I return the car at …?	ké yǐ zài … jiāo chē ma?

Word List: Car/Motorcycle/Bicycle

accident	gù zhàng
to add oil	shàng yóu
air conditioning	lěng qì shè bèi
air filter	kōng qì jìng huà qì
air pump	qì bèng
alarm	jǐng bào qì
alcohol content/level	jiǔ jīng hán liàng
antifreeze	fáng dòng qì
to apply the brake	shà chē
auto club	qì chē xié huì
automatic transmission	zì dòng pái dǎng, biàn sù huàn dǎng
axle	chē zhóu
backfire	gù zhàng zháo huǒ
backpedal/coaster brake	dào lún zhá
ball bearing	qiú zhóu chéng
bell (on bike)	chē líng
bicycle	zì xíng chē
bicycle chain	zhǐ liàn
bicycle lane/path	zì xíng chē zhuān yòng dào
to blind/to dazzle	cì yǎn
blinker	fāng xiàng zhǐ shì dēng
body; chassis	chē shēn
brake fluid	shà chē yóu
brake light	shà chē dēng
brake shoes	shà chē mó cā piàn
brakes	shà chē
broken; interrupted	duàn le
bumper (on car)	báo xiǎn gǎn
cable	diàn xiàn

car wash	xǐ chē
carburetor	qì huà qì
chain	chǐ lún
clutch	lí hé qì
clutch pedal	lí hé qì tà bǎn
comprehensive insurance	quán é báo xiǎn
construction site	shī gōng
coolant	lěng què shuǐ
cylinder	qì gāng
to dim headlights	dà dēng biàn xiǎo dēng
detour	rào dào
dimmer lights	xiǎo dēng
to disconnect; to uncouple	tuō gōu
distributor	pèi diàn pán
documents	wén jiàn
driver's license	jià shǐ zhí zhào
emergency telephone line	jí jiù tōng huà xiàn
exhaust pipe	pái qì guǎn
fan	gǔ fēng jī
fender	dǎng ní bǎn
fine	fá kuǎn
first gear	yì dǎng
flat tire	lòu tāi
foot brake	jiǎo shà chē
four lanes	sì xiàn dào
four-wheel drive	quán lún jǚ dòng
front axle	qián chē zhóu
front lights	qián dēng
front wheel	qián lún
fuse	bǎo xiǎn sī
garage (for repair)	xiū chē chǎng
gas can	qì yóu tǒng
gas gauge	yóu liàng biǎo
gas pedal	yóu mén tà bǎn
gas pump	chōu yóu jī
gas station	jiā yóu zhàn
gas tank	yóu xiāng
gasoline	qì yóu
gasoline coupon	qì yóu piào
gear	dǎng

gear (mechanism)	zhuán dòng jī
gearshift	biàn sù dǎng
generator	fā diàn qì
to give it the gas; to accelerate	jiā yóu
hand brake	shǒu shà chē
handle bar (bicycle)	bǎ shǒu
headlight flasher	chē dēng
heater	nuǎn qì shè bèi
high beams	yuǎn guāng dēng
highway	gōng lù
highway map	gōng lù dì tú
to hitchhike/catch a ride with	dā biàn chē
hitchhiker	dā biàn chē de
hood (engine)	mǎ dá hù gài
horn	lǎ bā
horsepower	mǎ lì
hub (of wheel)	lún gǔ
ignition	dián huǒ
ignition switch	dián huǒ kāi guān
injection	pēn yóu bèng
inner tube	nèi tāi
insurance card	báo xiǎn zhèng míng
jack (for lifting)	qǐ zhòng jī
jumper cables	fā dòng diàn lǎn
to knock (engine)	guài shēng
license plate	chē pái
moped	qīng xíng mó tuō chē
motor	mǎ dá
motor scooter	xiǎo xíng mó tuō chē
motorcycle	mó tuō chē
mountain bike	dēng shān xíng zì xíng chē
neutral	kōng dǎng
nozzle	pēn zuǐ
octane rating	xīn wǎn hán liàng
oil	lùn huá yóu
oil change	huàn lùn huá yóu
oil level check	lùn huá yóu cè liáng
to overtake another car	chāo chē
parking light	tíng chē dēng
parking lot	tíng chē chǎng

parking meter	tíng chē jì shí jì
parking place/spot	tíng chē wèi
pedal	tà bǎn
piston	huó sāi
racing bike	pǎo chē xíng zì xíng chē

You'll see these everywhere in China: A wastepaper container and a spittoon.

rack; stand	jiǎo jià
radiator; cooler	shuǐ xiāng
rear axle	hòu chē zhóu
rear lights	hòu dēng
rear wheel	hòu lún
rearview mirror	hòu shì jìng
red light	hóng lǜ dēng
rest stop	xiū xí zhàn
reverse	dào chē dǎng
rim, wheel	lún wǎng
road sign	lù biāo
roof-rack	zài wù jià
screw	luó sī
screw nut	luó sī tóu
screwdriver	luó sī qǐ zi
sealant; packing	mì fēng

seat/saddle	zuò diàn
seat/safety belt	ān quán dài
shift	qǐ zhòng gàng gǎn
shock absorber	huǎn chōng qì
short circuit	duǎn lù
snow tires	dōng jì lún tāi
socket wrench	kǎ pán bǎn shǒu
spare parts	bèi jiàn
spare tire	bèi tāi
spark plug	dián huǒ sāi
spoke	lún fú
to start (an engine, etc.)	fā dòng
starter	qǐ dòng zhuāng shì
steering wheel	fāng xiàng pán
superhighway	gāo sù gōng lù
suspension	tán huáng
tachometer/ speedometer	jì sù qì
three-/ten-speed bike	sān/shí dǎng zì xíng chē
tire	lún tāi
tire repair kit	bǔ tāi yòng jù
toll	gāo sù gōng lù fèi
tools	gōng jù
to tow a car; towing service	tūo chē
tow cable	tūo chē shéng
tow truck	tūo chē
towing station	gù zhàng tūo yùn zhàn
traffic jam	sāi chē
truck	kǎ chē
trunk	xíng lǐ xiāng
turbine	lún jī
to turn	zhuǎn wān
V-belt	sān jiǎo pí dài
valve	huó mén
warning light	jǐng gào dēng
wheel (on car/bike)	chē lún
windshield	dǎng fēng bō lí
windshield washer	yǔ shuā
wrench	luó xuán bǎn zi

Airplane   飞机

fēi jī

In China, an airport tax is collected at all airports. The amount of the tax varies by region.

At the Travel Agency/At the Airport   zài lǚxíng shè/fēi jī chǎng

Where is the … Airlines counter?	… háng kōng gōng sī de guì tái zài nǎ li?
When is the next flight to …?	xià yì bān dào … de fēi jī shén me shí hou fēi?
I want to book a one-way/roundtrip ticket to …	wǒ yào dìng yī zhāng dào … de dān chéng/lái hui jī piào.
Are there still seats available?	hái yǒu kòng wèi ma?
How much is an economy/a first-class ticket?	jīng jì/tóu děng zhāng duō shǎo qián?
How much baggage can one take?	ké yǐ dài duō shǎo xíng lǐ?
How much does the excess cost?	chāo zhòng měi gōng jīn duō shǎo qián?
I'd like to cancel/reschedule my reservation.	wǒ yào qǔ xiāo/dìng piào/wèi.
When do I have to be at the airport?	shén me shí hòu děi dào fēi jī chǎng?

起飞	qǐfei	takeoff
降落	jiàngluò	landing
抵达	dǐdá	arrival
登机门	dēngjìmén	check-in
出口	chūkǒu	exit/gate
入口	rùkǒu	entrance/arrival gate

Where is the information desk/ waiting room?	xún wèn chù/hòu jī shì zài nǎ li?
Can this be considered carry-on baggage?	ké yǐ bǎ zhè ge dāng shǒu tí xíng lǐ ma?
Is the plane to … late?	dào … de fēi jī wù diǎn le ma?
How late is it?	wù diǎn duō jiǔ?
Has the flight from … already landed?	cóng … fēi lái de bān jī yǐ jīng jiàng luò le ma?

On Board   zài fēi jī shàng

No smoking, please! Fasten your seat belts!	qǐng wù xī yān! jì shàng ān quán dài!
What river/mountain is that below?	xià miàn shì shén me hé/shān?
Where are we now?	wǒ men xiàn zài zài nǎ li?
When do we land in …?	shén me shí hou zài … jiàng luò?

Rice terraces, Sichuan Province

| We will land within ... minutes. | wǒ mēn zài ... fēn zhōng nèi jiàng luò. |
| What is the weather like in ...? | ... de tiān qì zěn me yàng? |

系上安全带	jìshang ānqúandài	Fasten seat belts.
请勿吸烟	qǐng wù xīyān	No smoking, please.
禁止吸烟	jìnzhǐ xīyān	No Smoking (on sign)
紧急出口	jǐnjí chūkǒu	Emergency Exit (on sign)

Arrival   dǐ dá

I can't find my baggage.	wǒ zhǎo bú dào wǒ de xíng lǐ.
My baggage has been lost.	wǒ de xíng lǐ diū le.
My baggage has been damaged.	wǒ de xíng lǐ bèi nòng huài le.
Whom shall I talk to (for help)?	wǒ yīng gāi zhǎo shéi?
Where can I get the bus to the city-center?	dào shì zhōng xīn de gōng chē zài nǎr dā chéng?

Word List: Airplane   ► See also Word List: Train, Ship

airline company	háng kōng gōng sī
airplane/airliner	fēi jī
airplane ticket	jī piào
airport	fēi jī chǎng
airport shuttle	jī chǎng bā shi
airport tax	jī chǎng fèi
aisle	zǒu dào
arrival	dào dá
arrival time	dǐ dá shí kè
baggage/bags	xíng lǐ
baggage cart	xíng lǐ chē
baggage check-in	bàn lǐ tuō yùn shǒu xù
baggage claim	tuō yùn xíng lǐ
boarding pass	dēng jī kǎ

business class	shāng yè cāng
to cancel	tuì piào
captain	jī zhǎng
carry-on baggage	shǒu tí xíng lǐ
to change one's reservation	gǎi dìng
to check in	bàn lǐ dēng jī
connection	jiē fēi jī
counter	guì tái
crew/steward(ess)	fú wù rén yuán
delay	wù diǎn
destination	mù dì dì
direct flight	zhí fēi
domestic flight	guó nèi háng xiàn
duty-free shop	miǎn shuì diàn
economy class	jīng jì cāng
emergency chute	jǐn jí huá dào
emergency exit	jǐn jí chū kǒu
emergency landing	jǐn jí jiàng luò
to fasten (seat belt, etc.)	jì hǎo
flight	fēi xíng
flight attendant	fēi jī fú wù yuán
flight schedule	háng chéng biǎo
gate/boarding gate	dēng jī kǒu
helicopter	zhí shēng jī
international flight	guó jì háng xiàn
jet plane	pēn shè jī
to land	jiàng luò
landing	jiàng luò
life vest	jiù shēng yī
No Smoking	bù xī yān
on board	zài jī shàng
on-time takeoff	àn shí qǐ fēi
passenger	lǚ kè
pilot	jià shǐ yuán
regularly scheduled flight	háng xiàn
reservation	dìng piào
to reserve/book	dìng
route	háng chéng
runway	pǎo dào
safety check	ān chuán jiǎn chá
seat belt	ān quán dài

smoking	xī yān
stopover	zhōng tú jiàng luò
tag (on baggage, etc.)	bīao qiān
tail section	fēi jī wěi bù
takeoff	qǐ fēi
terminal	dēng jī lóu
window seat	chuāng wèi

Train 火车

tiě lù

At the Travel Agency/ At the Railroad Station	**zài huǒ chē zhàn**

Where is the ticket window?	shòu piào chù zài nǎr?
Is this the place to line up for tickets to …?	dào … de chē piào zài zhèr pái duì ma?
One hard seat/soft seat, one-way to …	yì zhāng dào … de dān chéng yìng/ ruǎn zuò chē piào.

There are four different types of trains, ranging from the rather slow regional trains **(màn chē)** through the somewhat speedier express trains **(kuài chē)** to the rapid-express trains **(tè kuàichē)** and the super-express train **(tè tè kuài chē)**, which travels nonstop between Beijing and Shanghai exclusively.

There are two classes on the trains: a hard-seat (with some padding) class **(yìng zuò)**, usually taken by local Chinese and not recommended for foreign tourists, and a soft-seat class **(ruǎn zuò)**, more comfortable, more expensive, and often in short supply. The same two classes apply for the sleepers **(yìng/ruǎn wò)** as well.

Two round-trip tickets to …	liǎng zhāng dào … de lái huí piào.
Do you have children's/ student tickets?	yǒu ér tóng/xué shēng piào ma?
One 8 A.M. hard-seat/ soft-seat ticket to …	yì zhāng zǎo shàng bā diǎn dào … de yìng/ruǎn zuò chē piào.
Is it a window seat?	shì chuāng kǒu ma?

One 8 P.M. hard-seat/ soft-seat ticket to ...	yì zhāng wǎn shàng bā diǎn dào ... de yìng/ruǎn wò chē piào.
I'd like to book a seat on the 1 P.M. train to ...	wǒ yào dìng xià wǔ yì diǎn kāi wǎng ... de chē wèi.

In "soft seats" on the Shanghai–Waxi route

I'd like to check my baggage.	wǒ yào tuō yùn xíng lǐ.
Will the baggage be shipped along on the ... o'clock train?	xíng lǐ suí ... diǎn de huǒ chē yì qǐ yùn zǒu ma?
When will it arrive in ...?	shén me shí hou dào ...?
Is the train to ... late?	cóng ... lái de huǒ chē màn le ma?
Can I connect in ... with the train/ferry to ...?	zài ... jiē de dào wǎng ... de huǒ chē/ lún chuán ma?
Where do I change trains?	zài nǎr zhuǎn chē?
At which platform does the train to ... stop?	kāi wǎng ... de huǒ chē tíng zài nǎ ge zhàn tái?
The train from ... to ... is entering platform three.	cóng ... kāi wǎng ... de huǒ chē kāi jìn dì sān hào zhàn tái.

The number ... train from ... will be ten minutes late arriving in the station.	cóng ... kāi lái dì ... bān cì de huǒ chē màn shí fēn zhōng jìn zhàn.
The train to ... is about to depart; all aboard.	kāi wǎng ... de huǒ chē jiù yào kāi le, qǐng gǎn kuài shàng chē.
What is being announced over the loudspeaker?	zài guǎng bò shén me?

火车站	huǒchēzhàn	train station
询问台	xúnwèntái	information
服务台	fúwùtái	(passenger) service
广播处	guǎngbōchù	information (broadcasting station)
检票口	jiǎnpiàokǒu	ticket check-point
售票处	shòupiàochù	ticket booth/sales/booking
签票处	jiǎnpiàochù	ticket reservation window

On the Train   huǒ chē shàng

Is this seat taken?	zhè wèi zi yǒu rén ma?
Can you help me?	néng bù néng bāng wǒ yí xià?
May I open/close the window?	wǒ ké yǐ kāi/guān xià chuāng hù ma?
Pardon me, smoking is not allowed here.	duì bù qǐ, zhè lǐ jìn zhǐ xī yān.
Excuse me, this is my seat.	duì bù qǐ, zhè shì wǒ de wèi zi.
May I see your ticket?/ Tickets, please.	chá piào.
Did someone just get aboard?	yǒu rén gāng shàng chē ma?

Does the train stop at … ?	huǒ chē tíng … ma?	
Where are we now?	wǒ men zài nǎ li?	
How long are we stopping here?	zài zhè tíng duō jiǔ?	
Will the train arrive on time?	huì zhǔn shí dào dá ma?	

托运行李处	tuōyùn xínglǐchù	baggage check
行李寄存处	xínglǐ jìcúnchù	baggage room
贵宾室	guìbīnshì	waiting room for guests of honor
外宾候车室	wàibīn hòuchēshì	waiting rooms (for foreigners)
第一候车室	dì-yī hòuchēshì	Waiting Room Number One
第二候车室	dì-èr hòuchēshì	Waiting Room Number Two

Word List: Train   ▶ See also Word List: Airplane, Ship

aisle	guò dào
to announce	guǎng bò
to arrive; arrival	dào dá
baggage	xíng lǐ
baggage car	xíng lǐ chē
baggage check	bǎo guǎn dān
baggage check room	xíng lǐ jì cún chù
baggage check-in (for forwarding)	tuō yùn xíng lǐ chù
baggage locker	xiǎo jiàn cún fàng xiāng
baggage rack	xíng lǐ jià
to board (train, car)	shàng chē
to buy a better ticket en route	bǔ piào
car number	chē xiāng hào mǎ
children's ticket	ér tóng piào
compartment	chē xiāng

departure time	kāi chē shí kè
dining car	cān chē
discount	yōu dài
emergency brake	jǐn jí shà chē
express	kuài chē
extra charge	fù jiā fèi
free/no charge	miǎn fèi
to get off (train, car)	xià chē
group ticket	tuán tǐ piào
local escort	dì péi
local train	màn chē
locomotive	huǒ chē tóu
main station	zǒng zhàn
nonsmoking car	jìn zhǐ xī yān chē xiāng
occupied	yǒu rén
platform ticket	zhàn tái piào
porter	bān yùn gōng
rail(road)	tiě guǐ
railroad	tiě lù
reservation	yù dìng
round-trip ticket	huí chéng piào
sleeper ticket	wò chē piào
smoking car	xī yān chē xiāng
special express train	tè kuài chē
start; departure	kāi chē
station restaurant	tiě lù cān tīng
stop; stopover	tíng liú
subject to extra charge	yào jiā qián
super express (Beijing-Shanghai)	tè tè kuài
ticket	chē piào
ticket booking office	piào fáng
ticket counter	shòu piào chù
ticket inspection	jiǎn chá chē piào
ticket price	piào jià
timetable	shí kè biǎo
toilet	cè suǒ
tour-wide escort	quán péi
train	huǒ chē
train crew	suí chē fú wù yuán
train station	huǒ chē zhàn
waiting room	hòu chē shì
washroom	xǐ shǒu jiān
window seat	chuāng wèi

Ship 船

chuán

Information	**xún wèn**
Which boat is best to take to get to …?	dào … dā nǎ tiáo chuán zuì hǎo?
When does the boat to … leave?	wǎng …de chuán shén me shí hou kāi?
How long will it take?	yào zuò duō jiǔ?
Which ports does it call at?	kāi wǎng nǎ xiē gǎng kǒu?
When do we dock at …?	shén me shí hou dào … kào àn?
How long will we be in port in … ?	zài … kào àn duō jiǔ?
I would like one boat ticket to Shanghai.	wǒ yào yì zhāng dào Shànghǎi de chuán piào.
first-class cabin	tóu děng cāng
luxury-class cabin	háo huá cāng
special-class cabin	tè cāng
tourist-/economy-class cabin	pǔ tōng cāng
a single (not double) cabin	dān rén kè cāng
a two-bed cabin	shuāng rén chuáng kè cāng
I would like a round-trip ticket on the … o'clock boat.	wǒ yào yì zhāng … diǎn de huán yóu chuán piào.

On Board	**zài chuán shàng**
Where is cabin number …?	… hào kè cāng zài nǎ li?
Can I change to a different cabin?	ké yǐ huàn bié de kè cāng ma?

Where is my baggage?	wǒ de xíng lǐ ne?
Where is the dining hall/the entertainment center?	cān tīng/yu lè tīng zài nǎ li?
When do we eat?/ When is our meal served?	shén me shí hou kāi fàn?
Steward, please bring …	fú wù yuán, qǐng nǐ ná … lái, hǎo ma?
I'm not feeling well.	wǒ bù shū fu.
Please call a doctor.	qíng nǐ jiào yī shēng lái, hǎo ma?
Please give me something for seasickness.	qíng gěi wǒ yùn chuán yào.

救生设备	jiùshēng shèbèi	life-saving equipment
救生船	jiùshēng chúan	lifeboat

Word List: Ship ▶ See also Word List: Airplane, Train

anchor	máo
berth	kào àn chù
to board a boat	shàng chuán
boat ticket	chuán piào
bow	chuán tóu
cabin	chuán cāng
to call at	kāi wǎng
captain	chuán zhǎng
coast	hǎi àn
course	háng xiàn
crew	rén yuán
crossing/passage	héng dù
cruise	huán yóu háng xíng
deck	jiǎ bǎn
to dock	kào àn
ferry boat	dù chuán
gangplank	tiào bǎn
harbor	gǎng kǒu
harbor tax	gǎng wù fèi
hovercraft	qì diàn chuán
hydrofoil	shuǐ yì tǐng

knots	jié
land	lù dì
to land/to disembark	shàng àn
to leave port	lí gǎng
life jacket	jiù shēng yī
life belt	jiù shēng quān
lifeboat	jiù shēng chuán
lighthouse	dēng tǎ
motorboat	qì tǐng
on board	zài chuán shàng
passenger	lǚ kè
pier/dock/wharf	mǎ tóu
port (side)	zuǒ xián
promenade deck	jiá bǎn
reservation/booking	dìng
round-trip voyage	huán yóu
rowboat	huá chuán
rudder	huá jiǎng
sailboat	fān chuán
seaman/sailor	hǎi yuán
seasick	yūn chuán
ship's cabin	chuán cāng
shore	àn biān
starboard	yòu xián
steamship	lún chuán
stern	chuán wěi
steward	fú wù yuán
sun deck	lù tiān jiǎ bǎn
steerage	tǒng cāng
wave	hǎi làng
yacht	yóu tǐng

At the Border　边界

biān jiè

Passport Check　jiǎn chá hù zhào

Your passport, please!	nǐ de hù zhào!
Your passport is expired.	nǐ de hù zhào guò qī le.

出境	chūjìng	Departures
入境	rùjìng	Arrivals

Anyone wishing to enter the People's Republic of China is required to have a passport, which must be valid for at least six months after the date of your scheduled departure from China, as well as an entry visa. For group travel, the tour organizer is responsible for obtaining the visas. Visas for individual travel are easily obtained from Chinese embassies or consulates in most Western countries. In the United States the standard 30-day single-entry visa costs about $35 and takes about a week to get. In addition to the Chinese Embassy in Washington, D.C., there are consulates in Chicago, Los Angeles, New York, and San Francisco.

I have come with the … tour group.	wǒ shì gēn … lǚ xíng tuán yì qǐ lái de.
Do you have a visa?	ní yǒu qiān zhèng ma?
May I quickly arrange a visa?	ké yǐ mǎ shàng bàn qiān zhèng ma?

Customs   hǎi guān jiǎn chá

The usual customs regulations apply. Upon entry, a customs declaration listing any valuables you are bringing in must be filled out, and this form must be presented when you leave China. Upon departure, keep in mind that antiques may not be taken out of the country unless they bear the red lacquer seal of an official antique shop.
For domestic flights, there is no special processing for foreigners. Expect such procedures only at large airports, when you are leaving the country. The usual advice is to fly as little as possible in China; take the train instead.

Are you carrying anything subject to duty?	dài dǎ shuì de dōng xì ma?
No, I just have a few little gifts.	méi yǒu, zhǐ dài le jǐ jiàn xiǎo lǐ wù.
Please come to the right/left.	qǐng dào yòu/zuǒ biān lái.

Please open your luggage.	qíng dǎ kāi nǐ de xíng lǐ.
Must I pay duty?	yào dǎ shuì ma?
How much duty must I pay?	yào fù duō shǎo shuì?

Word List: At the Border

birthdate	chū shēng nián yuè rì
birthplace	chū shēng dì
border crossing point	biān jiè
characteristic	tè zhēng
customs	hǎi guān
customs duty	guān shuì
customs inspection	hǎi guān jiǎn chá
customs official	hǎi guān rén yuán
departure	chū jìng
driver's license	jià shǐ zhí zhào
duty-free	miǎn shuì
entry	rù jìng
export	chū kǒu
given name	míng
health certificate	jiàn kāng jiǎn chá zhèng míng
ID card	shēn fèn zhèng
immunization certificate	guó jì yù fáng zhèng míng shū
import	jìn kǒu
marital status	hūn yīn zhuàng kuàng
married	yǐ hūn
nationality	guó jí
passport	hù zhào
passport control	hù zhào jiǎn chá
place of residence	zhù sǔo
regulations	fǎ tiáo, guī dìng
single	wèi hūn
surname	xìng
tariff	guān shuì
tax; duty	shuì
valid	yǒu xiào
visa	qiān zhèng
widowed	guǎ jū

Local Transportation

gōng lù

May I ask, where is the ... stop?	qǐng wèn, ... zhàn zài nǎr?
bus	gōng gòng qì chē
street car	diàn chē
subway	dì tiě
minibus/van (for sharing cost)	xiǎo ba

Qian Men ("outer gate") Subway Station, Beijing

What means of transportation do I take to get to ...?	zuò shén me chē dào ...?
What line goes to ...?	jǐ lù chē kāi wǎng ...?
Is this the bus to ...?	zhè shì kāi wǎng ... de gōng chē ma?
When does it leave?	shén me shí hou kāi?
When does the first/last subway to ... leave?	dì yī/zui hòu yī bān wǎng ... de dì tiě shén me shí hou kāi?
Which direction should I take?	zuò nǎ ge fāng xiàng de chē?

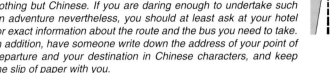

Going by bus is no easy matter, because the signs you see both upon departure and upon reaching your destination will have only Chinese characters, and the bus drivers usually speak nothing but Chinese. If you are daring enough to undertake such an adventure nevertheless, you should at least ask at your hotel for exact information about the route and the bus you need to take. In addition, have someone write down the address of your point of departure and your destination in Chinese characters, and keep the slip of paper with you.

How many stops (before I get off)?	zuò jǐ zhàn?
Where should I get off/ change buses?	zài nǎr xià/huàn chē?
When we get to my stop, please tell me.	dào zhàn shí, qǐng gào sù wǒ.
Where can I buy a ticket?	zài nǎr mǎi chē piào?
I'd like to buy one ticket to ...	mǎi yì zhāng dào ... de chē piào.

Taxi 出租汽车

chū zū chē

Taxis in China are usually yellow in color and impossible to miss; you can easily summon one from your tourist hotel. Be sure to insist that the driver turn on the taxi meter when the trip begins. Prices can be negotiated but, of course, only in Chinese. Ask at your hotel in advance to find out what local fares are.

In addition to the official taxis, off-duty drivers of official cars also are willing to carry passengers in their vehicles for a fee. With a little skill, you can negotiate a very favorable flat rate for your ride. For longer trips, it also is possible to use a group taxi (usually minibuses with fixed flat rates).

As with bus travel, when going by taxi you should always carry a piece of paper with the address written in Chinese characters, since the drivers are likely to speak only Chinese.

Please phone for a taxi.	qǐng dǎ ge diàn huà jiào chū zū chē.
To the train station.	dào huǒ chē zhàn.
To the airport.	dào fēi jī chǎng.
To the … Hotel.	dào … bīn guǎn.
To … Street.	dào … lù.
Drive to …	kāi dào …
How much to …?	dào … duō shǎo qián?
I charge according to the meter.	àn jì fèi biǎo suàn.
Stop for a moment!	zàn tíng yí xià!
Stop here.	zài zhèr tíng.
Wait a moment, I'll return in five minutes.	děng yí xià, wǒ wǔ fēn zhōng jiù huì lái.
Please drive slower/ faster.	qǐng kāi màn/kuài yì diǎn.
This is your tip.	zhè shì gěi nǐ de xiǎo fèi.

On Foot

bù hsíng

May I ask, where is …?	qǐng wèn, … zài nǎ li?
May I ask, how does one get to …?	qǐng wèn, … zěn me zǒu?
Sorry, I don't know.	duì bù qǐ, wǒ bù zhī dào.
What is the best way to get to …?	dào … zǒu nǎ tiáo lù zuì jìn?
How far is it to …?	dào … duō yuǎn?
Not too far.	(bù) hěn yuǎn.
It's nearby.	jiù zài fù jìn.
Go straight ahead.	yì zhí wǎng qián zǒu.
Go left/right.	wǎng zuǒ/yòu zǒu.
Turn left/right at the first/second intersection.	dì yī/èr ge shí zì lù kǒu zuǒ/yòu zhuǎn.
Go past … the bridge. the square. the road/street.	guò … qiáo. guǎng chǎng. mǎ lù.
Then ask again.	zài wèn yí xià.
You can't miss it.	nǐ bú hui cuò guò.
Take the … bus.	nǐ zuò … lù chē.

Word List: On the Go in Town

announce	guǎng bō
avenue	dà jiē
building	jiàn zhú
bus	ba shi, gōng gòng qì chē
bus station	gōng chē zhàn
bus stop	gōng gòng qì chē zhàn
to buy a ticket	mǎi piào
city bus	gōng chē

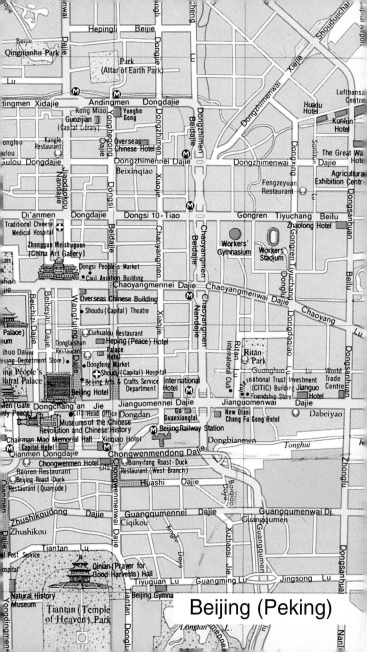

Beijing (Peking)

city sight-seeing tour	yóu lǎn shì qū
city-center	shì zhōng xīn
direction	fāng xiàng
district	shì qū
drive a car; drive; driving	kāi chē
to drive off; to depart	kāi
driver	sī jī
fare	chē fèi
to get on a bus/into a car	shàng chē
to get out of a car/bus	xià chē
house	fáng zi
house number	mén pái hào mǎ
intercity bus	cháng tú gōng gòng qì chē

Bus tickets should be purchased from the conductor on the bus. You need to show the ticket again when you get off the bus.

intersection	shí zì lù kǒu
intracity; within the city	chéng nèi
last stop	zhōng zhàn
minibus	xiǎo bā
park	gōng yuán
receipt	shōu jù
ring bell	àn líng
schedule	shí kè biǎo
sidewalk	rén xíng dào
to stop	tíng
street	mǎ lù
streetcar	diàn chē
subway	dì tiě
taxi	chū zū chē
taxi driver	sī jī
taxi meter	jì fèi biǎo
taxi stand	zhāo hū zhàn
ticket	chē piào
ticket seller/conductor	shòu piào yuán
tip	xiǎo fèi
traffic	jiāo tōng
traffic light	hóng lǜ dēng
train (local)	màn chē

4 **Accommodations**
住宿

Information

xúnwèn

Please recommend ...	qǐng gěi wǒ jièshào
a nice/fine hotel.	yì jiā hǎo de lǚguǎn.
a simple/economical hotel.	yì jiā jiǎndān yi diǎn de lǚguǎn.

China International Travel Service (CITS) can arrange hotels and accommodations at your destination for you, or provide you with the address of the regional CITS offices. In China, as elsewhere, there are various kinds of hotels. Rules determine which hotels foreigners may stay in. Usually the only hotels available for foreign tourists are the expensive ones. The rather large, government-run hotels, referred to as **bīnguǎn** *or* **fàndiàn,** *have been renovated and are open to foreigners. They are usually moderately priced. Hotels in the lower category usually do not meet international standards and are patronized mostly by the local population. Should you be the guest of a Chinese organization or institution or a participant in a course or conference, it is advisable to ask whether it is possible to stay in one of the affiliated guest houses—*zhāodàisuǒ *in Chinese—since they offer almost the same facilities as a hotel but are far more reasonably priced.*

In most hotels, it is still customary for an attendant to be stationed on every floor to be helpful to guests. When you leave the hotel, you can leave your room key with him, rather than at the reception desk.

Since the Chinese know very little privacy, the hotel staff often fail to understand that a foreign guest does not wish to be disturbed. Someone may burst unexpectedly into your room, even if the "Do Not Disturb" sign is hanging outside the door. Consequently, it is a good idea to fasten the chain. In addition, never leave valuables in your room. It is better to deposit them in the hotel safe.

Campgrounds, vacation apartments, and youth hostels are not yet customary in China.

Is it in the center of town?	zài shì zhōngxīn ma?
Is it quiet?	ānjìng ma?

Is it convenient to public transportation?	jiāotōng fāngbiàn ma?
Is shopping convenient?	gòuwù fāngbiàn ma?
Is it near the train station?	kàojìn huǒchēzhàn ma?
How much is it per night?	yì tiān duōshǎo qián?
How do I get there from here?	cóng zhèr zěnme qù?

Dongfang Hotel, Guangzhou

宾馆	bīnguǎn	guest house
饭店	fàndiàn	hotel
旅馆	lǚguǎn	hotel
旅社	lǚshè	inn
招待所	zhāodàisuǒ	guest house

Hotel

bīn-guǎn/lǚguǎn

At the Reception Desk	jiēdài chù/zǒngtái

My name is … I've reserved a room here.	wǒ xìng … wǒ zài nǐmen zhèr dìngle yí ge fángjiān.
I've telephoned and reserved a room.	wǒ dǎ diànhuà dìngle yí ge fángjiān.
Do you still have any rooms available?	hái yǒu kòng fáng ma?
How long will you be staying?	zhù duō jiǔ?
For one night.	yí ge wǎnshàng.
For two nights/one week.	liǎng tiān/yí ge xīngqī.
Sorry, no, we're full up.	duìbùqǐ, dōu mǎnle, méi kòng fáng le.
Can you recommend another hotel?	néng bù néng gěi wǒ jièshào lìng yì jiā lǚguǎn?
Can you help me telephone them (i.e., the other hotel)?	néng bù néng bāng wǒ dǎ ge diànhuà gěi tāmen?
What price category do you want?	nǐ yào shénme biāozhǔn de?
What sort of room do you want?	nǐ yào shénmeyàng de fángjiān?
A single.	dānrén fáng.
A double.	shuāngrén fáng.
A suite.	tàojiān.
A standard room.	biāozhǔn fáng.
A room for three/four persons.	sān/sì rén fáng.
A quiet room.	ānjìng diǎnr de.
A sunny room.	liàng yì diǎnr de.

A room ...	yì jiān ...
with hot and cold running water.	dài lěng rè shui de.
with a bath.	dài xǐzǎo jiān de.
with a bathroom/ toilet.	dài wèishēng jiān de.
with a terrace/ balcony.	dài yángtái de.
with a sea view.	chuānghù cháo hǎibiǎn de.
with air conditioning.	dài kōngtiáo de.
with heat.	dài nuǎnqì de.
on the ground floor.	zài dǐlóu de.
with a good view of the city.	kě-yǐ kàndào chéngshì quánjǐng de.

Is hot water supplied daily?	tiántiān gōngyìng rèshuǐ ma?
May I see the room?	wǒ xiān kàn xià fángjiān, hǎo ma?
I don't much like this room; may I see another?	wǒ bú tài xǐhuān zhè jiān, yǒu bié de ma?
This room is fine.	zhè jiān hén hǎo.
Can you supply another bed?	néng bù néng zài jiā yì zhāng chuáng?
How much will it cost?	děi jiā duōshǎo qián?
How much is the room?	fángfèi, duōshǎo qián?
Can I pay in foreign currency or in RMB?	fù wàibì háishì rénmínbì?
Does the hotel serve breakfast?	bāo zǎocān ma?
Is breakfast included?	zǎocān bāokuō zài nèi ma?
Does the hotel serve meals?	yǒu huǒshi ma?
Does it include three meals (daily)?	bāo sāncān ma?

| Meal charges are figured separately. | huǒshífèi lìngwài suàn. |

总台	zǒngtái	Reception
询问台	xúnwèntái	Information Desk
餐厅	cāntīng	Dining Room
咖啡厅	kāfēitīng	Cafeteria
酒吧	jiǔba	Bar

Please fill out the registration form.	qǐng zài zhèr dēngjì yíxìa.
May I see your passport?	duibùqǐ, ní de hùzhào ne?
Please have my baggage sent to my room.	qǐng bǎ wǒ de xínglǐ sòngdào wǒ de fángjiān qu.
This I'll take myself.	zhè ge wǒ zìjǐ ná.
Where can I park the car?	nǎli ké-yǐ tíngchē?
Park in our garage/ parking lot.	tíng zài wǒmen de chēkù./ tíngchēchǎng.
Does the hotel have a pool?	lǚguǎn yǒu yóuyǒng chí ma?

Talking to the Hotel Staff

gēn fúwù rényuán duìhuà

Please give me the key for room number …	qǐng géi wǒ … hào de yàoshí.
I'm staying in room number …, please help me open the door.	wǒ zhù … hào fáng, qǐng bāng wǒ kāi fángmén.
When do we eat breakfast?	shénme shíhou ké-yǐ chī zǎofàn?

Where is the dining room?	cāntīng zài nǎli?
Where do we have breakfast?	dào nǎli chī zǎocān?
Do you want to eat breakfast in your room?	nǐ yào zài fángjiān lǐ yòng zǎocān ma?

Tomorrow morning at ... o'clock, please bring breakfast to my room.	míngtiān zǎoshàng ... diǎn, qǐng bǎ zǎocān sòngdào fángjiān lái.
What's for breakfast?	zǎocān chī shénme?

For breakfast I would like ...   zǎocān wǒ yào ...

coffee.	kāfēi.
black tea.	hóng chá.
cocoa.	kěke.
fruit juice.	shuǐguǒ zhī.
a soft-boiled egg.	bàn zhú de dàn.
scrambled eggs.	chǎodàn.
ham and eggs.	huǒtuǐ jiāndàn.
bread/toast.	miànbāo/tǔsī.
ham.	huǒtui.
butter.	huángyóu.
cheese.	nǎilào.
sausage.	xiāngcháng.
honey.	fēngmì.
marmelade/jam.	guǒzijiàng.
fruit.	shuǐguǒ.

Please wake me at ... o'clock.	qǐng zài ... diǎn jiàoxǐng wǒ.

Please bring me ...   qǐng nǐ ná ... lái.

an electrical adapter.	yí ge liánjiē chātóu
a woolen blanket.	yì tiáo máotǎn
a glass.	yí ge bēizi
a glass of mineral water.	yí bēi kuàngquán shuǐ
a light bulb.	dēngpào
some clothes hangers.	jǐ ge yījià
a clean towel.	yì tiáo gānjìng de máojīn
a bar of soap.	yí kuài féizào

The electrical voltage in China is 220V. Since the wall sockets are different, however, your electric appliances require an appropriate adapter.

How does this work?/ How is this used?	zěnme yòng?
Please give me a little boiled water/green tea.	qǐng gěi wǒ yìdiǎnr rè kāishui/lǜchá.
Is there anyone looking for me?	yǒu rén zháo wǒ ma?
Is there any mail for me?	yǒu wǒ de xìn ma?
Do you have picture postcards/stamps here?	nǐmen zhèr yǒu fēngjǐng míngxìnpiàn/yóupiào ma?
Where can I mail a letter?	nǎli ké-yǐ jìxìn?
Where can I rent/ borrow …?	nǎli ké-yǐ zūdào/jièdào …?
Where can I make a phone call?	nǎli ké-yǐ dǎ diànhuà?
When I leave the hotel, do I leave my key at the reception desk?	líkāi lǚguǎn shí, yào bǎ yàoshí jiāo gěi fúwùtái ma?
May I leave my bags here with you for a while?	wǒ ké-yǐ bǎ dōngxī zànshí fàng zài nǐmen zhèlǐ ma?
May I leave valuables in the room?	ké-yǐ bǎ guìzhòng de dōngxī fàng zài fángjiān lǐ ma?
Where can I deposit/ store valuables?	nǎr ké-yǐ cúnfàng guìzhòng de dōngxī?
Can I leave my valuables in your safe?	ké-yǐ bǎ guìzhòng de dōngxī cúnfàng zài nǐmen de báoxiǎn guì ma?

请勿打扰	qǐng wù dǎrǎo	Do not disturb!
安静	ānjìng	Quiet
打扫中	dǎsǎozhōng	Cleaning in progress

Complaints   bù mǎn

The room has not been cleaned.	fángjiān hái méi dásǎo.
The shower ...	xǐzǎojiān ...
The toilet ...	mátǒng ...
The heat ...	nuǎnqì ...
The light ...	diàndēng ...
The radio ...	shōuyīnjī ...
The TV ... is broken.	diànshì ... huài le.
The faucet is leaking/ dripping.	shuǐlóngtóu dīshuǐ.
There's no hot water.	méi (rè) shuǐ.
The toilet/sink is clogged.	cèsuǒ/xǐshǒupén bù tōng.
The window does not close/does not open.	chuānghù guān bù qǐlái/dǎ bù kāi.
The key does not work.	yàoshi dǎ bù kāi.
Please be a bit quieter.	qǐng xiǎoshēng diǎnr.

Checking Out   líkāi

I will be leaving the hotel this evening/ tomorrow at ...	wǒ jīntiān wǎnshàng/míngtiān ... diǎn líkāi zhèlǐ.
What time must I vacate the room?	jídiǎn wǒ děi líkāi fángjiān?
Please figure out my bill.	qǐng suànhǎo zhàng.
We'd like separate bills, please.	fēnkāi suàn.
May I use US currency to pay?	ké-yǐ fù měiguó qian ma?
Can I use a credit card to pay the bill?	ké-yǐ yòng xìnyòngkǎ fùkuǎn ma?

Please have my mail sent to this address.	qǐng bǎ wǒ de xìnjiàn jìdào zhè ge dìzhǐ.
Please have someone take my bags down.	qǐng jiào rén bǎ xínglǐ ná xiàqù.
Please have someone send my bags to the train station/airport.	qǐng jiào rén bǎ xínglǐ sòngdào huǒchēzhàn/fēijīchǎng.
Please call a taxi.	qǐng jiào liàng chūzūchē.
Thank you very much! Good-bye!	fēicháng gǎnxiè! zàijiàn!

Word List: Hotel

air conditioning	lěngqì
ashtray	yānhuīgāng
bar	jiǔba
bathe; take a bath	xǐzǎo
bathroom	xǐzǎojiān
bathtub	xǐzǎopén
bed	chuáng
bedding	bèidān hé chuángdān
bedsheets	chuángdān
bedside lamp	chuángtóuguì xiǎodēng
bedspread	bèidān
blanket (woolen)	máotǎn
boiled water	kāishuǐ
breakfast	zǎocān
cafeteria	kāfēitīng
category	biāozhǔn
chair	yǐzi, shāfā
chambermaid	nǚ fúwù-yuán
clean	gānjìng
to clean	dásǎo
clotheshanger	yījià
cold water	lěngshuǐ
cupboard, closet	guìzi
detergent	xǐdíjì
dining room	cāntīng
dinner/supper	wǎncān
elevator	diàntī

entertainment program	yúlè jiémù
fan (electric)	diànshàn
floor/story	lóu
grill; grilled meat	kǎoròu
heat; heating	nuǎnqì
hot water	rèshuǐ
hotel bus	bīn-guǎn bāshi
key	yàoshí
lamp	diàndēng
light switch	kāiguān
lounge	dà tīng
lunch	wǔcān
mattress	chuángdiàn
mirror	jìngzi
nightstand	chuángtóuguì
off-season	dànjì
outlet; socket	chāzuò
overnight stay	guòyè, zhùsù
peak season	wàngjì
phone in one's room	fángjiān diànhuà
pillow	zhěntóu
plug (electric)	chātóu
porter	ménfáng
radio	shōuyīnjī
reception	jiēdàichù
reception hall	jiēdàitīng
registration	dēngjì
reservation	yùdìng
room	fángjiān
safe	báoxiǎnxiāng
shower	chōngzǎojiān
terrace	yángtái
toilet	cèsuǒ
toilet paper	wèishēngzhǐ
towel	máojīn
trash basket	lājīlǒu
TV	diànshì
TV room	diànshìtīng
ventilation	tōngfēng shèbèi

*You should drink only boiled water in China. Tap water is not safe to drink. "Boiled water," or **kāishuǐ,** is available everywhere, in private homes as well as in hotels and on trains.*

washbasin	xǐshǒupén
water	shuǐ
water faucet	shuǐlóngtóu
water glass	bēizi
window	chuānghu
youth bed	értóng chuáng

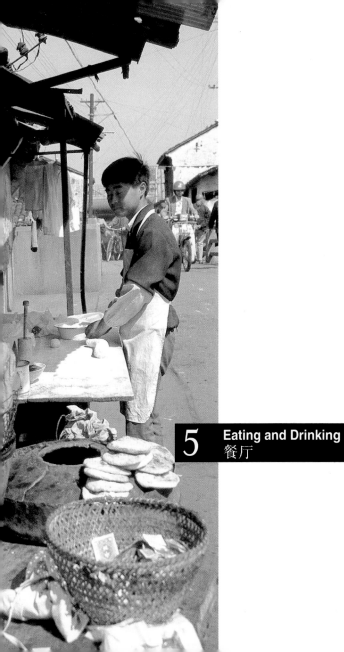

Eating Out

qù chīfan

Eating is one of the greatest passions of the Chinese. It is no surprise, then, that Chinese cuisine has such great variety, with pronounced regional differences as far as the seasoning and preparation of the foods are concerned. In Chinese restaurants in foreign lands, the dishes have been adapted to local tastes, but in China you have an opportunity to become acquainted with the various styles of cooking prepared in the original manner. In addition to the kitchens of the large hotels and state-operated restaurants, there are a great many small, privately run restaurants, which frequently offer a better selection of regional specialties than the larger establishments. Further, you will find a host of small cookstands on the streets, selling a wide range of Chinese snacks, such as seafood, noodles, and Chinese "pot stickers," or filled, steamed yeast buns. Since these stands offer all kinds of unusual dishes—things that are considered delicacies in many areas but that may not agree with your appetite (such as dog, snake, or lizard meat)—you need to take a close look before you order. If you take advantage of the offerings at street stands, keep in mind that the hygienic conditions there don't always meet Western standards and that you'll need to have a fairly sturdy digestive system.

Is there … nearby?	zhè fùjìn nǎr yǒu …
a good restaurant	hǎo de fàn-guǎn?
a Western-style restaurant	xīcān tīng?
an inexpensive restaurant	bú tài gui de fàndiàn?
a snack shop	xiǎochī diàn?
Where can I get a good meal in this area?	fùjìn nǎr yǒu hǎochī de dōngxī?

At the Restaurant

zài cāntīng

餐厅	cān tīng	
饭店	fàn diàn	restaurant
饭馆	fàn guǎn	
咖啡厅	kāfēi tīng	café
小吃店	xiǎochī diàn	snack shop
西餐厅	xīcān tīng	Western-style restaurant

> *In some higher-class restaurants it is customary for the staff to assign the customer a seat.*

Please help us reserve a table in the dining room.	qǐng bāng wǒmen zài cāntīng dìng ge wèizi.
Until what time is your restaurant open?	nǐmen de fàndiàn kāidào jǐ diǎn?
Is this place taken?	zhèr yǒu rén ma?
Do you have a table for two/three?	yǒu liǎng/sān ge rén de wèizi ma?
Where is the bathroom?	cèsuǒ zài nǎli?

厕所	cèsuo	toilet
洗手间	xǐshǒujiān	
化妆室	huàzhuāngshì	powder room
公共厕所	gōnggòng cèsuǒ	public toilet

This way.	wǎng zhèbiān zǒu.

Ordering

diǎncài

People often assume that a side dish of rice is an indispensable component of Chinese cooking. This is true only of the cuisine of the southern provinces, however, where rice is grown. In the north, where grain is cultivated, pasta or noodles are the preferred accompaniment. The Yangtze River divides the two areas, roughly speaking. As a rule, there are four main varieties in Chinese cuisine:

1. In the northern cuisine of **Peking/Beijing,** meat is frequently fried to a crisp. One example is the famous Peking duck. In addition, since this is China's wheat belt, there are a great many pasta dishes available, such as Chinese "pot stickers," filled, steamed yeast buns, and noodles in a great many variations. The style of preparation is basically quite simple: mainly, steaming or stir-frying.

2. In the southern cuisine of **Canton,** the dishes are often steamed, boiled, or stir-fried. Meat, for example, is first boiled, then roasted. Especially well known are the sweet-and-sour dishes. Food is lightly cooked and not highly spiced. In addition, Cantonese cooking is famed for a special kind of meal known as "Dim Sum" **(diǎnxīn),** a kind of snack-food feast. It begins in the late morning and continues through midday, and tea is served with it. A

great many different delicacies in steamer baskets and on small plates are ordered and served immediately from a serving cart, which is continually refilled and pushed around the restaurant. Cantonese cooking is famous for exotic specialties.

*3. The eastern cuisine of **Shanghai,** perhaps less known by foreigners, is famous for its dishes containing fish, shellfish, and other kinds of seafood. The taste tends toward the mild, and some dishes are high in fat content. Look especially for "red-cooked" dishes, prepared in a stock of soy sauce and rice wine.*

*4. The western Chinese cuisine of **Sichuan** is characterized by its spicy-hot, highly seasoned foods. This style of cooking is famed for its meat and tofu dishes with spicy peppers. Keep the ice water handy!*

Waiter!	fúwùyuán!
The menu, please.	càidān.
The wine list, please.	jiǔdān.
What house specialties do you have?	nǐmen yǒu shénme náshǒu cài?
What kind of food do you serve here?	nǐmen zhǔyào zuò shénmeyàng de cài?
Do you have vegetarian dishes?	yǒu sùcài ma?
Do you have small portions?	yǒu xiǎofèn de ma?
Are you ready to order?	diǎnhǎo le ma?
I would like …	wǒ yào …
Do you want soup?	yào tāng ma?
I don't want soup.	bú yào tāng.
We've run out of …/We don't have …	… méiyǒu le.
This dish must be ordered in advance.	zhè dào cài děi xiān yùdìng.
May I have … instead of …?	néng bù néng bǎ … huànchéng …
I can't eat … Could you prepare the dish without …?	wǒ bù néng chī …, qǐng bú yào fàng …

What will you have to drink?	hē shénme yǐnliào?
A glass of ..., please.	yì bēi ...
A bottle/half bottle of ..., please.	yì/bàn píng ...
With ice, please.	jiā bīngkuài.
Enjoy your meal!	màn chī!

*At an important dinner or a banquet, the guests are seated at several tables, with no more than eight to ten persons at each. As a general rule, the number of courses served is roughly equal to the number of people at the table. The dishes are placed on a turntable in the center of the table, so that each guest has easy access to the foods of his choosing. After the host has asked the guest of honor to start his or her meal, the banquet can get under way. Instead of "Bon appétit," the Chinese say **màn chī,** which literally means "enjoy slowly."*

Would you like anything else?	hái yào shénme?
What is the name of this dish?	zhè dào cài jiào shénme?
What sort of meat/vegetable is this?	zhè shì shénme ròu/qīngcài?
Please bring us some ...	máfán gěi wǒmen ...
We would like some more bread/rice/beer.	zài yào yìdiǎnr miànbāo/báifàn/píjiǔ.

Complaints

bù mǎn

We're still without a ...	hái shǎole yì ...
You have forgotten my ...	nǐ wàngle wǒ de ...
I did not order this.	wǒ méi dìng zhè ge.
This dish/food is too salty.	cài tài xián le.

The meat is too tough/fatty.	ròu tài lǎo/féi le.
The fish is not fresh.	yú bú tài xīnxiān.
Please take this dish back.	bǎ cài duān huiqù.
Tell the manager to come out.	jiào láobǎn chūlái, hǎo ma?

The Check
zhàngdān

Waiter, the check, please.	fúwùyuán suànzhàng!
I'm in a hurry. Please prepare the check.	wǒ gǎn shíjiān, qǐng mǎshàng suànzhàng.
One check for everyone, please.	yìqǐ suàn.
Separate checks.	fēnkāi suàn.
Is the tip included?	xiǎofèi suàn jìnqu le ma?
There appears to be an error in the check.	zhàng hǎoxiàng suàncuò le.
We didn't have this, we had …	wǒmen méi chīdào zhè ge. wǒmen zhǐ yǒu …
Was everything okay (delicious)? Satisfied?	hǎochī ma? mǎn-yì ma?
Everything was wonderful.	hǎojíle.
Here's your tip.	gěi nǐ de xiǎofèi.
No need to give change.	bú yòng zhǎo le.

Tipping is just one of those things generally not done in China. Almost no one asks for a tip. This is good news for tourists. But keep in mind that foreign tourists are often charged extra for many services, such as ticket purchases.

As a Dinner Guest

yànkè

Thank you for your invitation!	xièxie nǐ de yāoqǐng!
You're welcome!	bú yào kèqì!
Here's to you!	jìng nǐ!

*Alcohol usually is drunk in China only at a dinner or on festive occasions. The beverages of choice are either clear Chinese grain alcohols (such as the famous **Máotái**), Chinese rice wine (**Shàoxīng**, for example), or Chinese beer (such as the well-known **Qīngdǎo** brand). The host or perhaps one of the guests call for "drying of the cup—**gānbēi ("bottoms up")**—which doesn't always have to be taken literally, however. You should counter by asking the host or the other guests to do likewise.*

May I trouble you to …/ Please hand me a …	máfan bǎ … dì gěi wǒ.
Have a little more …?	zài chī diǎn …?
Thanks, I've had plenty.	xièxie, wǒ chī tài duō le.
I'm full, thanks.	wǒ tài bǎo le, xièxie.
May I smoke?	ké-yǐ xīyān ma?

Word List: Eating and Drinking

▶ See also Chapter 8, Word List: Groceries

alcohol-free	bù hán jiǔjīng
appetizer (on a menu)	qiáncān
ashtray	yānhuīgāng
bar	jiǔba
beef	niúròu
beer	píjiǔ
beverage/drink	yǐnliào

*The selection of breads available is not very large, as one would expect, since bread is not a staple food of the Chinese. Usually only white bread is served, since breakfast already includes rice, noodles, or pastry fried in deep fat **(yóutiáo)**, often accompanied by soy milk **(dòujiāng).***

boiled	zhǔde
boiled water	kāishuǐ
bone	gǔtóu
bone (fish)	yúcì
bowl (rice)	wǎn
bread	miànbāo
breakfast	zǎocān
butter	huángyóu
chef/cook	chúshīr
chicken meat	jīròu
chopsticks	kuàizi
cold	lěngle
cold beverage	lěngyǐn
to cook/boil	zhǔ
course (of food)	dào
dessert	tiándiǎn, diǎnxīn
diabetic	tángniàobìng
dinner	wǎnfàn, wǎncān
dish (of food)	cài
dish, plate	pánzi
done	shúle
dressing (salad)	shālajiàng
to drink	hē
duck meat	yāròu
to eat	chī
fat, oil	féi, yóu
filling	xiànr
fish	yú
fixed menu in restaurant	hétsài
flavor	wèidào
flavoring/seasoning	tiáowèi/hsiāngliào
food/dish of food	cài
fork	chāzi
french fries	shǔtiáo
fresh	xīnxiān
fried	chǎode
garlic	dàsuàn
glass	bōlíbēi
glass, tumbler	bēizi
gravy (meat)	ròuzhī
grilled	kǎo de
hard	yìng
homemade specialties	náshǒu cài, jiācháng cài
hot	rè

hot beverage	rè de yǐnliào
hot pepper/chili	làjiāo
to be hungry	èle
juice	guǒzhī
juicy	zhī hěn duō
knife	dāozi
lean	shòu de
lemon	níngméng
lunch	wǔfàn,wǔcān
meat	ròu
menu	càidān
mineral water	kuàngquán shuǐ
napkin	cānjīn
noodles	miàntiáo
oil	yóu
onion	yángcōng
order	diǎncài
paprika	jīngjiāo
pepper	hújiāo
pepper shaker	hújiāoguàn
plate	pánzi
pork	zhūròu
portion	fèn
pot/pan	guōzi
potato	tǔdòur
raw	shēng de
to reserve	dìng
rice (cooked)	fàn, báifàn
rice (uncooked)	mǐ
roasted	kǎode
salad	shālā
salt	yán
salt shaker	yán-guàn
saucer	dǐpán
to season	tiáowèi
seasoning	tiáowèiliào
to serve oneself	zìjǐ lái
sesame oil	máyóu

Since the Chinese eat with chopsticks, travelers from the West have the choice of knife, fork, and spoon or chopsticks usually only in the larger hotels. Everywhere else, only chopsticks are available. If you can't eat with chopsticks, you should bring along your own tableware, if at all possible. Even if you can

manage chopsticks, however, it is a good idea to carry your own pair of sticks since disposable chopsticks are not yet available everywhere in China, and in many parts of the country there is a risk of contracting hepatitis from sticks that have seen repeated use.

slice	piàn
smoked	xūnde
soda pop	qì shuǐ
soft	ruǎn
soup	tāng
soup spoon	tāngchír
sour	suān
sour/acidy/tart	suānde
soy sauce	jiàngyóu
specialty of the house	náshǒucài
spicy hot	là
stain/spot	wūdiǎn
steamed	zhēngde
steamed dumplings	bāozi
steeped	mènde
stewed/boiled	áode
straw	xīguǎn
stuffed (contains a filling)	bāo xiànr
sugar	táng
sweet	tián
tablecloth	zhuōjīn
tableware	cānjù
to taste	chángcháng
teaspoon	cháchír
tender	nèn
tip	xiǎofèi
toasted	kǎode
tofu	dòufǔ
toothpick	yáqiān
tough	lǎo
vegetables	shūtsài, qīngcài
vegetarian	sùshí
vinegar	cù
waiter/waitress	fúwù-yuán
water	shuǐ
water glass	bōlíbēi
well-done	quán shú
wine	jiǔ
wine glass	jiǔbēi

Menu

A Chinese meal consists of:

a soup, three to four dishes made of various types of meat, such as beef, pork, lamb, poultry, and fish, as well as an omelette and a vegetable platter. Normally the dishes are brought to the table at the same time (except at banquets, where they are served in a certain prescribed order). In northern China the soup generally is served after the other dishes, while in southern China it is served along with them.

*At home, it is not usual to drink alcohol with meals. When invited out to dinner or attending company parties or business dinners—especially if men are in the majority—the Chinese consume large quantities of beer, **shàoxīng** (a kind of rice wine), and high-proof spirits. Wine made from grapes, however, is rare in China.*

*Instead of rice, in some provinces you may be served **xiǎo mì zhōu** (barley soup), **yǐnshí juǎn** (pan-fried yeast dumplings), **mán tou** (salty yeast dumplings), or **cōng yóubǐng** (flatbread with scallions) as an accompaniment.*

In addition, the Chinese enjoy innards, such as intestines, stomach, kidneys, or liver.

Typical Chinese Dishes

bāozi	Steamed yeast buns filled with meat or sweet beans
jiǎozi	Dumplings stuffed with various kinds of meat, with crab, or prepared vegetarian style with tofu (either steamed or boiled in water)
gúotiē	Pan-fried dumplings, also called "pot-stickers," with pork and vegetable filling
húndùn	Small meatballs wrapped in a thin pastry, added to soup
níuròu miàn	Noodles with beef and some vegetables, usually served in broth
dāoxiāo miàn	Thick noodles mixed with various meats and vegetables
chǎo miàn	Thin noodles fried to a crisp, served with various kinds of meat
chǎo fàn	Crispy fried rice mixed with various meats and vegetables
huóguo	Mongolian "hotpot," a kind of fondue, with various accompaniments such as raw, thinly sliced meat, various vegetables, etc., prepared by the customer at his or her own table, in a pot with broth
shuān yángròu	Similar to huóguo, but the only meat used is thinly sliced lamb
huángyú sān chī	A fish served in three ways: 1. in soup, 2. boiled, 3. pan-fried
Běijīng kǎoyā	Duck roasted to a crisp in the Peking manner, also served in three ways (skin, meat, and soup), accompanied by leeks, a thick, black sauce, and thin pancakes in which the slivers of meat are wrapped
tāng	Among the soups are specialties prepared with abalone, sea urchin, turtle, and shark fin, as well as soups made with various mussels or clams

Vegetarian Dishes

Fó tiào qiáng	"Buddha leaps over the convent wall"
Luóhàn zhāi	Dish eaten by Lohans (Buddhist saints) during periods of fasting

Types of Dishes

shíjǐn	Chop suey containing various kinds of meats and vegetables
hóngshāo	Dishes boiled or braised in soy sauce
tángcù	Sweet-and-sour dishes

Special "Dim Sum" Dishes

chāshāo bāo	Steamed noodles with meat marinated in chashao sauce
shāo mai	Round, filled dumplings, open on top
fēng zhuā	Chicken feet

Chinese Desserts

bā bǎofàn	Sweet, sticky rice with "eight treasures"
xíngrén dòufu	Almond tofu with stewed fruit
zhīmá tángyuán	Sweet sesame balls in sauce
hóngdòu tāng	Sweet red bean soup
And of course, the world-wide favorite,	
bīng qī lín	Ice cream

Fish and Shellfish

bàngké	mussel; clam	jìyú	crucian carp
cǎoyú	grass carp	lǐyú	carp
fēiyú	herring	mányú	eel
guīyú	salmon	mòyú	cuttlefish/inkfish
huángyú	yellow croaker	mǔlì	oyster
jīngyú	whale	qīngyú	black carp
jīnqiāngyú	tuna	shādīngyú	sardine

shāyú	shark	yúchì	shark's fin
xiā	shrimp	yúròu	fish roe
xuěyú	cod	zūnyú	trout

Vegetables

báicài	Chinese cabbage	mógū	mushrooms
bōcài	spinach	mùěr	"tree ears" (edible fungus)
bōlícài	white cabbage		
cōng	onions; scallions	qiézi	eggplant
dòuyár	soy bean sprouts	qíncài	celery
fānshǔ	sweet potato	qīngjiāo	paprika
hǎidài	kelp	huángguā	cucumber
hóngluóbo	carrot	sìjìdòu	stringbeans
huācài	cauliflower	suàn	garlic
huángdòu	soy bean	zhúsǔn	bamboo shoots
jièlán	broccoli	tǔdòu	potato
jiāng	ginger	wǎndòu	peas
jīnzhēn	dried day lily (flower)	xiānggū	*xianggu* mushroom
luóbo	radish	xīhóngshì	tomato
lúsǔn	asparagus	yùtóu	taro root

Fruits

cǎoméi	strawberry	mùguā	papaya
fènglí	pineapple	píngguǒ	apple
hāmìguā	Hami muskmelon	pútáo	grapes
		shíliú	pomegranate
jīnjú	kumquat	táozi	peach
júzi	mandarin orange	xiāngjiāo	banana
liǔchéng	orange	xīguā	watermelon
lìzhī	lichee	xìngzi	apricot
lízi	pear	yīngtáo	cherry
lìzi	chestnut	yòuzi	grapefruit
lǐzi	plum	zǎozi	Chinese figs
mángguǒ	mango		

Beverages

Nonalcoholic Beverages

bīng hóngchá	iced (black) tea
bīng kāfēi	iced coffee
guǒzhī	fruit juice
júzizhī	orange juice
kāfēi	coffee
kāishuǐ	water (boiled)
kěkǒu kělè	Coca-Cola
kuàngquánshuǐ	mineral water
lǜchá	tea (green)
niúnǎi	milk
qìshuǐ	soda pop

Alcoholic Beverages

jiǔ	wine, liquor
báijiǔ, lièjiǔ	spirits; strong drink (distilled from grain)
báilándì	brandy
fútèjiā	vodka
mǐjiǔ	rice wine
píjiǔ	beer
shàoxīng huángjiǔ	Shaoxing rice wine
xiāngbīn jiǔ	champagne
wēishìjì jiǔ	whiskey
zā píjiǔ	draft beer

dàqǔ	
máotái	native Chinese spirits
wǔliángyì	

6 Culture and Nature
文化和自然环境

At the Tourist Information Office

lǔxíngshè

I'd like a map of …	wǒ yào yì zhāng … de dìtú.
Do you have a brochure that describes …?	yǒu méiyǒu jièshào … de shuōmíngshū?
Do you have this week's calendar of events/ program of cultural activities?	yǒu méiyǒu zhè xīngqī de wénhuà huódòng jiémùbiǎo?
Are there tours of the city?	yǒu méiyǒu yóulǎn chéngshì de jiémù?
How much does the tour cost?	cānjiā huányóu huódòng yào duōshǎo qián?
When does the tour bus leave?	yóulǎnchē shénme shíhou kāi?
May I trouble you to phone and inquire?	máfán nǐ dǎ diànhuà wèn yíxià, hǎo ma?

Places of Interest/Museums

míngshèng gǔjī/bówùguǎn

Are there places of interest to tourists nearby?	zhèr fùjìn yǒu shénme míngshèng gǔjī?
We would like to visit …	wǒmen xiǎng cān-guān …
the exhibition.	zhǎnlǎn.
the historical/cultural museum.	wénwùguǎn.
the museum.	bówùguǎn.
the palace.	huánggōng.
the park.	gōng-yuán.
the temple.	miàoyú.
When does the museum open?	bówùguǎn shénme shíhou kāi?
Admission is free!	miǎnfèi!
When will the guided tour begin?	shénme shíhou yǒu dǎoyóu jiěshuō?

Opening and closing times of Chairman Mao's mausoleum

Is there an English-speaking tour?	yǒu shuō yīngwén de jiěshuōyuán ma?
May we take photos?	ké-yǐ zhàoxiàng ma?
What is the style of this building?	zhè shì shénme fēnggé de jiànzhù?
Is this ...?	zhè shì ... ma?
When was it built/renovated?	shénme shíhou gài de/zhěngxiū de?

What period does this ... date from?	shì shénme shíhou de ...
building	jiànzhù?
work of art	zuòpǐn?
pottery	táoqì?
ink painting	shǔimò huà?

Are there other buildings in this same style?	hái yǒu tóngyàng fēnggé de jiànzhù ma?
Has the excavation work been completed?	fājué gōngchéng yijīng jiéshù le ma?
Where are the cultural artifacts on display?	fājué de wénwù chéngliè zài nǎr?

What artist did this painting?	nǎ wèi huàjiā huà de?
Is there a catalog for the exhibition?	yǒu méiyǒu zhǎnlǎn mùlù?
Are there reproductions/ postcards/slides available for ...?	yǒu méiyǒu ... de fùshì pǐn/míngxìn piàn/huàndēng piàn?

观光游览区	guānguāng yóulǎn qū	Tourist Area
博物馆	bówùguǎn	Museum
展览馆	zhǎnlǎnguǎn	Exhibition
名胜古迹	míngshèng gǔjī	Scenic and Historical Sites

Word List: Places of Interest/Museums

age-old culture	yōujiǔ wénhuà
altar	shéntán
ancient	gǔdài de
ancient city	lǎo chéng
ancient grave	shízhǒng
antique	gǔdǒng
antiquity	gǔdài
archaeology	káogǔ xué
architect	jiànzhú shī
architecture	jiànzhú wù
art	yìshù
artist	huàjiā
arts and crafts	gōng yì měishù
believer	jiàotú
bell/clock	zhōng
birthplace	chūshēngdì
bridge	qiáo
bronze	tóng
bronze age	tóngqì shídài
brush (for calligraphy)	máobǐ
Buddha	fó
Buddhism	fójiào
Buddhist	fójiàotú

building	jiànzhú
calligrapher	shūfǎjiā
calligraphy	shūfǎ
carpet/rug	dìtǎn

Buddhism, unlike China's other great religions, Taoism and Confucianism, is not Chinese in origin, but came to China through Central Asia in the first century A.D. Its development took an independent course, by integrating Taoist ideas into its teachings, for example. This variety of Buddhism is widespread in many different schools of thought in China and, in varying forms, throughout East Asia. Alongside it, however, there exist other schools of Buddhism, such as Lamaism, which is of Tibetan origin.

Buddha entering into Nirvana, at Mount Baoding near Dazu in Sichuan Province

castle	chéngbǎo
Catholic	tiānzhǔjiào
ceiling	tiānhuābǎn
century	shìjì
ceramics/pottery	táoqì
Chinese ink painting (no color)	shǔimò huà
Chinese lantern	huādēng
church	jiàotáng

city hall	shì zhèng
collection of paintings	shōucáng
column/pillar	yuánzhù

Guan Yu, the god of war, Luoyang, Shaanxi Province

A chronological listing of the dynasties will help you fit the buildings and events you learn about on your travels into a historical pattern.

Xia Dynasty	about 21st–16th century B.C.
Shang Dynasty	about 16th–11th century B.C.
Western Zhou Dynasty	about 11th century–770 B.C.
Eastern Zhou Dynasty	
Spring and	
Autumn era	770–476 B.C.
Warring States	
era	475–221 B.C.
Qin Dynasty	221–207 B.C.
Han Dynasty	206 B.C.–220 A.D.
Three Kingdoms	220–265
Jin Dynasty	265–420
Northern and	
Southern Dynasties	420–589

Sui Dynasty	*581–618*
Tang Dynasty	*618–907*
Five Dynasties	*907–960*
Song Dynasty	*960–1279*
Yuan Dynasty	*1271–1368*
Ming Dynasty	*1368–1644*
Qing Dynasty	*1644–1911*
Republic of China	*1911–1949*
People's Republic of China	*1949–*

Confucian	rújiā
Confucianism	rújiào
Confucius	kǒngzi
copy	mófǎng
cult of ancestors	jìsì
culture	wénhuà
customs and habits (of a people)	fēngsú xíguàn
design	shèjì
to destroy by fire	shāohǔi
dome	yuándǐng
domed building	yuándǐng jiànzhú
drum-tower	gǔlóu
dynasty	cháodài
embroidery	cìxiù
emperor	huángdì
empress	huánghòu
engraving; block print	bǎnhuà
entrance	dàmén
epoch	shídài
etching	tóngbǎnhuà
European opera	gējù
excavations	fājué
exhibit item	chénlièpǐn
exhibition	zhánlǎn

Chinese painting differs from that of Europe principally in that a painting is not slowly and gradually composed and developed, but is executed relatively quickly, in a single session, according to precisely defined models and with varying brush strokes. This requires that one master the individual steps perfectly and have some notion ahead of time of how the finished pic-

ture should look. The execution requires great ability to concentrate and often the painting process has to be repeated several times before the picture is in accordance with the artist's conception. The finished pictures usually are not framed, as in Europe, but wound on a roll.

There are three different subject areas in Chinese painting:

1. **Landscape painting** *is the most popular category, in which the landscapes generally are not based on a real example, but represent pure fantasy scenes, into which tiny towns, farms, ships, and individual people are integrated.*

2. **Flower and bird painting,** *in which arrangements of various flowers, bushes, and rocks, as well as birds, insects, and the like, are depicted, or individual motifs such as orchids, bamboo, plum blossoms, and chrysanthemums are singled out.*

3. In **figure and portrait painting,** *the subjects are chosen from historical personages like emperors and famous scholars or from the sphere of religion and philosophy (such as images of Confucius, Laotse, or famous Buddhist masters). An additional subject category includes figures from Chinese mythology, such as Fu Xi, to whom great cultural accomplishments are ascribed, or Zhong Kui, the destroyer of demons.*

facade	fángwū zhèngmiàn
fashionable	shímáo, liúxíng
feudal lord	zhūhóu
find/discovery	chūtǔwù
flying buttress	zhùtou
fortification	yàosài, guānkǒu
foundation	dìjī
frieze	bìzhuān
gallery	huàláng
garden	tíngyuán

Cave paintings, sculptures, and reliefs are found in the famous grottoes of Dunhuang, Yungang, and Longmen. These are Buddhist shrines that date from the time of Buddhism's gradual spread through China. They were established during the rule of the Toba, a non-Chinese tribe from Central Asia, at the time of the so-called Northern Wei Dynasty (386–534). The Toba declared Buddhism the state religion and thus contributed substantially to its spread. The caves and grottoes contain China's oldest and most beautiful Buddhist works of art. If you like art on a grand scale, don't miss them.

garden architecture	yuánlín jiànzhú
gardening	yuán-yì
Great Wall of China	chángchéng
grotto/cave painting	shíkū huìhuà
handicrafts	shǒu-yì
historic site	gǔjī
history	lìshǐ
Huns	xiōngnú
illustration	tújiě
incense/joss stick	xiāng
influence	yǐngxiǎng
ink	mòshǔi
ink stone	yàntái
inner-city	chénglǐ
inscription	bēiwén

Calligraphy *(shūfǎ),* the art of fine handwriting, is a recognized art form in China. Like Chinese painting, it is done with ink and brush, and the technique of rapid brush strokes is the same as well. The four principal styles of writing are: 1. The seal script, *zhuànshū,* 2. the official script, *lìshū,* 3. the cursive script, *cǎoshū,* and 4. the regular script, *kǎishū.*

insurrection/revolt	nèiluàn
king	guówáng
lantern	tídēng
library	túshūguǎn
lithograph	shíbǎn huà

Confucius (551–479 B.C.), China's best-known philosopher and sage, was the founder of Confucianism, a system of moral philosophy that seeks to teach mankind according to fixed rules and rituals. Among the chief virtues it promotes are humanity, love of one's parents, piety toward the spirits of one's ancestors, and righteous behavior toward one's fellow man. One who observes these rules of behavior is in harmony with heaven and can be termed a "noble human"; other people, in contrast, are considered "ordinary humans." This applies also to the rulers of the state, for harmony between heaven and earth and within society can result only from virtuous rule.

The influence of Confucius upon the religious life of the Chinese lies chiefly in the sphere of veneration of one's ancestors, which continues to occupy an important place in the life of every Chinese *family. Although his teachings went unrecognized during his lifetime, they have formed the basis of almost every dynasty since the Han era (221 B.C.–220 A.D.). The teachings of Confucius are presented principally in the "Analects" (Lunyu), the conversations of Confucius recorded by his pupils.*

In contrast, the Taoists, whose doctrine is based on the "Tao-te Ching" of Laotse, reject the notion of a life lived according to strict rules of behavior and rituals. Instead, they strive—with the help of mushrooms and herbs and through diet and exercises in breathing and meditation—to lead a "long life," in order to finally become "immortal." They consciously forsake dignity and the security of position in society and seek their salvation in "non-action," that is, in the passive life of a recluse who seeks to be in harmony with nature. From the mystical concepts of the early Taoists there developed two schools of religious thought. The southern school can be assigned to the category of folk religion; it involves magical, shamanistic, and exorcistic practices. This school can be described as a Taoist church with a leader, a well-developed liturgy, and a priesthood that conducts complicated ceremonies. The northern school consists largely of communities of monks, who live by self-imposed ascetic monastic rules and are heavily influenced by Buddhism. While Confucianism has determined the course of social life from time immemorial, Taoism has had a strong influence on the fine arts in China.

main gate	zhèngmén
marble	dàlǐshí
market	shìcháng
material	cáiliào
mayor	shìzhǎng
memorial/ commemorative area	jì-niàn dì
model	móxíng
modern	xiàndài
Mongols	ménggǔrén
monk	héshàng
monument/memorial	jì-niàn bēi
mosaic	mǎsàikè
moslem	húijiào
mosque	jīngchēnsì
mould pottery	niē táo
mural painting	bìhuà
museum	bówùguǎn

museum of ethnography	mínzú bówùguǎn
natural history museum	zìrán kēxué bówùguǎn
nun	nígū
opera (Peking)	jīngjù
Orient	dōngfāng

Monastery on the side of a cliff near Datong, Shanxi Province

Oriental	dōngfāng de
original	zhēnjī
pagoda	báotǎ
painter/artist	huàjiā
painting	huà, huìhuà
palace	huánggōng, gōngdiàn
pavilion	liángtíng
photocopy	yǐngyìn
to photograph	zhàoxiàng
photography	shèyǐng

The Peking Opera, **jīngjù** cannot be compared with a Euro-
pean-style opera. Although singing plays a major role, the
Peking Opera is more like a musical stage play that includes
dancing, acrobatics, and the Chinese art of boxing. Moreover, the
actors must master a repertoire of expressions and gestures and,
since few props are used, they must express activities like horse-
back riding or climbing by means of certain fixed movements. Important components of the Peking Opera are the clothing and

heavily made-up masks of the actors, which allow the audience to recognize the position and character of each figure. The orchestra, which consists chiefly of percussion and rhythm instruments, along with a few string instruments, plays only a secondary role.

The subjects treated by the Peking Opera are drawn from history or based on folk tales and religious legends. Usually the spectators have known them since youth.

*In addition to the Peking Opera, there are local operas, such as the Cantonese Opera **(yèujù)** and the Sichuan Opera **(chuānjù)**, in almost all the provinces.*

When you visit the Peking Opera, there is no need for evening wear, and the atmosphere and behavior tend to be rather relaxed. You can, for example, leave and re-enter the auditorium at any time, which probably is unavoidable, since a presentation can last up to six hours.

pilgrim	jìnxiāng de
pilgrimage	jìnxiāng
pillar	zhùzi
place of worship	zōngjiào shèngdì
playbill/poster	hǎibào

"Great Gander" Pagoda, Xi'an

plunder	huǐhuài
porcelain/china	cíqì
portrait	rénwùxiàng
pottery figure	táotǔ rénxiàng
prehistoric	shànggǔ
prime/chief minister	shǒuxàng
Protestant	jīdū jiàotú
public square	guángchǎng
realism	xiànshí zhǔ-yì
to reconstruct	chóngzào, chóngjiàn
relics/ruins	yízhǐ
relief (sculpture)	fúdiāo
religion	zōngjiào
religious service/worship	lǐbài

The best-known and most valuable Chinese porcelain dates from the Song era (960–1279) and the Ming period (1368–1644). While the pale green-hued porcelain of the Song Dynasty represents an early high pitch of perfection in Chinese ceramics, the art of making porcelain reached a truly advanced stage of development in the Ming Dynasty. By the middle of the sixteenth century, the East Indies Trading Company had begun to bring the famous blue and white porcelain to Europe.

Today, antique shops in China continue to offer so-called Ming porcelain, which can be only a forgery, of course, since genuine Ming porcelain is rarely available on the open market, and if it were to be put up for sale, its cost would be prohibitive.

replica/copy/imitation	fùshìpǐn
to restore/renovate	xiūfù
roof	wūdǐng
ruin	fèixū
sarcophagus	shíguān
school (of thought, creativity)	xuépài
sculptor	diāokējiā
sculpture	diāosù
sculpture/plastic art	diāosù/sùliào
sights/places of interest	míngshèng gǔjī
sketch	sùmiáo
statue	sùxiàng
statue of Buddha	fóxiàng
still-life	jìngwù huà

Stone Age	shíqì shídài
style	fēnggé
tapestry (used as wall decoration)	bìtǎn
temple	sìmiào
theater	xìjù
time of chaos	luànshí
tomb	fénmù
tombstone	mùbēi
tour	dǎoyóu, huányóu
tour companion/guide	quánpéi
tourist guide	dǎoyóu

*Temples usually are designated as **miào**, which refers chiefly to the temples of folk religion, in which extreme syncretism prevails; that is, both Buddhist and Taoist divinities are venerated in the same temple. The Confucian temples too, though less heavily frequented and used for a large ceremony only on the birthday of Confucius, are generally called **miào**.*

*Specifically Buddhist temples are called **si,** and specifically Taoist temples are known as **guàn** (shrine) or **gōng** (palace).*

庙	miào	
寺	sì	temple
观	guān	
宫	gōng	

tourist map	dǎoyóutu
tower	tǎlóu
travel/trip	lǚxíng
treasury/treasure vault	bǎokù
turret/corner tower/ watchtower	jiǎolóu
university	dàxué
vase	huāpíng
village arts/handicrafts	xiāngjiān shǒu-yì
visit	cānguān
wall	chéngqiáng
water color	shuǐcǎi

weaving	fǎngzhī
well	jǐng
window	chuānghu
wood carving	mùdiāo
woodcut	mùkē
work of art/literature	zuòpǐn
Zen Buddhism	chánzōng

Excursions

jiāoyóu

Can you see ... from here?	cóng zhèr kéyǐ kàndào ... ma?
In what direction is ...?	... zài nǎ ge fāngxiàng?
Do we pass by ...?	jīngguò ... ma?
Are we also visiting ...?	wǒmen yě cānguān ... ma?
How much free time do we have?	zìyóu huódòng duōcháng shíjiān?

Pavilion of Pure Sound in the Emei Mountains, Sichuan Province

When do we go back?	wǒmen shénme shíhou huíqu?
What time/When do we get back?	shénme shíhou huídào?

Word List: Excursions

amusement park	yóulèyuán
botanical garden	zhíwùyuán
canyon/gorge	xiágǔ
cave	dòngxuè
embankment walk/ promenade	yán-àn jǐngsè

Lotus blossom

excursion	jiāoyóu
farming family	nóngjiā
fireworks	yānhuǒ
fishing port/harbor	yúgǎng
forest	shùlín
forestry	shùlínxué
inland	nèilù
island tour	huándǎo lǚyóu
lake	hú
lookout/vantage point	guānjǐngtái
man-made lake	rén-gōng hú

market	shìcháng
mountains	shān

national park	guójiā gōngyuán
nature preservation area	zìrán bǎohù qū
observatory (astronomy)	tiānwéntái
ocean	hǎiyáng
passport	hùzhào
place	dìfāng
place of pilgrimage	jìnxiāng shèngdì
pond/pool	chítáng
reef	jiāoshí
rock	yánshí
scenery/landscape	fēngjǐng
stalactite cave	chōngrǔshí dòngxuè
suburb	shìjiāo
surroundings/environs	fùjìn
valley	shān gǔ
village in the mountains	shāncūn
volcano	huǒshān
waterfall	pùbù
wild bird sanctuary	yě-niǎo bǎohùqū
wildlife preserve	zìrán bǎohùqū
windmill	fēngchē
zoo	dòngwùyuán

Events/Entertainment

yúlè húodòng

Theater/Concerts/ Movies	jùchǎng/yīn-yuè huì/diànyǐng-yuàn
What movie is being shown today?	jīntiān yǎn shénme diànyǐng?
Where can I go to see the Peking Opera?	dào nǎr kàn jīngju?
What movie is playing tomorrow?	míngtiān wǎnshàng yǎn shénme diànyǐng?
What good play/movie can you recommend?	yǒu shénme hǎo de huàjù/diànyǐng?
When does the show start?	shénme shíhou kāiyǎn?
Is it being held in the temple?	zài miàolǐ jǔxíng ma?
Where can I buy tickets?	dào nǎr mǎi piào?
Two tickets for tonight.	liǎngzhāng jīntiān wǎnshàng de piào.
Your seat is in the middle/on the right/on the left.	wèizi zhōngjiān/yòubiān/zuǒbiān yìdiǎn!
Two adults, one child.	liǎng ge dàrén, yí ge xiǎohái.
The show is sold out.	kèmǎnle.
Is there a program?	yǒu jiémùdān ma?
When does the show end?	shénme shíhòu yǎnwán?
Where is the checkroom?	yīmàojiān zài nǎr?

售票处	shòupiào chù	ticket office
售完/客满	shòuwán/kèmǎn	sold out
电影院	diànyǐngyuàn	movie house
音乐会	yīnyuèhuì	concert
表演中	biǎoyǎn zhōng	performance in progress

Word List: Theater/Concerts/Movies

accompaniment	péibàn
act (of a play)	mù
advance sale	yùgòu
ballet	bāléiwǔ
box (in theater)	bāoxiāng
checkroom	yīmàojiān
choir	héchàngtuán
circus	mǎxìtuán
comedy	xìjù
composer	zuòqǔjiā
concert	yīn-yuèhuì
curtain	mù
dance hall; ballroom	wǔchǎng
dancer	wǔdào jiā
direction (play, movie, etc.)	dáoyǎn
director	zhǐhūi
drama	xìjù
fair; market fair	jíshì
festivity	qìngzhù huódòng
folk play	mínjiān xìjù
front row	qiánpái
intermission	xiūxi
jazz concert	juéshì yuè
leading role	zhǔjué
movie/film	diànyǐng
movie actor	yǎn-yuán
movie house	diànyǐng yuàn
musical	gēwǔjù
opera (European-style)	gējù

operetta	gēwǔjù
orchestra	yuètuán
outdoor movie theater	lùtiān diànyǐng-yuàn
outdoor theater	lùtiān jùchǎng
performance	yǎnchü, biǎoyǎn
performer/actor	yǎn-yuán
play/drama	xìjù
pop concert	liúxíng gēqǔ
premiere	shóuyǎn
program	jiémù
role (in play, drama, etc.)	juésè
script	jùběn
singer	gēxīng
soloist	dúzòu
stage	wǔtái
symphony concert	jiāoxiǎng yuè
ticket counter/ box office	shòupiào chù
ticket of admission	ménpiào
title	biāotí
tragedy	bēijù

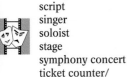

Bar/Discotheque/Nightclub jiǔba/dísīkē/yèzǒnghuì

酒吧	jiǔba	bar
迪斯科	dísīkē	disco
夜总会	yèzǒnghuì	nightclub
KTV	keitivi	TV
卡拉 OK	kǎlā o kei	karaoke
咖啡馆	kāfēi guǎn	café

What is there to do in the evening here?

zhèr wǎnshàng yǒu shénme yúlè xiāoqiǎn?

Is there a place that serves drinks/liquor nearby?

fùjìn nǎr yǒu hējiǔ de dìfāng?

Where can we dance?	nǎr ké-yǐ tiàowǔ?
Is it a place for young people or older people?	shì niánqīng rén háishì lǎo yìdiǎn de rén qù de dìfāng?
Must we wear formal dress?	děi chuān zhèngshì de wǎnlǐfú ma?
The entrance fee includes a drink.	rùchǎngfèi bāokuo yì bēi yǐnliào.
A beer, please.	lái yì bēi píjiǔ.
One more of the same.	tóngyàng de zài lái yì bēi.
I'll pay the check.	wǒ lái fùzhàng.
Would you like to dance (again)?	yào bú yào (zài) tiàowǔ?
Would you like to walk around a bit?	yào bú yào zǒu yì zǒu?

Word List: Bar/Discotheque/Nightclub

band	yuèduì
bar	jiǔbā
casino	dǔchǎng
to dance	tiàowǔ
dance band	yuètuán
dance hall	wǔtīng
dance music	wǔqǔ
disc jockey	liúxíng gēqǔ guǎngbòyuán
disco	dísīkē
doorman	shǒumén
fashion show	fúzhuāng biáoyǎn
fashionable place	gāojí yúlè chǎngsuǒ
folk activities	mínsú huódòng
folk customs; folkways	mínsú
folk music	mínsú yīn-yuè
to go out	chūqù
karaoke	kǎlā o kei
live music	xiànchǎng yǎnzòu

nightclub	yèzǒng huì
party	wǔhuì
show	biǎoyǎn
tavern/bar	jiǔguǎn
video game center	diàndòng wánjù yóulèchǎng

7 **On the Beach/Sports**
海滩/体育活动

At the Swimming Pool/On the Beach

zài yǔyǒngch/hǎibīn

Is there ... nearby?	zhè fùjìn yǒu ...
a swimming pool	yóuyǒngchí ma?
an indoor swimming pool	shìnèi yóuyǒngchí ma?
a hot water pool	rèshuǐ yóuyǒngchí ma?
One ticket, please.	mǎi yì zhāng ménpiào.
Deep water area!	shēnshuǐqū!
No diving!	jìnzhǐ tiàorù!
No swimming!	jìnzhǐ yóuyǒng!

禁止游泳	jìnzhǐ yóuyǒng	Swimming Prohibited
禁止乱丢垃圾	jìnzhǐ luàndiū lājī	Discarding of Rubbish Prohibited

Is the beach sandy or rocky?	hǎitān shì shāshí háishì yánshí?
Are there jellyfish in the water?	shuǐli yǒu shuǐmǔ ma?
Are the waves strong?	hǎilàng qiáng bù qiáng?
How far out is swimming allowed?	kěyǐ yóu duó yuǎn?
Is it dangerous for children?	dui xiǎohái wéixiǎn ma?
When is low tide/high tide?	shénme shíhou tuìcháo/zhǎngcháo?
I would like to rent ...	wǒ xiǎng zū ...
a boat.	yì tiáo chuán.
a sun umbrella.	yì bǎ chēyángsǎn.
a chair.	yí ge zuòwèi.
How much is it per hour/day?	měi xiǎoshí/tiān duōshǎo qián?

Although cultural highlights are the focus of tourism in China, anyone interested in a vacation at the beach can arrange such a stay at several beaches: Beidaihe in Hebei Province (the most accessible from Beijing), Qingdao in Shandong Province in the north, or Sanya, in the tropical climate of Hainan Island in China's extreme south.

海滨浴场	hǎibīn yùchǎng	bathing area
运动场	yùndòngchǎng	stadium/playing field
更衣室	gēngyī shì	changing/dressing room
冲澡间	chōngzǎo jiān	shower room
厕所	cèsuǒ	toilet
男	nán	men
女	nǚ	women

Sports

yùndòng

Among the indigenous Chinese sports, which were played predominantly at the imperial court, are a type of soccer (zúqíu), polo (mǎqíu), archery (gǒngjiàn) and Chinese boxing (quánfǎ).
Today, however, almost all the Western sports are played in China, with the most popular being table tennis, basketball, volleyball, and soccer, which were introduced by the English around the turn of the century.

What sort of sports events are there?	yǒu shénme tǐyu huódòng?
What sort of sports are available here?	yǒu shénme yùndòng shèbèi?
Is there a golf course/tennis court/race course here?	zhèr yǒu gāoérfū qiúchǎng/wǎngqiú chǎng/páomǎ chǎng ma?
Where can I fish nearby?	fùjìn shénme dìfāng ké-yǐ diào-yú?
I would like to see a soccer match/horse race.	wǒ xiǎng kàn zúqiúsài/sàimǎ.
When/Where will it be held?	shénme shíhou/zài nǎr jǔxíng?

How much is a ticket?	ménpiào duōshǎo qián?
I would like to go climbing.	wǒ xiǎng qù páshān.
Which route would be most fun to take?	nǎ tiáo lù bǐjiào hǎowán?
Where can I borrow/learn ...?	nǎr ké-yǐ jièdào/xué ...?
I would like to join a ... class.	wǒ xiǎng cānjiā ... de kèchéng.
What sport do you play?	píngcháng zuò shénme yùndòng?
I play ...	wǒ huì ...
I'm a ... fan.	wǒ zui ài ...
I enjoy going ...	wǒ xǐhuān qù ...
I like to play ...	wǒ xǐhuān dǎ ...
May I join in?	wǒ ké-yǐ cānjiā ma?

Word List: Beach/Sports

advanced class	gāojíbān
aerobics	yóuyǎng tǐcāo
air mattress	qìdiàn
athlete	yùndòngyuán
badminton	yǔmáo qiú
badminton racket	yúmáo qiúpāi
ball	qiú
basketball	lán qiú
bay	hǎiwān
beach towel	máojīn
beginner	chūxuézhě
boat rental	zūchuán
bowling	bǎolíng qiú
canoe	dúmùzhōu
changing room	gēng-yī shì
Chi-gong (Chinese form of exercise)	qìgōng
competition	bǐsài
course (of study)	kèchéng

deck/lounge chair	tǎng-yǐ
deep-sea fishing	yuǎn diào
defeat/lose	shū
to dive	qiánshuǐ
diving board	tiàobǎn
diving equipment	qiánshuǐ shèbèi
diving suit	qiánshuǐ yī
doubles	shuāngrén
draw/tie	píngshǒu
fencing	jiànshù
figure skating	huāshì huábīng
fishing; to fish	diàoyú
game	yóuxì
gliding	huáxiáng fēixíng
goal post	qiúmén
goalie	shǒumén
golf	gāoérfū qiú
golf clubs	gāoérfū qiúgùn
golf course	gāoérfū qiúchǎng
gymnastics	tǐcāo
half (of a game)	bànchǎng
handball	shǒu qiú
hiking path	jiànxíng lùxiàn
hockey	qǔgùn qiú
hockey stick	qǔgùnqiú qiúgùn
horse	mǎ
horse race	sàimǎ
hot springs	wēnquán
ice hockey	bīngchǎng jǔgùn qiú
ice skates	liūbīngxié
ice-skating rink	huábīngchǎng

Among the best-known of the Chinese sports that have found adherents in the West are the Chinese forms of competitive sport involving two contestants, which are known in the West under the name **gōngfu** *(kung fu, training), but in China are known collectively as* **wǔshù** *(martial arts).*
The origin of all these combative sports lies in the famous Shaolin Monastery in Henan, where, tradition tells us, the techniques were developed under the influence of Chan Buddhism (Japanese Zen). During the Tang Dynasty, a large number of monks were trained in the martial arts, and they are said to have saved the life of the Tang Emperor Tai Zong during an enemy raid.

Wushu

to jog	mànpǎo
jogging	mànpǎo
judge/referee	cáipàn
Judo	róudào
karate	kōngshǒudào
kung fu	gōngfu
lie down	tǎng-xialai
life preserver	yóuyǒng quān
lifeguard	jiùshēngyuán
long-distance running	chángpǎo
to lose (a game)	shūle
man-made lake; artificial lake	réngōng hú
martial arts	wǔshù
midpoint (station/stop)	zhōngtú zhàn
mini-golf	xiǎoxíng gāoérfū qiú
motorboat	qìtǐng
mountain climbing/ hiking	dēngshān
net (for tennis, etc.)	wǎng
parachute-jumping	tiàosǎn
pebble	xiǎo shítou
Ping Pong/table tennis	pīngpāng qiú
Ping Pong paddle	pīngpāng qiúpāi
private beach	sīrén hǎitān

program	jiémù
race	sàipǎo
racquet	wǎngqiú pái
result/outcome/score	chéngjī
to ride a bike	qí zìxíngchē
to ride a horse	qí mǎ
to row	huáchuán
row a boat	húachuán
rubber boat/raft	xiàngpí tǐng
sailboat	fánchuán
saltwater swimming pool	hǎishui yù
sand	shā
sand dune	shāqiū
sauna	sān wēnnuǎn
sea-water pool	hǎishui yóuyǒngchí
seaside bathing resort	hǎibīn yùchǎng
shower bath	chōngzǎo
singles	yí ge rén
ski	huáxuě
snorkel (for diving)	yǎngqì guǎn
soccer	zú qiú
soccer field	zú qiúchǎng
soccer game	zú qiúsài
soccer team	zú qiúduì
sports arena/stadium	yùndòng chǎng
starting time	qǐdiǎn
sun umbrella	yángsǎn
sunburn	shàishāng
to surf	chōnglàng
surfboard	chōnglàng bǎn
to swim	yóuyǒng
swimming pool	yóuyǒngchí
Tai Chi/Chinese shadow boxing	tàijíquán
team	tuántí sài
tennis	wǎng qiú
ticket	ménpiào
ticket office	shòupiào chù
title/championship match	guànjūnsài
track and field events	tiánjìng yùndòng
underwater goggles	qiánshuǐ jìng

victory	shènglì
volleyball	páiqiú
to walk/to hike	jiànxíng
water polo	shǔi qiú
to win (a game)	yíngle
windscreen	dǎng fēng píng
wrestling	shuāijiāo

齐备

公用电话
代办长途直拨

只售

8 **Shopping/Stores**
购物/商店

Questions/Prices

xúnwèn/jiàgé

Business hours	yíngyè shíjiān
Open/closed	kāimén/guānmén
Closed for vacation	xiūyè

营业中	yíngyè zhōng	open
暂停营业	zàntíng yíngyè	closed
休息中	xiūxí zhōng	on a break

Specially priced item	tèjiàpǐn
20% discount	dǎ bāzhé
Where can I find ...?	nǎr yǒu ...?
Where may I buy ...?	nǎr ké-yǐ mǎidào ...?
Can you recommend a ... store?	qǐng jièshào yì jiā hǎo de ... diàn gěi wǒ, hǎo ma?

What are you looking for?	nǐ yào shénme?
I'm just looking.	wǒ zhǐ yào kànkan.
I'd like to buy ...	wǒ yào mǎi ...
I'm looking for ...	wǒ zhǎo ...
Do you have ...?/Do you sell ...?	nǐmen yǒu méiyǒu ...?
May I see ..., please?	qǐng gěi wǒ kàn ...
a pair of ...	yì shuāng ...
a ...	yí ge ...
Please let me see something else.	qǐng ná biéde gěi wǒ kànkan.
Do you have a better grade/cheaper one?	yǒu méiyǒu hǎo/piányí yìdiǎn de?
I'd like this/I'd like to buy this.	wǒ yào zhè ge.
How much is it?	duōshǎo qián?
Can you make it a bit cheaper?	kéyǐ piányí yìdiǎn ma?

May I pay with …	wǒ kéyǐ fù…
US dollars?	měijīn ma?
a check?	zhīpiào ma?
a credit card?	xìnyòng kǎ?
a traveler's check?	lǚxíng zhīpiào ma?

Please wrap it up.	máfán nǐ bāo qǐlái.
I'd like to return something.	wǒ yào tuìhuàn dōngxī.

Although the Foreign Exchange Certificates (FEC), the only currency valid for foreigners, were eliminated in 1994 and only a single currency—**rénmínbì**—is in circulation today, there continue to exist state-run "friendship stores" set up for tourists, in which native arts and crafts are for sale at affordable prices.

In state-operated stores in China, the service usually is not very gracious. Don't let that irritate you, however; persist in your efforts, and with a little patience you will get the item you want. In addition to the state-run stores, private markets now offer a large selection of goods. The service here is friendly, but you need to bargain for lower prices.

Word List: Stores

antique store	gúdǒng diàn
art dealer	yìshùpǐn shāng
art shop	yìshùpǐn shāngdiàn
articles of daily use	rìcháng yòngpǐn
arts and crafts	yìshùpǐn
bakery	miànbāo diàn
barber shop/hairdresser	lǐfà diàn
beauty shop	měiróng yuàn
bookstall/newspaper vendor	shūbào tān
bookstore	shū diàn
boutique	fúzhuāng diàn
butcher shop	ròu diàn
candy store	tángguǒ diàn
cosmetics store/ perfumery	huàzhuāngpǐn diàn
department store	bǎihuò dàlóu
dry cleaners	gānxǐ diàn

*In the vicinity of temples or other places of interest, souvenirs such as sandalwood fans (Careful! Usually not made of genuine sandalwood!), silk, Chinese rolled paintings (scrolls), and traditional clothing, including quilted silk jackets and coats **(mianao)** and Chinese slit skirts **(qipao),** often are sold at market stands. At markets held by ethnic minorities, you can buy their carvings and native costumes, and at antique markets you will find Mao suits and caps, revolutionary devotional articles, and curiosities such as old coins from the era of the Republic (Careful! Usually counterfeit!) offered for sale.*

electrical appliance store	diànjì háng
fair/bazaar	shìjí
fish store	yú diàn
flea market	shìchǎng
florist	huā diàn
Friendship Store	yǒu-yí shāngdiàn
fruit store	shǔiguǒ diàn
furniture store	jiājù háng
grocery store	záhuò diàn, fùshí diàn, shípǐn diàn
hardware store	wǔjīn diàn
housewares	záhuò diàn
jewelry shop	zhūbǎo diàn
laundromat/laundry	xǐ yī diàn

Souvenirs/Keepsakes

bambooware	zhú shìr pǐn
cloisonné	jǐngtàilán
scrolls	juǎnzhóu
sandalwood fans	tánxiāng shàn
bicycle bells (bought for their unique sound)	chēlíng
lacquerware	qīqì
pearls	zhēnzhū
satin	chóu
silk	sī
quilted silk jacket	sīchóu mián-áo
rug	dìtǎn
ink painting (without color)	shǔimò huà

leathercraft store	píhuò diàn
mall	bǎihuò zhōngxīn
market	shìchǎng
musical instruments store	yuèqì háng
optician	yǎnjìng háng
pastry shop	gāodiǎn háng
pharmacy	yào diàn
photo shop	zhàoxiàng guǎn
record shop	chàngpiàn háng
second-hand stand/store	jiùhuò tān, jiùhuò diàn
shoe store	xié diàn
shoemaker	xié jiàng
souvenirs/keepsakes	jì-niànpǐn
sports equipment store	tǐ-yù yòngpǐn
stationery store	wénjù diàn
supermarket	chāojí shìchǎng
tailor	cáiféng
tobacconist	yānjiǔ diàn
toy store	wánjù diàn
travel agency	lǚxíng shè
vegetable stand	shūcài tān
watch repair	xiū zhōngbiǎo de

Groceries

shípǐn

What would you like?	yào shénme?
Please give me ...	qǐng gěi wǒ ...
one kilo of ...	yì gōngjīn ...
a pound of ...	yì jīn ...
100 grams of ...	yì bǎi gōngkè ...
10 slices of ...	shí piàn ...
a piece of ...	yí kuài/ge ...
a package of ...	yì bāo ...
a glass of ...	yì bēi ...
a can of ...	yí guàn ...
a bottle of ...	yì píng ...
a plastic bag.	yí gé sùliào dài.

What is this?	zhè shì shénme?
Is it edible?	kéyǐ chī ma?
How does one eat it?	zěnme chī?
Can one eat it raw?	kéyǐ shēng chī ma?
Must it be peeled?	děi bōpí ma?
A bit more, OK?	duō yìdiǎn, hǎo ma?
What else do you want?	hái yào shénme?
May I try it?	wǒ kéyǐ shìshi kàn ma?

Visitors are fascinated by the huge selection of fruits and vegetables available in such abundance, especially in southern China. Along with mangoes *(mángguǒ),* lychees *(lìzhī),* and guavas, which now are familiar in the West as well, at regional markets in the provinces of Guangxi, Guangdong, or Fujian you can find exotic fruits like Chinese dates *(zǎozi),* dragons' eyes *(lóngyǎn),* wax apples *(liánwǔ),* and many other kinds of fruits and vegetables that one rarely or never gets to see in the West.

Word List: Groceries

almond	xìngrén
apple	píngguǒ
apricot	xìngzi
asparagus	lúsǔn
baby food	yīng-er shípǐn, értóng shípǐn
bamboo	zhúzi
bamboo shoots	zhúsǔn
banana	xiāngjiāo
beans	dòuzi
beef	níuròu
beer	píjiǔ
bread	miànbāo
brown bread	hēi miànbāo
butter	huángyóu
cake	dàn-gāo
can	guàntóu
candy	tiánshí
carrot	hóng lúobo
cauliflower	huācài
celery	qín cài
champagne	xiāngbīn
cheese	nǎilào, qǐsī
cherries	yīngtáo
chestnuts	lìzi
chicken	jī
chicken meat	jīròu
Chinese cabbage	báicài
Chinese grapefruit	yòuzi
chocolate	qiǎokèlì
coconut	yézi
coffee	kāfēi
cooked rice	fàn
cookie	bǐnggān
corn	yù mǐ
crab	xiā
cream	nǎiyóu
cucumber	huáng guā
dark plum	suānméi
dates	zǎozi
dried fruit	mìjiàn

Poultry market in Guangzhou

dried mushroom	xiānggū
dried squid	yóu yú
eel	màn yú
egg	jīdàn
eggplant	qiézi
fish	yú
flour	miànfěn
fresh	xīnxiān
fruit	shuǐguǒ
garlic	dà suàn
ginger	jiāng
grapefruit	pútáoyòu
grapes	pútáo
green beans	lǜdòu
ground meat	jiǎoròu
ham	huǒtuǐ
herring	qīngdāo yú
honey	fēngmì
honeydew melon	hāmìguā
hot pepper/chili	qīngjiāo, làjiāo
ice	bīng
jam/marmalade	guǒjiàng
lamb (meat)	yángròu
leeks	suàn

lemon	níngméng
lemonade	júzi shǔi
lentils	bīndòu
liver	gān
lobster	lóngxiā
mackerel	qīng yú
margarine	shíwu yóu
meat	ròu
milk	niúnǎi
mineral water	kuàngquán shǔi
mushrooms	mógū
mussels	bànggé
mustard	jièmò
nectarine	mìtáo
noodles/macaroni	miàntiáo
nuts	hétáo
oatmeal	màipiàn
oil	yóu
olives	gǎnlán
onions	yángcōng
orange	liǔdīng
orange juice	liǔdīng zhī
orangeade	liǔdīng shǔi
organically grown	bù shǎ nóngyào de
oyster	mǔlì
parsley	xiāngcài
pastries/small cakes	xiǎo dàn-gāo
peach	táozi
peanuts	huāshēng
pear	lízi
peas	dòuzi
pepper	hújiāo
peppermint	bóhé
peppery; hot	là
pineapple	fènglí
plum	lǐzi
pork	zhūròu
pork chop	zhūpái
potato	tǔdòu
pumpkin	nán-guā
rabbit	tùzi
raisins	pútáo gān

red (grape) wine	hóng pútáo jiǔ
rice	mǐ
rice wine	mǐjiǔ
salad	shēngcài shāla
salt	yán
sardine	shādīng yú
sausage	xiāngcháng
scallions	cōng
shrimp	xiāren
smoked meat	xūnròu
soup	tāng
spinach	bō cài
spirits	báijiǔ, lièjiǔ
squid	mò yú
strawberries	zǎoméi
sugar	táng
tangerine	júzi
tea	chá
tea bag	chábāo
tea caddy	cháguàn
tea leaves	cháyè

Rice plants

toast	tǔsī
tomato	xīhóngshì
tuna	jīnqiāng yú
vegetables	shūcài
vinegar	cù
watermelon	xīguā
white (grape) wine	bái pútáo jiǔ
white cabbage	bōlícài
wine	jiǔ

Drugstore Items

shūxǐ yòngpǐn

Word List: Drugstore Items

anti-dandruff shampoo	qù tóupí de
baby bottle	nǎipíng
Band-aid	xiàngpí gāo
brush	shuāzi
cleansing lotion	rùn miàn rǔ-yì
clothes brush	yī shuā
cologne	gǔlóng shuǐ
comb	shūzi
condom	bì-yùn tào
cotton	miánhuā
cream	rùnfūgāo
deodorant	chúchòu jì
detergent	xǐdí jì/fěn
diaper	niàobù
dry skin/normal skin/ oily skin	gānxìng/pǔtōng/yóuxìng de pífu
electric razor	diàndòng guāhú dāo
eye shadow	yǎnliǎn gāo
eyebrow pencil	méi bǐ
eyeliner	yánbǐ
face towelette	qīngjié xǐmiàn zhǐ
hair band	xiàngpí jīn
hair curlers	fájuǎn
hair spray	pēnfǎ jì
hairbrush	shūzi
laundry detergent/ powder	xǐ-yī fěn

lipstick	kǒuhóng
lotion (body)	rùnfū jì
mirror	jìngzi
mouthwash	shùkǒu shuǐ
nail	zhǐjia
nail clippers	zhǐjia dāo
nail file	zhǐjia módāo
nail polish	zhǐjia yóu
nail polish remover	qù zhǐjia yóu
pacifier	nǎizuǐ
perfume	xiāng shuǐ
powder	xiāngfěn
Q-tip	miánhuā bàng
razor blade	guāhú dāopiàn
rouge	kǒuhóng
safety pin	bié zhēn
sanitary napkin	wèishēng mián
shampoo	xǐfǎ jīng
shampoo for dry/	gānxìng de/pǔtōng de/yóuxìng de
normal/oily hair	xǐfǎjīng
shaving lotion	guāhú shuǐ
shaving soap	guāhú zào
soap	féizào
sponge	hǎimián
spot remover	qù wū shuǐ
sunscreen factor	fángshài qiángdù
sunscreen lotion	fángshài gāo
sunscreen oil	fángshài yóu
tissue	miànzhǐ
toilet paper	wèishēng zhǐ
toothbrush	yáshuā
toothpaste	yágāo
tweezers	qiánzi
wash cloth	mǒbù

Tobacco Products

yāncǎo

One package of American cigarettes, with/without filters.	yì bāo měiguó de xiāng-yān, dài/méi yānzuǐ de.
Do you have American cigarettes?	yǒu měiguó de xiāng-yān ma?
Which brand is ... lighter? stronger?	nǎ zhǒng páizi bǐjiào ... bù qiáng? qiáng?
10 cigars/small cigars.	shí zhī xuějiā/xiǎo xuějiā.
One pack/package/can of tobacco.	yì bāo/yì hé/yí guàn yāncǎo.
One box of matches/A lighter.	yì hé huǒchái/yí ge dáhuǒjī.

Clothing/Leather Goods/Dry Cleaning

fúzhuāng/píhuò/xǐ-yī

Can you show me …?	qǐng géi wǒ kànkan …
What color?	shénme yánsè de?
I would like something in …	wǒ yào … sè de.
One to go with this.	pèi zhège de.
Can I try it on?	kéyǐ shìshi kàn ma?
What size do you take?	chuān duódà de?

On me it's too …
  tight/loose.
  short/long.
  small/large.

dui wǒ lái shuō tài …
  jǐn/kuān.
  duǎn/cháng.
  xiǎo/dà.

It fits. I'll take this one.	hěn héshì. wǒ yào zhè jiàn.
This is not what I want.	zhè bú shì wǒ xiǎng yào de.

I would like to buy a pair of … shoes.	wǒ yào mǎi yì shuāng … xié.
I wear size … shoes.	wǒ chuān … hào de.
They're too tight in the front/back.	qiántou/hòutou yǒu dián jǐn.
They're too narrow/wide.	tài jǐn/dà.
I'd also like some shoe polish/shoe laces.	hái yào xiéyóu/xiédài.
I would like to have the soles replaced.	wǒ yào huàn xiédǐ.
I would like to have the heels replaced.	wǒ yào huàn xiégēn.
I would like to have these clothes washed.	wǒ yào xǐ zhè xiē yīfu.
When can I pick them up?	shénme shíhou lái ná?

Word List: Clothing/Leather Goods/Dry Cleaning

artificial/synthetic fabric	rénzào xiānwéi
backpack	bèibāo
bathing hat/cap	yóuyǒng mào
bathrobe	yùpáo
belt (leather)	pídài
bikini	bǐjīní yóuyǒng yī
blouse	chènshān
boots	pí xuē
bow tie	lǐngdài jié
bra	nǎizhào
button	kòuzi, niǔkòu
cap	màozi
children's shoes	tóng xié
coat	dà yī
collar	lǐngzi
color	yánsè
cotton	mián de
cotton shorts	mián duǎn kù
dressing gown	chén páo
to dry-clean	gānxǐ
ethnic clothing	mínzú fúzhuāng
exercise clothes	yùndòng yī
formal dress; evening clothes	wǎn lǐfú
fur coat	diāopí dà yī
fur jacket	diāopí jiákè
gloves	shǒutào
handbag	shǒutí bāo
handkerchief	shǒupa
hat	màozi
to iron clothes	yùn yīfu
jacket	jiákè
jeans	niúzǎi kù
jogging pants	yùndòng kù
knitted jacket (cardigan)	máo yī jiákè
lady's handbag	nǚ yong píbāo
leather coat	pí dà yī
leather jacket	pí jiákè

leather pants	pí kù
linen	má de
lining	lǐzi
man's handbag	nányòng píbāo
miniskirt	mínǐ qún
muffler	wéijīn
pajamas	shùi yī
panties	sānjiǎo kù
pants/trousers	kùzi
parka	wàitào
plaid	fānggé de
pullover	máo yī
raincoat	yǔ yī
rubber boots	yǔ xié
sandals	liángxié
scarf	wéijīn
shirt	chènshān
shoe brush	xiéshuā
shoe polish	xiéyóu
shoe size	dàxiǎo
shoes	xiézi
shorts	duǎn kù
silk	sī
silk stockings	sīwà
skirt	qúnzi
sleeve	xiùzi
slip	chèn qún
slippers	tuō xié
sneakers	yùndòng xié
socks	duǎn wà, wàzi
sole (of shoe)	xiédǐ
stockings	wàzi
straw hat	cǎo mào
striped	tiáowén de
suit	xīzhuāng, tào chuāng
suitcase	xínglǐ xiāng
summer dress	xiàtiān de yángzhuāng
swim shoes/sandals	yóuyǒng xié
swim trunks	yóuyǒng kù
swimsuit	yóuyǒng yī
T-shirt	tīxu shān
terry cloth	máojīn bù

tie	lǐngdài
travel bag	lǚxíng dài
umbrella	sǎn
underpants	nèi kù
undershirt	nèi yī
underwear	nèi yīkù
vest	bèixīn
Western-style	xīshì
Western-style clothing	yáng zhuāng
woolen	máo de
workout clothes	yùndòng yī
zipper	lāliàn

Books and Stationery   书店/文具店

shūjí/wénjù

Do you have American newspapers or magazines?	nǐmen yǒu měiguó de bàozhǐ huò zázhì ma?
I want to buy a travel guide.	wǒ yào mǎi yì běn lǚyóu zhǐnán.

Word List: Books and Stationery

adhesive tape	jiāo dài
ball-point pen	yuánzi bǐ
city map	shìqū dìtú
colored pencil	sèbǐ
coloring book	túhuà běn
cookbook	shípǔ
envelope	xìnfēng
eraser (rubber)	xiàngpí cā
evening paper	wǎn bào
fountain pen	gāngbǐ
guidebook	lǚyóu zhǐnán
letter paper; stationery	xìnzhǐ
magazine (illustrated)	huàbào, zázhì
map	dìtú
newspaper (daily)	rì bào

note pad	xiǎo bǐjì běn
notebook	bǐjì běn
novel	xiǎoshuō
paper	zhǐ
paper clip	huìwén zhēn
paste	jiànghú
pencil	qiānbǐ
pencil sharpener	xiāo bǐ jī
playing cards	zhǐ pái
postcard (scenic)	fēngjǐng míngxìn piàn
road map	gōnglù dìtú
rubber band	xiàngpí jīn
sketchbook	huìhuà běn
spy novel	zhēntàn xiǎoshuō
stamp (for letters)	yóupiào
thumbtack	dà tóu chēn
wrapping paper	bāozhuāng zhǐ

Housewares

rìcháng yòngpǐn

Word List: Housewares

aluminum foil	xízhǐ
bottle opener	kāi píng jì
broom	sàobǎ
can opener	kāi guàn jì
candle	làzhú
chopsticks	kuàizi
dusting brush	xiǎo sàobǎ
dustpan	běnjī
garbage can	lājī tǒng
glass	bēizi
napkin	cānjīn
plastic bag	sùliào dài
pocket knife	xiǎo dāo
pot/pan	guōzi
silverware/cutlery	dāochā
sun umbrella	tàiyáng sǎn
thermos	bǎowēn píng

Electrical Goods and Photographic Supplies

diànjì/shèyǐng

I'd like to buy ...	wǒ yào mǎi ...
a roll of film.	yì juǎn jiāojuǎn.
color film/slide film.	cǎisè jiāojuǎn/huàndēngpiàn jiāojuǎn.
a 36/20/12 film roll.	sānshíliù/èrshí/shíèr zhāng de jiāojuǎn.
Please help me load the film.	qǐng bāng wǒ zhuāng jiāojuǎn.
Please develop this film.	wǒ yào xǐ jiāojuǎn.
Please make one copy of each negative.	měi zhāng dǐpiàn xǐ yì zhāng.
I would like to have this enlarged.	wǒ yào fàngdà.
What size?	shénme chǐcùn?
Do you want glossy or matte finish?	xǐ guāngmiàn háishì píngmiàn de?
When can I pick them up?	shénme shíhou lái ná?
The sooner the better.	yuè kuài yuè hǎo.
The release is broken.	kuàimén huài le.
The ... is broken. Can it be fixed?	... huài le. néng xiūlǐ ma?

Word List: Electrical Goods and Photographic Supplies

adapter (electrical)	biànyā qì, liánjiē chātóu
automatic release/ self-timer	zìdòng shèyǐng zhuāngzhì
battery	diànchí
black-and-white film	hēibái jiāojuǎn
bulb	dēngpào
calculator	jìsuàn jī
camera	zhàoxiàng jī
camera film	shèyǐng jī

cassette	lùyīn dài
CD/compact disc	xīdī piàn, jīguāng cípiàn
to develop film	xǐ dǐpiàn
dryer	chūi fēng jī
earphones	ěr jī
film	jiāo juǎn
flash unit	shǎn guāng dēng
flashlight	shǒudiàn tǒng
lens	jìngtóu
light meter	pùguāng biǎo
loudspeaker	lǎbā, guǎngbò
negative	dǐpiàn
passport photo	hùzhào zhàopiàn
plug	chātóu
Polaroid camera	pāi lì dé zhàoxiàng jī
positive	zhèngpiàn
record	chàngpiàn
release	kuàimén ànniǔ
shutter	guāngquān, kuàimén
slide film	huàndēngpiàn
tape recorder	lù yīn jī
telephoto lens	shè yuǎn jìngtóu
tripod	sānjiǎo jià
video camera	lùxiàng shèyǐng jī
video film	lùxiàng
video recorder/VCR	lùxiàng jī
videotape	lùxiàng dài
viewfinder	qújǐng qì
Walkman	suí shēn tīng

At the Optician

yǎnjìng háng

Please repair these eyeglasses.	qǐng xiūlǐ zhè ge yǎnjìng.
My eyeglasses are broken.	wǒ de yǎnjìng pòle.
I am nearsighted/ farsighted.	wǒ jìn/yuǎn shì.

What is the strength of your lenses?	duōshǎo dù?
The right/left is … strength.	yòu/zuǒ yǎn … dù.
When can I pick them up?	shénme shíhou lái ná?
I need …	wǒ xūyào …
contact lens storage solution.	yǐnxíng yǎnjìng báoyǎng jì.
contact lens cleaning solution.	yǐnxíng yǎnjìng yàoshuǐ.
I wear …	wǒ dài …
hard/soft contacts.	yìng/ruǎn de yǐnxíng yǎnjìng.
I'm looking for a pair of sunglasses/binoculars.	wǒ zhǎo yí fù tàiyáng yǎnjìng/wàngyuǎn jìng.
Please make out a receipt.	qǐng kāi zhāng shōujù.

At the Watchmaker/Jeweler

Biǎo diàn/zhūbǎo diàn

My watch is broken. Please have a look.	wǒ de biǎo huài le. qǐng nǐ kàn yí kàn.
I would like to buy a nice gift.	wǒ xiǎng mǎi yí ge hǎokàn de lǐwù.
What sort of stone/jewel is this?	shì shénme bǎoshí?
Is it a genuine …?	shì zhēn de … ma?
How much do you want to spend?	nǐ yào mǎi duōshǎo qián de?
I'd like something not too expensive.	bú tài guì de.

Word List: Watchmaker/Jeweler

18-carat gold	shíbā ke jīn
24-carat gold	(èrshísì ke) jīn
bracelet	shǒu zhuó
brooch	xiōng zhēn
coral	shānhú
crystal	shǔijīng
cultured pearls	réngōng péiyǎng de zhēnzhū
earrings	érhuán
gold-plated	dùjīn
jewelry	shǒushì
natural pearls	tiānrán zhēnzhū
necklace	xiàngliàn
pearls	zhēnzhū
pendant	xiàngliàn chüi shì
real/genuine	zhēn de
ring	jièshǐ
silver	yín
silver-plated	dùyín
turquoise	lánbǎo shí
wristwatch	shǒu biǎo

At the Hairdresser/Barber

zài lífǎ tīng

May I have my hair done right away?	mǎshàng kéyǐ zuò tóufǎ ma?
How long must I wait?	yào děng duōjiǔ?
May I make an appointment for tomorrow?	kéyǐ dìng ge míngtiān de shíjiān ma?
What hairstyle do you want?	yào shū shénmeyàng de fǎxíng?
A shampoo and a tint/set.	xǐ hé rán/tàng fǎ.
Shampoo and cut, please.	jiǎn hé xǐ.
Just a cut, no shampoo.	zhǐ jiǎn bù hsǐ.

I'd like …	wǒ yào …
a perm.	tàng tóufǎ.
a tint/dye.	rán fǎ.
Leave it long, please.	cháng yìdiǎn.
Just the ends.	zhǐ jiǎn shàngmian de yìdiǎn.
Not too short/A bit short.	búyào tài duǎn/duǎn yìdiǎn.
Take a little more off the back/front/top/sides.	hòu/qián/shàng/pángbiānr (zài) jiǎn yìdiǎn.
Don't cover the ears/Cover the ears.	búyào gàizhù ěrduō shàngmiàn/gàizhù ěrduō.
Part it on the left/right.	zuǒ/yòu fēn.
Tease it a little.	shū gāo yìdiǎn.
No hair spray/A little hair spray, please.	búyào/yào yìdiǎnr pēnfǎjì.
A shave, please.	wǒ yào guā húzi.
Trim my beard a bit shorter.	bǎ húzi jiǎn duǎn yìdiǎn.
I want a manicure.	wǒ yào xiū zhǐjia.

Thank you. This is fine.	xièxie. zhè yàng hén hǎo.
A bit shorter.	zài duǎn yìdiǎn.

Word List: Hairdresser/Barber

bangs	liúhǎi
barber	lǐfǎshī
beard	húzi
blond	jīnhuáng
to blow-dry hair	chūi tóufǎ
to color hair	ránfǎ
to comb	shū
curls	juánfǎ
dandruff	tóupí
dry hair	gānxìng de
eyebrow	méimáo
to get a shave	guā húzi
hair	tóufǎ
hair cut	fǎxíng
hair loss	diàofǎ
hair spray	pēnfǎ jì
mustache	bāzi hú
oily hair	yóuxìng de
part (in hair)	fēnxiàn
permanent	tàngfǎ
shampoo	xǐfǎjīng
to style hair	zuò tóufǎ
to tint hair	ránfǎ
trim	jiǎnduǎn
wig	jiáfǎ

9 **Services**
   日常事务

Money Matters 财务

cáiwù

Is there a bank nearby?	fùjìn nǎr yǒu yínháng?
When does the bank open/close?	yínháng shénme shíhou kāi/guān?

Branch office of a bank, Wuxi

I want to change US dollars/English pounds/ marks/schillings/ Swedish francs into Chinese currency.	wǒ yào bǎ … měijīn/yīngbàng/mǎkè/ xiānlìng/ruìshì fǎláng huànchéng Rénmínbì.
What is today's exchange rate?	jīntiān de huìlǜ shì duōshǎo?
One hundred US dollars is how much in Chinese currency?	yì bǎi měijīn huàn duōshǎo Rénmínbì?

The Chinese currency, rénmínbì, is divided as follows: 1 yuán (colloquially: kuài) = 10 jiǎo (colloquially: máo) = 100 fēn. You can exchange currency in the branch offices of the bank of China (Zhōngguo Rénmín Yínháng) and in all large hotels, which also accept internationally recognized credit cards.

I want to cash this traveler's check/bank check.	wǒ yào duìxiàn zhe zhāng lǚxing zhīpiào/yínháng zhī-piào.
What is the most I can make out a check for?	yì zhāng zhīpiào zui duō xiě duōshǎo qián?
Your withdrawal card/passbook, please.	nǐ de yínháng tíkuǎnkǎ.
Here's your passport!	nǐ de hùzhào!
Please sign here.	qǐng zài zhèr qiānmíng.
I would like to withdraw ... US dollars from my account.	wǒ yào cóng wǒ de zhànghù tí ... měijīn.
Have my funds/Has my money been transferred?	wǒ de qián huídào le ma?
Please go to the counter/window.	qǐng dào guìtái.
I ... only want bills. would also like some change.	wǒ ... zhǐ yào chāopiào. yě yào yì xiē língqián.
Give me four ... bills and the rest in change.	sì zhāng ... yuán chāopiào, qíta huànchéng língqián.
I have lost my traveler's check/passbook (withdrawal card).	wǒ bǎ lǚxíng zhīpiào/tíkuǎnkǎ nòngdiū le.
I want to report the loss of my traveler's checks/passbook and stop payment.	wǒ yào bào zhīpiào/tíkuǎnkǎ yishī zhīfù.

银行	yínháng	bank
柜台	guìtái	counter
付款	fùkuǎn	payment
提款	tíkuǎn	to withdraw
外汇	wàihuì	foreign exchange
储蓄	chúxù	deposit
贷款	dàikuǎn	loans/credit

Word List: Money Matters

account	zhànghù
American money	meijīn
amount (in an account, etc.)	jīn yé
ATM machine	zìdòng tíkuǎn jī
bank	yínháng
bank account	yínháng zhànghù
bank ID code	yínháng dàihào
bank remittance/ banker's order	fùkuǎn dānjù
bill (paper money)	chāopiào
cash/in cash	xiànjīn
to cash (a check, etc.)	duìxiàn
to cash a check	duìxiàn zhīpiào
cashier's/bank check	yínháng zhīpiào
change (coins)	língqián
check	zhīpiào
check charges	shǒuxù fèi
checkbook	zhīpiào bù
code	mìmì dàihào
coin	yìngbì
counter/teller's window	guìtái
credit/loan	dàikuǎn
credit card	xìnyòng kǎ
credit co-op bank	xìnyòng hézuò yínháng
currency	wàihuì
to deposit	cún rù
exchange foreign currency	wàibì duìhuàn
exchange office	duìhuàn suǒ
exchange rate	huìlǜ, duìhuàn lǜ
foreign currency exchange	wàihuì duìhuàn
foreign exchange	wàihuì
form	biǎogé
to make out a check	kāi zhīpiào
money/funds	qián
money order	huìkuǎn
to pay	fù
payment	fùkuǎn
postal money order	yóujú huìkuǎn
postal savings book	yóujú cúnkuǎn bù

receipt	shōujù
remittance	huìkuǎn
savings account	cúnkuǎn zhànghù
savings book	cúnkuǎn bù
service charge	shǒuxù fèi
to sign one's name	qiānmíng
signature	qiānmíng
telegraph remittance	diànbào huìkuǎn
traveler's check	lǚxíng zhīpiào
to withdraw	tíkuǎn

At the Post Office   邮局

zài yóujú

Where is the nearest post office/mail box?	fùjìn nǎr yǒu yóujú/yóutǒng?
How much is it to mail an air mail letter/a postcard to …	jìdào … de hángkōng xìn/ míngxìnpiàn yào duōshǎo qián?
the United States?	měiguó
Canada?	jiānádà
Three … yuan stamps, please.	sān zhāng … kuài de yóupiào.
This letter is to be mailed …	zhè fēng xìn jì …
registered.	guàhào.
air mail.	hángkōng.
express.	tèkuài.
How long does it take to get to America?	jìdào měiguó yào duōjiǔ?
Do you have commemorative stamps?	yǒu jì-niàn yóupiào ma?
This set of stamps, please.	zhè tào yóupiào.
One (stamp) of each kind.	měi yàng yī zhāng.

General Delivery

dàilǐng yóujiàn

Is there any mail for me? My name is …	yǒu wǒ de xìnjiàn ma? wǒ jiào …
No, there's no mail for you.	méiyǒu nǐ de xìnjiàn.
Yes, there is. Please let me see your ID.	yǒu. qǐng géi wǒ kàn nǐ de zhèngjiàn.

Telegrams/Faxes

diànbào/diànchuán

I'd like to send a telegram.	wǒ yào fā yì fēng diànbào.
Can you help me fill out the form?	nǐ néng bāng wǒ tián xià biǎogé ma?
How much is each word?	měi ge zì duōshǎo qián?
The basic fee is … yuan; for each word add …	jīběn fèi … yuán, měi ge zì jiā …
Can it get there today?	jīntiān huì dào ma?
Can I send a fax from here?	ké-yǐ zài nǐ zhèr fā chuánzhēn ma?

Word List: Post Office

address	dìzhǐ
automatic stamp dispensing machine	zìdòng fànmài jī
blank/form	biǎogé
charge	fèiyòng
COD	yóujú dàishōu huòkuǎn
collection	shōu yóujiàn
commemorative stamp	jì-niàn yóupiào
counter	guìtái
counter service times	guìtái yíngyè shíjiān
customs declaration	bào guān
declared value	jiàzhí
destination	mùdìdì
envelope	xìnfēng
express letter/mail	kuàixìn

fax	chuánzhēn
to fill out	tiánxiě
form	biǎogé
to forward	zhuǎnjì
hold until called for	dàilǐng yóujiàn
letter	xìn
mailbox	yóutǒng
mailman	yóudì yuán
main post office	yóuzhèng zǒngjú
package	bāoguǒ
parcel	xiǎobāo
parcel bill	bāoguǒ dān
post office	yóujú
postage/postal rate	yóufèi
postcard	míngxìn piàn
printed matter	yìnshuā pǐn
receipt (for mail, etc.)	shōujù
recipient (of mail)	shōuxìn rén
registered letter	guàhào xìn
to send (telegram, fax, etc.)	jì, fā
sender	jìxìn rén
stamp	yóupiào
to stamp	tiē
telegram	diànbào
telex	diànchuán
via air mail	hángkōng
weight	zhòngliàng
zip code	yóuzhèng dàihào

Telephoning 打电话

dǎ diànhuà

May I use your telephone?	ké-yǐ yòng nǐ de diànhuà ma?
Where is the nearest public telephone?	nǎr yǒu gōnggòng diànhuà?
May I purchase a phone card?	mǎi zhāng diànhuà kǎ?
Can you make change? I'd like to make a phone call.	néng huàn ge língqián ma? Wǒ yào dǎ diànhuà.

Do you have the phone book for …?	nǐ yǒu … de diànhuà bù ma?
What is the area code for …?	… de dìqū diàn huà hàomǎ shì duōshǎo?
Information, please look up the number for …	xúnwèntái, máfán chá xià … de diànhuà hàomǎ.
I'd like to place a long distance call to …	máfán nǐ jīe xìa … de chángtú diànhuà.
I want to make a collect call.	wǒ yào dǎ duìfāng fùfèi de diànhuà.
Please connect me to …	máfán jiē …
Please go to phone booth number …	qǐng dào dì … hào diànhuàtíng.
The line is busy.	zhàn xiàn.
There's no answer.	méi rén jiē.
Please hold the line.	qǐng shāo děng.
Hello, this is …	wéi, zhè lǐ shì …

*Chinese telephone subscribers usually don't identify them- selves when they answer the phone; like Americans, they simply say **Wéi** (Hello).*

Hello, who is this?	wéi, nín shì nǎwèi?
May I speak to Mr./ Miss …, please?	qǐng … xiānshēng/xiáojiě tīng diànhuà?

Telephoning in China is getting easier and easier. Both international calls and local calls can be dialed from most mid- range to top-end hotels, and card phones are even more wide- spread. In fact, card phoning is probably the cheapest way to place calls in China.
There are public pay phones on the street, similar to those we used to see at U.S. street intersections. If you are expecting a call, it's a good idea to tell the caller your room number or inform the operator that you're expecting a call and write down your name and number. The international access code is 011. To reach your party, add the country code, then the city code (remember to omit the 0 before it), and then the local number.

Dialing codes for international calls from China:

Country	Direct dial number
Australia	108-61
Canada	108-1
Japan	108-81
UK	108-44
USA	108-11 (AT&T), 108-12 (MCI), 103-13 (Sprint)

City codes for the major cities (all usually prefixed by 0; omitted when dialing):

Beijing:	10	Xian:	29
Shanghai:	21	Chengdu:	28
Tianjin:	22	Kunming:	871
Guangzhou (Canton):	20	Hangzhou:	571
Wuhan:	27	Fuzhou:	591
Nanjing:	25	Shenzhen:	755
Shenyang:	24		

Remember: To make a telephone call to China, you need to dial the international access code (011), then the code for China (86), then the city code (see above list), and, finally, the local number. Despite the country's size, there are no time zones in China. When it's noon in Beijing, it's noon all over China, but when it's noon in Beijing, it's 8 P.M. in Los Angeles and 11 P.M. in New York City.

This is he/she.	wǒ jiù shì.
I'll go and call him/her.	wǒ qù jiào tā.

Sorry, he/she is not in at the moment.	duìbùqǐ, tā xiànzài bú zài.
When will he/she return?	tā shénme shíhou huílái?
Would you like him/her to return the call?	yào tā huí diànhuà ma?
Yes, my phone number is …	hǎo, wǒ de diànhuà hàomǎ shì …
Do you want to leave a message?	yào liú huà ma?
Please tell him/her that I called.	qǐng gàosù tā, wǒ dǎ le diànhuà.
Please give him/her a message.	máfán nǐ gàosù tā, hǎo ma.
I'll call back later.	wǒ děng yí xià zài dǎ.
Wrong number.	dǎ cuò le.
The number you have dialed is not in service.	nǐ dǎ de hàomǎ shì kōnghào.

Word List: Telephoning

to answer the phone	jiē diànhuà
area code	diànhuà dìqū hàomǎ
business telephone directory	gōngsī diànhuà hàomǎ bù
busy	zhànxiàn
busy signal	wōngwong shēng
charge	fèiyòng
coin/change machine	yìngbì duìhuàn jī
collect call	duìfāng fùfèi
connection	xiànlù
to dial a number	bō diànhuà
to dial direct	zhí bō
information	xúnwèn chù
international call	guójì diànhuà
local call/in-city call	shìnèi diànhuà
long-distance call	chángtú diànhuà
to make a telephone call	dǎ diànhuà
operator	jiēxiàn yuán
pay phone	tóubì diànhuà jī
person-to-person call	gēn zǒngjī yùjiē de diànhuà
phone fax	diànhuà chuánzhēn
repair service	gùzhàng xiūjiǎn bùmén

telephone	diànhuà
telephone answering machine	zìdòng lùhuà jī
telephone book	diànhuà bù
telephone booth	diànhuà tíng
telephone box/call box	diànhuà jiān
telephone call	diànhuà
telephone calling card	diànhuà kǎ
telephone company office	dìanhuà jú
telephone number	diànhuà hàomǎ
telephone switchboard	diànhuà zǒngjī
unit of charge	fèiyòng jìsuàn dānwèi

At the Police Station

jǐngchájú

▶ See also Chapter 3, A Traffic Accident

Where is the nearest police station?	fùjìn nǎr yǒu jǐngchá jú?

Police station in Guangzhou (Canton)

I want to report a theft/ loss/car accident.	wǒ yào bào tōuqiè/yíshī/chēhuò bàojǐng.

If something is stolen, get the advice of the hotel staff about reporting the theft to the local office of the Foreign Affairs Branch of the Public Security Bureau (that is, the police). Be prepared for a good deal of red tape.

In any event, it is worthwhile to purchase travel insurance before you start your trip. Try to obtain a loss report from the Foreign Affairs Branch so that you can claim compensation if the stolen articles are not recovered.

警察局	jǐngchájú	police
公安局	gōngānjú	public security office
交警队	jiāojǐngduì	traffic corps
交通警察	jiāotōng jǐngchá	traffic police
派出所	pàichūsuǒ	police substation
大使馆	dàshǐguǎn	embassy
领事馆	lǐngshìguǎn	consulate

My ... has been stolen.	wǒ de ... bèi tōu le.
handbag	shǒutíbāo
wallet	qiánbāo
camera	zhàoxiàngjī
car/bicycle	qìchē/zìxíngchē
I've been assaulted.	wǒ bèi qiǎng le.
The ... in my car has been stolen.	chē lǐ de ... bèi tōu le.
My ... has been lost.	wǒ de ... diū le.
My son/daughter has been missing for two days.	wǒ de érzi/nǚér yǐjīng liǎng tiān shīzōng le.
This person is bothering me.	zhè ge rén zhǎo wǒ máfán.
Please help.	bāngbang máng.

When did it occur?	shénme shíhou fāshēng de?
We will investigate.	wǒmen huì diàochá de.
I have nothing to do with this.	wǒ gēn zhè ge méi shénme guānxi.
Write down your name and address.	xiě xià nǐ de xìngmíng hé dìzhǐ.
Please contact the US/German/Austrian/Swiss consulate/embassy.	qǐng gēn meiguo/déguó/àodìlì/ruìshì lǐngshìguǎn/dàshǐguǎn liánluò.

Word List: Police

to annoy	zhǎo máfán
to arrest	bèibǔ
to beat up	ōudǎ
to break open/in	tōuqiè
car license	qìchē zhízhào
check (drawn on a bank)	zhīpiào
to confiscate	mòshōu
court	fǎtíng
crime	fàn zuì
custody/detention	jūliú
documents/papers	wénjiàn
drugs/narcotics	dúpǐn
fault	guòcuò
ID	shēnfèn zhèng
jail/prison	jiān-yù
judge (in court of law)	fǎguān
key	yàoshi
lawyer	lǜshī
to lose	diū le
money	qián
passport	hùzhào
pickpocket	páshǒu
police	jǐngchá
police car	jǐngchē
rape	qiángjiān
to report to the police	bàojǐng

robbed	bèi qiǎng
smuggling	zǒusī
theft	tōuqiè
thief	xiǎotōu
wallet	píjiā, qiánbāo

Lost and Found Office

shīwù zhāolǐngchù

Where is the lost and found office?	nǎr yǒu shīwù zhāolǐngchù?
I have lost ...	wǒ diū le ...
I've left my handbag on the train.	wǒ bǎ shǒutíbāo wàng zài huǒchē lǐ.
If you find it, please notify me.	rúguǒ zhǎodào le, qǐng tōngzhī wǒ.
Here is my hotel/home address.	zhè shì wǒ fàndiàn/jiāxiāng de dìzhǐ.

10 Health
保健

At the Pharmacy	药房/药店

zài yàodiàn

Where is the nearest pharmacy?	fùjìn nǎr yǒu yàodiàn?
Do you have a medicine to cure …?	yǒu méiyǒu zhì … de yào?
Chinese medicine or Western medicine?	zhōngyào háishì xīyào?

*In China there are both Western pharmacies that also carry Chinese remedies and purely traditional Chinese pharmacies that purvey Chinese medications exclusively. These are preparations of plant, animal, and mineral origin, as described by the great physician and pharmacologist **Li Shizhen** at the end of the Ming era in his famous pharmacological work "**Běncǎo Gāngmù.**" Many travelers find it a good idea to assemble a basic first-aid kit of common medications and take it along to China.*
Generally, larger cities like Beijing and Shanghai have adequate medical facilities. That is not true of remote areas like Mongolia or Tibet.

How much should I take (per dose)?	yào chī duōshǎo?
Does it also come in pill form?	yǒu méiyǒu yàowán?
Is the medicine very strong?	yàolì hěn qiáng ma?

Word List: Pharmacy ▶ See also Word List: Doctor/Dentist/Hospital

after eating	chīfàn hòu
anti-diarrhea medicine	zhǐ xiè yào
antibiotic	kàngshēng sù
antidote	jiědú yào
aspirin	ā sī pǐ lín
Band-Aid	gāoyào
bandage	bēngdài
before eating	chīfàn qián
burn salve	shāoshāng yàogāo
capsule	jiāonǎng
chamomile tea	gānjú chá

Chinese medicine shop	zhōngyào diàn
circulation	xúnhuán xìtǒng
condom	bì-yùn tào
contraceptive/the "pill"	bì-yùn yào
cough lozenge	zhǐké táng
cough medicine	zhǐké yào
cough syrup	zhǐké yàoshuǐ
disinfectant	xiāodú yàoshuǐ
drops	yàoshuǐ, yàojì
ear drops	ěrduō yàojì
external use	wàiyòng
eyedrops	yǎnyào shuǐ
gauze	shābù
glucose	pútáo táng
headache medicine	tóutòng yào
herbal medicines	yàocǎo
insect repellent (ointment)	fáng chóng gāo
insulin	yídǎo sù
internal use (only)	nèiyòng
iodine	diǎnjiǔ
laxative	xièyào
let dissolve in the mouth	hán zài kǒulǐ
medicinal powder	yàofěn
medicine	yào
medicine to cure ...	zhì ... de yào
mosquito bite	wénchóng yǎoshāng
mouthwash (bacterial)	xiāodú sùkǒu shuǐ
on an empty stomach	jìn shí
painkiller	zhǐtòng yào
prescription	yàofāng
salve	yàogāo
side-effects	fù zuòyòng
sleeping pill	ānmián yào
sterilized cotton	yàomián
suppository	yàosāi
stomach medicine	wèiyào
sunburn	shàishāng
tablet	yàowán, yàopiàn
to take (medicine)	fú, chī
talcum powder	shuǎngshēn fěn
thermometer	tǐwēn jì
throat lozenge	hóu piàn
tranquilizer	zhènjìng yào
Western pharmacy	xīyào diàn

At the Doctor   看病

kànbìng

In an emergency you can reach the following emergency services by telephone:

Ambulance, Tel: 120
(bilingual, English and Chinese)
International SOS First Aid Center, Tel: 5003419
(bilingual, English and Chinese)
International First Aid Center for Asia, Tel: 5053521-5
(bilingual, English and Chinese)

Alternatively, you can contact one of the following embassies:
United States Embassy, Beijing
3 Xiushui Beijie (Tel: 532 3831; fax: 532 6057)
Canadian Embassy, Beijing
19 Dongzhimenwai Dajie (Tel: 532 3536; fax: 532 40725)
British Embassy, Beijing
11 Guanghua Lu (Tel: 532 1961; fax: 532 1939)
Swiss Embassy, Beijing
3 Sanlitun Dongwujie, Beijing (Tel: 532 2736; fax: 532 4353)
The United States, Canada, France, Germany, Japan, and Britain, among others, also maintain consulates in Shanghai.

Would you please recommend a good …	máfán nǐ jièshào yí ge hǎo de …
doctor.	yīshēng.
eye doctor.	yǎn kē yīshēng.
obstetrician and gynecologist (OB-GYN).	fùchǎn kē yīshēng.
ear, nose, and throat doctor.	ěr bí hóu kē yīshēng.
dermatologist.	pífū kē yīshēng.
herbalist/herbal specialist.	cǎoyào shī.
internist.	nèi kē yīshēng.
pediatrician.	xiǎoér kē yīshēng.
neurologist.	shénjīng kē yīshēng.
urologist.	mì-niào kē yīshēng.
dentist.	yá yī.

Where is his clinic?	tā de zhěnsuǒ zài nǎr?
What are the clinic hours?	shénme shíhou ménzhěn?
Where do you hurt?	yǒu shénme téngtòng?
I am not feeling well.	wǒ bù tài shūfu.

内科	nèi kē	internal medicine
外科	wài kē	surgery
牙科	yá kē	dentistry
耳鼻喉科	ěrbíhóu kē	ear, nose, throat department
妇产科	fùchǎn kē	gynecology and obstetrics
小儿科	xiǎoér kē	pediatrics
中医	zhōngyī	Chinese medicine
急诊	jízhěn	emergency

I have a fever.	wō fāshāo.
I can't sleep.	wǒ shùi bù zháo.
I often feel nauseous/ dizzy.	wǒ cháng xiǎng tù/tóu yūn.
I fainted.	wǒ hūn le guòqù.
I have a bad cold.	wǒ gǎnmào hěn lìhài.
My head/throat hurts./ I have a cough.	wǒ tóutòng./hóulóng tòng/késòu.
I've been stung/bitten.	wǒ bèi dīng/yǎo le.
I have an upset stomach.	wǒ wèi bù shūfu.
I've got diarrhea/ constipation.	wǒ fùxiè/biànmì.
I'm not used to the food/climate here.	wǒ bù xíguàn zhèlǐ de shíwù/ tiānqi.
I've been hurt.	wǒ shòushāng le.
I've fallen.	wǒ diédǎo le.
I'm afraid that I've broken/twisted my ...	wǒ pà wǒ bǎ ... diéduàn/niǔshāng le.

Where does it hurt?	nǎr tòng?
It hurts here.	zhè lǐ tòng.
Does it hurt here/Does this hurt?	zhèr tòng ma?
I've got high/low blood pressure.	wǒ yǒu gāo/dī xuěyā.
I've got diabetes.	wǒ yǒu tángniào bìng.
I'm pregnant.	wǒ huái yùn.
I've just …	gānggāng wǒ …
Please pull up/roll up your clothes/sleeve.	qǐng bǎ yīfu/xiùzi lā qǐlái.
Breathe deeply. Then hold your breath.	shēn hūxī, tíng.
Open wide.	dǎkāi zǔi.
Let me see your tongue.	ràng wǒ kànkan nǐ de shétóu.
Please cough.	qǐng ké jǐ shēng.
How long have you felt like this?	zhèyàng yijīng duōjiǔ le?
How's your appetite?	wèikǒu zěnmeyàng?
I have no appetite.	méi wèikǒu.
Have you been inoculated against …?	nǐ dǎguò … yùfáng zhēn le ma?
I have been inoculated against …	wǒ dǎguò … yùfáng zhēn.
You must have an X ray.	nǐ děi zhào X-guāng.
I want to test your blood/urine.	wǒ yào yàn xuě/niào.
I have to send you to a specialist.	wǒ děi bǎ nǐ sòngdào zhuānkē yīyuàn.

You need an operation.	wǒmen bìxū kāidāo.
You ought to rest for a few days.	nǐ yīnggāi jìngyǎng jǐ tiān.
It's nothing serious.	bú shì shénme yánzhòng de.
Would you please prescribe a medicine for …?	máfán nǐ kāi diǎn zhǐ … de yào, hǎo ma?
Normally I take …	píngcháng wǒ fúyòng …
Before going to bed take one pill/tablet/package.	shuì qián fú yí lì/piàn/bāo.
Would you please write out a certificate?	máfán nǐ kāi ge zhèngmíng?

At the Dentist 看牙医

kàn yáyī

My tooth hurts.	wǒ yáchǐ hěn tòng.
The upper/lower/front/back tooth hurts.	shàng/xià/qián/hòu miàn de nà kē zài tòng.
The filling has fallen out.	bǔyá tiánliào diào le.
A tooth has broken.	yì kē yá duàn le.
You must have a filling.	děi bǔ yá.
We'll fix it temporarily.	zànshí chǔlǐ.
The tooth must be pulled.	děi bá yá.
We must do a crown.	děi zuò chǐguàn.
I would like anesthesia./I don't want anesthesia.	wǒ yào mázuì./bú yào mázuì.
Please rinse.	qǐng sùkǒu.
Can you repair my denture?	máfán nǐ xiū xià jiǎyá?

Please come back in a couple of days for a follow-up.	liǎng tiān hòu zài lái zuò jiǎnchá.
As soon as you get back home, please see your dentist.	huíguó hòu mǎshàng qù kàn yīshēng.

In the Hospital   在医院

zài yìyuàn

How long must I stay in the hospital?	wǒ děi zài yī-yuàn dāi duōjiǔ?
What tests are to be done?	yào zuò nǎxiē jiǎnchá?
I can't sleep./It hurts.	wǒ shuì bù zháo./tòng de bùnéng shuìjiào.
Please give me a tablet to stop the pain/help me sleep.	qǐng gěi wǒ yí lì zhǐtòng/ānmián yào.
When may I get out of bed/go out?	shénme shíhou ké-yǐ xià chuáng/chūqù?
Please give me a certificate stating the diagnosis and the length of my hospital stay.	máfán nǐ kāi ge zhěnduàn zhùyuàn zhèngmíng.

收费处	shōufèi chù	billing
挂号室	guàhào shì	registration
药房	yàofáng	pharmacy

Word List: Doctor/Dentist/Hospital

In all large Chinese hospitals, along with the departments of Western medicine there is also a department of traditional Chinese medicine. Every hospital has its own affiliated pharmacy, where you can pick up the medicines prescribed after paying at the cashier's desk. The medicines are also prepared and mixed here.

*The basis of Chinese medicine is the diagnosis, which is made by a special method of feeling the pulse and examining the tongue. Then treatment with medicines, acupuncture, moxibustion, cupping, or pressure massage (**àn mó**) ensues. The use of **acupuncture,** in which a healing process is induced by insertion of needles at the so-called acupuncture points, is now widely known in the West as well. **Moxibustion** involves the use of meadow mugwort, dried and formed into small pellets, which are placed on the acupuncture points and burned. That causes a skin irritation that sets the healing effect in motion. In **cupping,** these points are stimulated by the application of small hollow glass cups and the vacuum resulting when the cups are partially evacuated by heating. That produces a therapeutic effect. In **pressure massage,** again, certain acupuncture points on the body (for example, points on the feet) are pressed and massaged with the fingers in order to intensify the healing process.*

abdominal pain	fù tòng
abortion	duòtāi
abscess	nóngzhǒng
ache/pain	tòng
acupuncture	zhēn jiū
addicted	yǒu yǐn
addicted to drugs	xīdú
AIDS	àizī bìng
alcoholic	xùjiǔ
to be allergic to	dui ... guòmǐn
allergy	guòmǐn
anesthesia	chuánshēn mázui
angina	jiǎo tòng
anklebone	huáigǔ
apoplectic fit	nǎo chōng xuě
appendicitis	mángcháng yán
appendix	mángcháng

arm	shǒubèi
artery	dòngmài
artificial heart	réngōng xīnzàng
asthma	qì chuǎn
attack/seizure	fāzuò
back	bèi
backache	bèi tòng
bandage	bēndài
to bandage	bāozā
bite	yǎoshāng
to bleed	liú xuě
blister	shuǐpào
blood	xuě
blood transfusion	shū xuě
blood type	xuěxíng
blood vessel	xuéguǎn
bone	gǔtóu
bone fracture	gǔ zhé
bowel movement	páibiàn
brain	tóunǎo
break	duànlìe
breast	xiōng bù
to breathe	hūxī
broken/fractured	duàn le
bronchial tubes	chīqì guǎn
bronchitis	chīqìguǎn yán
bruise/contusion	jīngchǒng
burn injury	shāo shāng
cancer	ái zhèng
cardiac defect	xīnzàng bànmó bìng
cardiac infarct	xīnqī gěngsài
to catch cold/flu	gǎnmào
chicken pox	fēng zhěn
cholera	huòluàn
circulatory disorder	xuěyì xúnhuán shītiáo
clinic/doctor's office	zhénsuǒ
cold	liú bítì, shāngfēng
collarbone	suǒ gǔ
concussion	nǎo zhèndàng
constipation	biànmì
convulsion/spasm/ cramp	jìngluán
cough	késòu
cut (injury)	gē shāng

diabetes	tángniào bìng
diagnosis	zhěnduàn
diarrhea	fùxiè
diet	jié shí
difficulty in breathing	hūxī bú shùn
digestion	xiāohuà
diphtheria	báihóu
disease	jíbìng
to disinfect	xiāodú
dizziness	tóu yūn
ear	ěrduō
eardrum	gǔ mó
elbow	zhóuzi
epilepsy	diānxián bìng
esophagus	shídào
examination	jiǎnchá
eye	yǎnjīng
face	liǎn
faint/unconsciousness	hūnmí
false teeth/denture	jiǎ yá
to fester	huà nóng
fever	fāshāo
filling (tooth)	bǔ zhùyá
finger	shóuzhǐ
flatulence/gas	zhàngqì
flu	liúxíng xìng gǎnmào
food poisoning	shíwù zhòngdú
foot	jiǎo
gall bladder	dǎnnáng
German measles	fēng zhěn
gland	fēnmì
hand	shǒu
hay fever	huāfěn rè
head	tóu
headache	tóu tòng
health insurance certificate	jiànkāng báoxiǎn dān
heart	xīnzàng
heart attack	xīnzàng bìng fāzuò
heart specialist	xīnzàng bìng zhuānjiā
heart trouble	xīnzàng bìng
heartburn	wèi suān tòng
hematoma	xuézhǒng
hemorrhoids/piles	zhìchuāng

high/low blood pressure	gāo/dī xuěyā
hip	yāobù
HMO/health insurance company	jiànkāng báoxiǎn gōngsī
to be hoarse	shā yǎ
hospital	yīyuàn
to hurt/to ache	tòng
infantile paralysis/polio	xiǎoér mábì
infection	gánrǎn
infectious/contagious	chuán rǎn
inflammation	fā yán
infusion	guàn diǎndī
injection	dǎ zhēn
to injure	shòu shāng
injury	shòushāng
insomnia	shīmián
intestines	chángzi
itch(ing)	fāyǎng
jaundice	huángdǎn bìng
jaw	xiàba
joint	guānjié
kidney	shèn
kidney inflammation	shèn yán
kidney stone	shèn jié shí
knee	xīgài
leg	tuǐ
leukemia	báixuě bìng
lip	zǔichún
liver	gānzàng
lower abdominal region	xià tǐ
lumbago	yāobù fēngshī bìng
lung	fèi
malaria	nuè jí
to massage	ànmó
measles	má zhěn
medical vaccination certificate	jíbìng zhèngmíng
menstruation	yuè jīng
middle-ear inflammation	chōng ěr yán
migraine	chōngqí xìng tóutòng
miscarriage	liúchǎn
mouth	zǔi
muscle	jīròu

nausea	ě xīn
neck	bózi
nerve	shénjīng
nervous	jǐnzhāng
nose	bízi
nosebleed	liú bí xuě
nurse	hùshì
office/clinic hours	zhěnliao shíjiān
operation	dòng shǒushù, kāidāo
pacemaker	xīnzàng qǐbó qì
paralysis	mábì
to perspire/to sweat	liú hàn
plaster/cast	shàng shígāo
pneumonia	fèi yán
poisoning	zhòngdú
poor appetite	shí yù bú zhèn
pregnancy	huái yùn
to prescribe	kāi yàofāng
prosthesis	jiǎ chǐ
to pull/to extract tooth	bá yá
pulse	màibó
rash	bānzhěn
rheumatism	fēngshī
rib	xiōng gǔ
salmonella	shāmén shì jùn
scar	bā
scarlet fever	xīng hóng rè
sciatica	zuògǔ shénjīng tòng
sense of hearing	tīngjué
septicemia/blood poisoning	bàixuě zhèng
sexual organ	xìng qìguān
shinbone	jìng gù
shivering fit/chill	fā dǒu
shoulder	jiānbǎng
sick/ill	bìng le
skin	pífu
skin disease	pífu bìng
skull	tóu gài gǔ
smallpox	tiānhuā
sore throat	yānhóu tòng
specialist	zhuān kē yīchēng
spine	jǐ zhuī
splint	shàng shígāo jiábǎn

sprain	niǔ shāng
stab wound	cì shāng
stomach	dùzi, wèi
stomachache	wèi tòng
stroke	zhòng fēng
sunstroke/heatstroke	zhòng shǔ
surgeon	wài kē yīshēng
to suture/to sew/to stitch	féng
sweat/perspiration	hàn
swelling	zhǒngdà
swollen	zhǒngdà
teeth/tooth	yá
tetanus	pò shāng fēng
toe	jiǎo zhǐ
tongue	shétou
tonsillitis	biǎntáo xiàn yán
tonsils	biǎntáo xiàn
tooth/teeth	yá chǐ
toothache	yá tòng
torn ligament	gǔgé rèndài sīliè
typhoid fever	shāng hán
ulcer	kuèiyáng
ultrasound exam	chāoyīnpō jiǎnchá
unconscious	hūnmí
urinary bladder	pángguāng
urine	niào-yì
to vaccinate	dǎ yùfáng zhēn
vaccination	zhùshè yìmiáo
vaccination certificate	yùfángzhēn zhèngming
vein	jìngmài
venereal disease	xìng bìng
virus	bìngdú
visiting hours	tànbìng shíjiān
to vomit	ǒutù
waiting room	hòu zhěn shì
ward (in hospital)	bìngfáng
whooping cough	bǎirì ké
wound	shāng kǒu
to x-ray	zhào X-guāng
yellow fever	huángrè bìng

11 A Business Trip
商务往来

On the Way to a Business Meeting

shāngwù bàifǎng

Which is the main entrance?	nǎ ge shì zhèngmén?
What floor is … company on?	… gōngsī zài jǐ lóu?
Which of you is Mr./Miss …?	nǎ wèi shì … xiānshēng/xiǎo jiě?
What room is Mr./Miss … in?	… xiānshēng/xiǎojiě zài nǎ ge fángjiān?
How do I get to …?	… zěnme zǒu?
My name is … I'm from … company.	wǒ jiào … wǒ shì cóng … gōngsī lái de.
Here is my business card.	zhè shì wǒde míngpiàn.
I'm looking for Mr./Miss …	wǒ zhǎo … xiānshēng/xiǎojiě.
Please tell Mr./Miss … that I'm here.	máfán nǐ gàosù … xiānshēng/xiǎojiě yǒu rén zhǎo ta.
I have an appointment with Mr./Miss …	wǒ hé … xiānshēng/xiǎojiě yuēhǎo le.
Mr./Miss … is expecting you.	… xiānshēng/xiǎojiě zhèng děngzhe nín.
He/She is still in a meeting.	tā zhèngzài kāihuì.
Please come with me.	qǐng gēn wǒ lái.
Sorry I'm late.	duìbùqǐ, wǒ lái wǎn le.
Please sit down.	qǐng zuò.
Would you like something to drink?	hē diǎnr shénme?
You've come a long way/had a hard trip.	yí lù xīnkǔ le.
How much time do we have (left)?	wǒmen (hái) yǒu duōshǎo shíjiān?

| When does your plane leave? | fēijī shénme shíhou qǐfēi? |
| I need an English interpreter. | wǒ xūyào yí wèi yīngwén fān-ì. |

Business travelers in China should always have business cards with them when meeting Chinese associates. The Chinese will give you their card; make sure you return the courtesy. Having your card translated into Chinese, with English on one side and Chinese on the other, is a nice touch that will be appreciated by your Chinese friends.

Avoiding loss of face is important in the social behavior of the Chinese. If, for example, you are treated to lavish dinners or receive "splendid" gifts, all this is done in order to preserve face and show respect. Consequently, you should take part in this custom and not refuse the honor. Instead, express your pleasure and admiration and return the favor.

Word List: Business Meeting

building	dàlóu
company/firm	gōngsī
conference center	huì-yì zhōngxīn
conference room	huì-yì shì
date (on a calendar)	rìqī
department	bùmén
doorman	ménfáng
entrance	dàmén
floor	lóu
interpreter	fān-yì
manager	jīnglǐ
meeting/conference	huì-yì
office	bàn-gōngshì
person in charge/ contact person	fùzé rén
reception	jiēdài
responsible person	fùzé rén
secretary	mìshū
secretary's office	mìshū chù

公司	gōngsi	company
有限公司	yǒuxiàn gōngsī	limited company
集团公司	jítuán gōngsī	holding company
秘书处	mìshū chù	secretary's office

Negotiations/Conferences/Trade Fairs

xiéshāng/huìtán/jiāo-ì huì

I'm looking for the ... company product booth.	wǒ zhǎo ... gōngsīde zhǎnchū tānwèi.
Please go to hall ..., booth number ...	qǐng dào ... tīng, dì ... hào tānwèi.
We produce ...	wǒmen shēngchǎn ...
We deal in ...	wǒmen jīngyíng ...
Do you have material about ...?	nǐmen yǒu ... de zīliào ma?
We will mail you detailed information about ...	wǒmen jì gěi nǐmen ... xiángxì de zīliào.
Who's in charge of ...?	nǎ wèi fùzé ... de shìwù?
Can you give us a price quote, please?	máfán nín bàojià gěi wǒmen?
Let's make an appointment to talk it over!	wǒmen yuē ge shíjiān tántan ba!
Here's my card.	zhè shì wǒde míngpiàn.
Let's keep in touch.	bǎochí liánluò.

展览会	zhǎnlánhuì	exhibition
交易会	jiāoyì huì	trade fair
商展	shāngzhǎn	fair

Word List: Negotiations/Conferences/Trade Fairs

5% discount	dǎ jiǔwǔ zhé
20% discount	dǎ bā zhé
advertising	guǎnggào
advertising campaign	guǎnggào huódòng
agenda	yìchéng
agent/representative	dàilǐ

authorized dealer	dàilǐ rén
bill/invoice	zhàngdān
business card	míngpiàn
business partner	kèhù
business relations/ dealings	shāngwù wǎnglái
business representative	shāngwù dàibiǎo
catalog	mùlù
conditions	tiáojiàn
conference	huì-yì
contract	héyuē
contract of sale	mǎimài hé-yuē
contract terms/ conditions	jiānyuē tiáojiàn
cooperation	hézuò
cost	chéngběn
cost estimate	gūjià
customer	gùkè
delivery	jiāohuò
delivery terms/ conditions	jiāohuò tiáojiàn
department	bùmén
department head	bùmén zhǔrèn
discount	zhékòu
discount price	yōudài jià
entrust/trust	wěituō
exhibitor	zhǎnchūzhě
export	chūkǒu
exporter	chūkǒu shāng
factory	gōngchǎng
factory manager	chǎngzhǎng
fair center	jiāoyì huì zhōngxīn
fair service	jiāo-yì huì fúwù
fair/show	jiāo-yì huì
fund	zìjīn
general agency	dàilǐ
general agent/ representative	zǒng dàilǐ shāng
group	qìyè, jítuán
guarantee	bǎozhèng
hall	tīng, guǎn
hall map/exhibition map	wèizhì tú

headquarters/head office	zhōngxīn
identity papers/ID/ proof	zhèngjiàn
import	jìnkǒu
importer	jìnkǒu shāng
industrial fair	gōngyè jiāo yì huì
information	zīliào
information booth	xúnwèn chù
insurance	báoxiǎn
to be interested in	duì … yǒu xìngqù
joint venture	hézī gōngsī
leasing	fēnqī fùkuǎn
lecture/talk	yǎnjiǎng
letter of trust	wěituō shū
licensing agreement	dàilǐ xúkě
list of exhibitors	cān chǎn mùlù
list of goods/manifest	shāngbiāo
manufacturer	zhìzào shāng
marketing	shìchǎng
meeting	huìmiàn
meeting point	huiwù zhōngxīn
merchandise	shāngpǐn
minutes/proceedings	bǐlù
model/sample	yàngběn
packaging	bāozhuāng
person in charge/ contact person	fùzé rén
price	jiàgé
price list	jiàgé biǎo
price quote	bàojià
price reduction	yōudài jiàgé
pro forma invoice	gūjià dān
production	shēngchǎn
promotional material	guǎnggào cáiliào
prospectus/brochure	mùlù, shuōmíng shū
public relations	gōngguān shìwù
retailer	jīngxiāo shāng, língshòu shāng
sales	jīngxiāo, xiāoshòu
sales department	jīngxiāo bùmén
sales network	xiāoshòu wǎng
sales promotion	tuēixiāo
sales tax	yínglì
salesman	shòuhuò yuán

service person	fúwùyuán
shipping	huò yùn
small room/cubicle	xiǎo fángjiān
staff member	zhíyuán
stand/booth at a fair	zhǎnchū tānwèi
subsidiary	fēn gōngsī
supplier	gōngyìng shāng
terms of payment	fùkuǎn tiáojiàn
time of delivery	jiāohuò shíjiān
trade fair director	jiāo-yì huì fùzé rén
trade fair/show	zhuānyè jiāo-yì huì
training	péixùn
transportation	yùnshū
transportation cost	yùn fèi
value-added tax (VAT)	huòwù zēngzhí shuì
wholesaler	pīfā shāng

Business Equipment

shèbèi

Please make several copies of this.	máfán nǐ fùyìn yí xià.
I need a slide projector.	wǒ xūyào yì jià huàndēngjī.
Please arrange for ...	qǐng shèfǎ nòngdào ...

Word List: Business Equipment

catalog	mùlù
color photocopier	cǎisè yǐngyìn jī
copy	fùběn, yǐngyìn běn
disk	cí piàn
exhibition materials	zhánlǎn zīliào
extension line	fēnjīxiàn
fax	chuánzhēn
fax number	chuánzhēn hàomǎ
microphone	màikèfēng
modem	mōdēng diànchuán
notebook	bǐjì běn
office telephone number	bàn-gōng shì diànhuà hàomǎ
overhead projector	huàndēng jī

PC	jiāyòng diànnǎo
pencil	bǐ
photocopier	yǐngyìn jī
printer	yìnshuā jī
private telephone number	zhùjiā diànhuà hàomǎ
rostrum/speaker's platform	jiǎngtái
telephone	diànhuà
telephone number	diànhuà hàomǎ
telex	diànchuán
VCR	lùxiàngjī
word processing system	wénshū chǔlǐ xìtǒng

A Short Grammar

Sentence Structure

A simple Chinese sentence has the following structure:

Subject	Predicate	Object
I wǒ	am shì	American. Měiguó rén.
I wǒ	eat chī	apples. píngguǒ.

This sentence order is the most frequent and customary. It expresses the plain form of a sentence.
There are other orders, such as the **ba** construction, that can place **particular emphasis on a particular object.**

Subject	ba	Object	Predicate
I wǒ	bǎ	the apple píngguǒ	have eaten. chīle.

Alternatively, the object can be put at the beginning, giving it greater prominence:

Object	Subject	Predicate
Apple píngguǒ	I wǒ	have eaten. chīle.

Sentence order also is not altered by **adverbs of time** or **negation.**
Along with other appropriate terms, they are placed before the verb:

Subject	Adverb of Time	Verb	Object
I wǒ	yesterday zuótian	eat chī	apple. píngguǒ.

Subject	Negation	Verb	Object
I wǒ	not bù	eat chī	apple. píngguǒ.

Alternatively, both may appear in combination:

Subject	Adverb of Time	Negation	Verb	Object
I wǒ	yesterday zuótian	not méi	eat chī	apple. pingguǒ.

Sentences with the Verb "yǒu" (there is, there are) Expressing Existence or Presence:

In this case, the position of the subject is occupied by an adverb of place or time that states "where" or "when" something is in existence:

Adverb of Place	you	Object
In the room fángjiānlǐ	there is yǒu	television. diànshì.
Up ahead qiánmiàn	there is yǒu	bookstore. shūdiàn.

Adverb of Time	you	Object
Tomorrow míngtian	there are yǒu	tickets of admission. ménpiào.

The negation of **you** is **mei you**:

Tomorrow míngtian	there are no méi you	tickets of admission. ménpiào.

With **interrogative sentences (questions),** too, the sentence order remains unchanged. Chinese has several alternative ways of asking a question:

1. By attaching the particle **ma**

You	come?	
nǐ	lái	ma?

2. Simple alternative question

You	come	not	come?
nǐ	lái	bù	lái?

3. Full alternative question

You	come	or	not	come?
nǐ	lái	háishi	bù	lái?

4. Question with supplement

You	come,	ok	not	ok?
nǐ	lái,	hǎo	bu	hǎo?

In questions containing the interrogative particles **how much, where,** or **what,** these words constitute the object:

Subject	Verb	Interrogative Particle (Object)
You nǐ	would like yào	how much? duōshǎo?
You nǐ	would like to go yào qù	where? nǎr?
You nǐ	would like yào	what? shénme?

The interrogative particle **when,** like the adverbs of time, precedes the verb:

Subject	when	Verb	Object
You nǐ	when shénme shíhou	go qù	China? Zhōngguó?

The interrogative particle **who** forms the subject:

Interrogative Particle (Subject)	Verb	Object
Who shéi	go qù	China? Zhōngguó?

Nouns

1. In Chinese there is neither a definite nor an indefinite article. The gender of nouns often can be determined only from the overall context.

2. Noun plurals are expressed by terms of quantity, such as "how many," "some," "few," and the like.

3. In Chinese, numerals and demonstrative pronouns normally cannot directly precede a noun. A classifier known as a **measure word** has to be inserted, as in the English expressions "two sheets of paper" or "four bottles of milk":

This is a book.   That student is Chinese.
zhè shi yì **běn** shū.   nà **ge** xúesheng shì Zhōngguó rén.

The most important measure words are these:

gè	the most common measure word, used generally for persons and many other objects
běn	for volumes of books, notebooks, etc.
zhāng	for sheets of paper, cards, and the "flat" objects
jiàn	for articles of clothing
tiáo	for long, slender objects like poles, rods, rivers, etc.
bēi	for cups/glasses of such liquids as coffee, tea, beer, etc.
liáng	for vehicles
zhī	for small, elongated objects such as brushes, pencils, etc.
fēng	for letters (to be mailed)

This is only a small selection from the huge number of measure words, which you have to discover for each noun as you learn it. In case you can't think of the correct one right off the bat, you can use the neutral **gè.**

4. There is no declension in Chinese. The nominative and the accusative (direct object) are identical in form. The genitive is expressed with **de,** and the dative (indirect object) usually is expressed with **gěi** or **gēn.**

Personal Pronouns

	Singular		Plural	
First person	wǒ	I	wǒmen	we
Second person	nǐ	you	nǐmen	you
Third person	tā	he/she	tāmen	they

Possessive Pronouns

	Singular		Plural	
First person	wǒ de	my	wǒmen de	our
Second person	nǐ de	your	nǐmen de	your
Third person	tā de	his/hers	tāmen de	their

Example:

Our friends	with us	go (to) China.
wǒmen **de** péngyou	**gēn** wǒmen	qù Zhōngguó.

Adjectives

As in English, adjectives precede the noun they modify. They never change in either gender or number.

Examples:

An	interesting	book
yí gè	**yǒuyìsi de**	shū.

Chinese	tea
Zhōngguó	chá

Adjectival Predicate

In Chinese there are sentences in which adjectives alone can form the predicate of the sentence. Usually the adverb **hěn** (very) has to precede and support the simple adjective in this type of sentence.

Example:

Chinese tea	(is) very good.
Zhōngguó chá	**hěn hǎo.**

Comparison

In comparisons, the **bǐ** construction is used:

A	bǐ	B	Adjective
This	than	that	better.
zhèi ge	**bǐ**	nà ge	hǎo.

Adverbs

There are two kinds of adverbs: (1) words that originally are adverbs and (2) adverbs that are formed from adjectives by attaching the auxiliary word **de.**

Original adverbs:

chángcháng	often
yídìng	absolutely

Adverbs formed from adjectives:

gāoxìng de	happily, cheerfully
xiǎoshēng de	softly, gently, quietly

Sample sentences:

He	often	travels.
tā	**chángcháng**	lǚxíng

He	quickly	walked.
tā	**kuàikuāi**	zǒu.

Verbs

In Chinese, verbs are not conjugated; they always retain the infinitive form. **Past, present,** and **future** are expressed by means of adverbs of time such as yesterday, today, tomorrow, this evening, this morning, in 1983, this year, next year, and so forth.

Since such adverbs of time play an important role in the sentence, they are placed before the predicate or even at the beginning of the sentence.

Sample sentences:

I	year before last	went	(to) China.
wǒ	**qiánnián**	qù	Zhōngguó.
I	today	am going	(to) China.
wǒ	**jīntian**	qù	Zhōngguó.
I	tomorrow evening	(will) go	(to) China.
wǒ	**míngtian wǎnshang**	qù	Zhōngguó.

Tenses

To emphasize the time, or tense, the Chinese use three so-called **aspect words:**

1. The **experiential aspect,** formed by attaching the particle **guo** to the verb, expresses that some event has been experienced.

I	have been	(in) China.
wǒ	qù**guo**	Zhōngguó.

2. The **durative aspect,** formed by attaching the particle **zhe** to the verb, expresses that the action is going on now.

I	am now reading	(a) book.
wǒ	kàn**zhe**	shū.

3. The **completed aspect,** formed by attaching the particle **le** to the verb, expresses that the action has been completed.

I	have read	a/some book(s).
wǒ	kàn**le**	shū.

Passive

To form the passive voice, the auxiliary word **bèi** is used:

I	just	was	robbed.
wǒ	gānggāng	**bèi**	qiǎngle.

The passive using **bèi** is very rare in Chinese, because Chinese has many other ways to express the passive voice.

Compound Sentences

In Chinese, two simple clauses are joined with a **conjunction**, which is placed between the two clauses (or rather, at the end of the first clause) or at the beginning of the first clause:

because	yīnwèi/suóyǐ	**yīnwèi** tài guì, **suóyǐ** wǒ bù mǎi. Because it's too expensive, I won't buy it.
before	yǐ qián	wǒmen chīfàn **yǐ qián,** xiān qù kàn diànyǐng ba. Before we go to dinner, let's go to the movies.
after	yǐhòu	wǒ húi lǚguǎn **yǐhòu,** cái fāxiàn dīule qián. After I came back to the hotel, I noticed that I had lost money.
when	dāng ... shí	**dāng** wǒ tīngdao xiāoxi **shí,** wǒ jiu hěn nánguò. When I heard the news, I was saddened.
and then	ránhòu	chīwán le wǎnfàn, **ránhòu** kāihuí lǚguǎn qù le. After eating dinner, we then drove back to the hotel.
if	rúguǒ	**rúguǒ** ni zuò chūzūchē, jiu yào xiān wèn jiàqián. If you take a taxi, ask about the fare first.
but	dànshi	wǒ hěn xiǎng lái, **dànshi** jīntian méiyou shíjiān. I'd very much like to come, but I don't have time today.

Numerals

Almost all the numerals from 1 to 100 billion can be formed from a total of 15 words:

0	zero	líng
1	one	yī
2	two	èr
3	three	sān
4	four	sì
5	five	wǔ
6	six	liù
7	seven	qī
8	eight	bā
9	nine	jiǔ
10	ten	shí
100	one hundred	yì bǎi
1,000	one thousand	yì qiān
10,000	ten thousand	yí wàn
1 yì	100 million	yí yì

Compound Numerals (two to nine places):

21	èrshí yī
321	sān bǎi èrshí yī
4,321	sì qiān sān bǎi èrshí yī
54,321	wǔ wàn sì qiān sān bǎi èrshí yī
654,321	liùshíwǔ wàn sì qiān sān bǎi èrshí yī
7,654,321	qī bǎi liùshíwǔ wàn sì qiān sān bǎi èrshí yī
87,654,321	bā qiān qī bǎi liùshíwǔ wàn sì qiān sān bǎi èrshí yī
987,654,321	jiǔ yì bā qiān qī bǎi liùshíwǔ wàn sì qiān sān bǎi èrshí yī

Some Ways of Reading Numerals:

Telephone **number:** 654798	diànhuà **hàomǎ**	liù wǔ sì qi jiǔ bā
Lecture hall/Auditorium **No.** 865	bā liù wǔ	**hào** jiàoshì
(The **year**) 1998	yī jiǔ jiǔ bā	**nián**

English–Chinese Dictionary

As in the preceding parts of this book, the *pinyin* system, now standard throughout the world, has been used in the following dictionaries.

A

a moment ago; just now gānggāng
able to néng, nénggòu, kěyǐ
able; skilled nénggàn
above shàngmiàn
absolutely impossible jué bù kěnéng de
absorbent/sterilized cotton yàomián
abundant; enough zúgòu
abuse; misuse lànyòng; **mistreat** nüèdài
academic subject xuékē
academy; institute xuéyuàn
accept; receive jiēshōu
accident; mishap yìwài
accident, have an chūshì
accidentally; by chance ǒurán de
accompany; escort péitóng; **accompany back** sònghuí
accomplishment; self cultivation xiūyǎng; **training** xiūyǎng
according to ànzhào
account (in a bank, etc.) zhànghù
accountant kuàijì
accurate zhèngquè
accustomed to; used to; habit xíguàn
ache; pain; soreness téngtòng
achieve dádào
achievement; gain chéngguǒ
acquaintance; friend shúrén
act (section of a play) mù
act as agent; proxy dàilǐ
acting... dàilǐ...
action; operation; move about xíngdòng
activity; maneuver huódòng
actor/actress yǎnyuán
acupuncture zhēnjiǔ
adapter (electrical) biànyà qì; liánjiē chātóu
add; increase jiā; **add to** jiā shang
addiction yǐn
additional; extra é wài de
address (of a house, etc.) dìzhǐ; **address, write an** xiě dìzhǐ
administrative organ xíngzhèng jīguān; **administrative unit** xíngzhèng dānwèi

admission ticket ménpiào
adult; grown up chéngrén
advanced class gāojí bān
advantage; good point hǎochù
advantageous yǒulì de
advertisement guǎnggào
advise, to; counsel quàngào
after... ...yǐhòu; **after that; and then** ránhòu
after eating fànhòu
afternoon xiàwǔ
afterwards hòulái
again yòu; zài; **again; anew; afresh** chóngxīn
against, be fǎnduì
age (of a person) niánjì
agenda yìchéng
agree, to tóngyì; **agree upon** yuēdìng
agreement; contract héyuē
AIDS àizībìng
air kōngqì
air blower sòngfēngjī
air conditioner lěngqì
air mail hángkōng xìn
air out, to tōngfēng
air pressure qìyā
airline company hángkōng gōngsī
airline flight hángxiàn
airplane fēijī
airport jīchǎng; **airport tax** jīchǎngfèi
alarm clock nàozhōng
alcohol jiǔjīng
alike, be; resemble xiāngxiàng
all dōu; **all of the...** suǒyǒude...; **all; entire** quánbù; **all people/persons** suǒyǒu rén
allergy guòmǐn
alley xiàngzi
allocate; allot fēnpèi
allow; to let zhǔnxǔ
almond xìngrén
almost chàbùduō
already yǐjīng
also yě
altar shénwèi
alter; change gēnggǎi
although suīrán
always zǒngshi

A/Z

amazed at; surprised at jīngqí
ambassador dàshǐ
ambiguous; vague hánhú
ambulance jiùhù chē
America; United States měiguó; American měiguó rén
amount shù'é; amount to; add up to zǒngjì
amusement; recreation yúlè; amusement park yóulèyuán
analyst (psychology) xīnlǐ fēnxī jiā
analyze fēnxi
ancient times gǔdài
anesthesia mázuì
anger qì
angina jiǎoxīn tòng
angle jiǎodù
Anglo-American yīngměi
angry, be; get mad shēngqì
animal dòngwù
annual meeting niánhuì
annually měi nián
another/different place bié de dìfang
answer, an; reply, a dáfù
answer, to; make a reply huídá; answer the phone jiē diànhuà
antagonistic duìlì de
antibiotic tèxiàoyào
antidote; remedy jiědú yào
antiques gǔdǒng
anywhere bùguǎn zài nǎli; anywhere you go bùguǎn qù nǎli
apartment gōngyù
apologize dàoqiàn
apparently; seemingly kàn qǐlái
appear chūxiàn; appears to be hǎoxiàng
appearance; style; manner yàngzi
appendix mángcháng; appendicitis mángcháng yán
appetite wèikǒu; shíyù; appetite, have no méi wèikǒu
appetizer; hors d'oeuvre (on a menu) qiáncān
applaud gǔzhǎng
apple píngguǒ
appointment yuēhuì
appreciate; admire zànshǎng
apprehensive, to be dānyōu
approach, to kàojìn
approve of; endorse zàntóng
approximately dàyuē
apricot xìngzi
arbitrate píngduàn
archeology kǎogǔ
architecture jiànzhù
area dìqū

argue chǎojià
arise; get up from bed qǐchuáng
arm shǒubèi
armchair zuòyǐ
arouse, to yǐnqǐ
arrival date dàodá shírì; arrival time dàodá shíjiān
arrive; reach dàodá; art yìshù; artist yìshù jiā
art academy yìshù xuéyuàn
art dealer yìshùpǐn màoyìshāng
art gallery huàláng
art history yìshù shǐ
art object yìshù pǐn
article; thing dōngxi
artificial réngōng de
artificial heart rén gōng xīnzàng
artificial leather rénzào pí
artificial limb yìzhī
artificial teeth jiǎyá
as long as zhǐ yào
as one pleases suíyì
as you wish suí nide biàn
Asia yàzhōu; Asian person yàzhōu rén; Asiatic yàzhōu de
ask, to wèn
asparagus lúsǔn
aspirin yǎsīpílín
asthma qìchuǎn
at first shǒuxiān
at home zài jiā
at least zhìshǎo
at present; before one's eyes yǎn qián
at the most zuì duō
athlete yùndòng yuán
athletic field yùndòng chǎng
ATM (money machine) zìdòngtíkuǎn
attain; reach dédào
attempt; try chángshì
attend; be present chūxí
attentive; careful xìxīn
audience; spectator guānzhòng
aunt āyí; bómǔ
Austria àoudìlì; Austrian person àoudìlì rén
authority; power quánlì
automatic zìdòng
autumn qiūtiān
average; equally píngjūn
avoid bìmiǎn
awake, to be; wake up xǐng
awaken jiàoxǐng
away; gone; left líkāi le; away from; be apart jùlí

B

baby; infant yīng ér
baby bottle nǎipíng
baby food yīng ér shípǐn
bachelor dānshēn
back (spine) bèi; **backbone; vertebra** jǐzhuī gǔ
backdoor connections; pull guānxi
bad huài; bùhǎo; **bad one** bùhǎo de; **bad tempered; aggressive** pōlà
bag (for holding things) dàizi
baggage cart xíngli tuīchē
baggage room tuōyùn xíngli chù
bakery miànbāo diàn
ball (for playing) qiú
ballet bāléiwǔ
ballpoint pen yuánzi bǐ
banana xiāngjiāo
bandage bēngdài
bank yínháng; **bank account** zhànghù
banknote; bill chāopiào
bar; tavern jiǔba
barber lǐfà shī
bargain over price jiǎngjià
base; foundation jīchǔ
basket (bamboo) zhúlán
basketball lánqiú
bathe; clean, to xǐ; **take a bath** xǐzǎo
bathroom (for bathing) xǐzǎojiān
bathtub zǎopén
battery diànchí
bay hǎiwān
be; is shì
beach hǎitān; **bathing beach** hǎibīn yùchǎng
beans dòuzi
bear; endure rěnshòu
beard; moustache húzi
beauty; beautiful měilì; **beauty parlor** měiróng yuàn
because yīnwèi
become; turn into chéngwéi
bed chuáng
bee mìfēng
beef niúròu
beer píjiǔ
begin; start; beginning kāishǐ
behavior xíngwéi
behind hòumiàn/tou
beige; cream color mǐsè
belief; faith xìnyǎng
believe, to; believe in; trust in xiāngxìn
bell (on a bike, etc.) chēlíng
belly dùzi

belong to shǔyú
below xiàmiàn/tou; **below zero** língxià
belt, leather pídài; **belt; strap** pí dàizi
beneficial; profitable yǒuyì de
bent; curved; crooked; turn/curve wān(r)
best, the zuì hǎo de
bet; make a bet; gamble dǎdǔ
beyond; outside of … zhī wài
bicycle zìxíngchē; **bicycle race** zìxíngchē bǐsài
bicycle, to ride a qí zìxíngchē
big; large; grand dà
bill; paper money chāopiào
bill, figure out a suànzhàng
biology shēngwù
bird niǎo(r)
birth; born, be chūshēng; **birthdate** chūshēng niányuèrì
birthday shēngrì
bitter; hard to endure kǔ
black hēi sè; **black and white** hēibái
blame; reprove zébèi
bleed liúxuě
blind person xiā zi
blister; bubble shuǐpào
blockade; block; seal off fēngsuǒ
blocked up; stopped sāizhù
blood xuě; **blood type** xuěxíng
blood pressure xuěyā; **high/low blood pressure** gāo/dī xuěyā
blood test; do a blood test yànxuě
blood transfusion shūxuě
blossom; bloom; flower; feel elated kāihuā
blow-dry hair, to chuī tóufa
blue lánsè
blueprint; plan píngmiàn tú
board a boat shàng chuán; **board a bus/car/train** shàngchē; **board a plane** shàng fēijī
boat chuán
body shēntǐ
bone gǔtóu
book shū; **book store** shūdiàn
booth; cabin xiǎo fángjiān
boots xuēzi
border checkpoint/crossing biānjiè jiǎnchá zhàn
boring; uninteresting wúliáo
born, to be chūshēng
boss lǎobǎn
botanical gardens zhíwùyuán
bottle píngzi
boundary; border biānjiè
bowling bǎolíng qiú

box hézi
boy nánhái
bra năizhào
brain tóunăo; **brains; mental power** năolì
brain concussion năo zhèndàng
brake a car; brakes shàchē
branch/affiliate store fēndiàn
brand name shāngbiāo
bread miànbāo
break off; suspend zhōngduàn
break; smash dăpò
breakdown; stoppage gùzhàng
breakfast zăocān
breathe; breathing hūxī
bridge qiáo
brief note tiáozi
briefcase gōngshì bāo
bright; brilliant liàng
bring along, to dài
broadcast; air guǎngbō
broken; damaged; torn pò le
broken; gone bad huài le
broken; split duàn le
bronchial tube zhīqìguǎn
bronze tóng
brooch xiōngzhēn
broom sàobǎ
brother (older) gēge; (younger) dìdi; brother-in-law (of older sister) jiěfū; (of younger sister) mèifū
brown zōngsè
bruise qīngzhǒng
brush; to brush shuāzi
Buddha fó; Buddhism fójiào; Buddhist fójiào tú; Buddhist statue fóxiàng
build; construct; cover; conceal gài
building; construct; build jiànzhù
bump into, to pèngzhuàng
burden; load; bear fùdān
burdensome, troublesome máfán de
bureaucrats; bureaucratic guānliáo
burlesque (Chinese) xiàngsheng
burn medicine/cream/ointment shāoshāng ruǎngāo
burn; heat; roast; stew shāo
burst, to; split pòliè
bus gōnggòng qìchē; bus stop chēzhàn
business; trade shēngyì
business card míngpiàn
business class shāngyè cāng
business connections shāngyè wǎnglái
business hours yíngyè shíjiān

business manager jīnglǐ
business partner kèhù
business; enterprise qǐyè
but dànshì
butcher shop ròupù
butter huángyóu
button niǔkòu
buy, to; purchase mǎi; buy a ticket mǎi chēpiào
buyer mǎifāng

C

cabbage juǎnxīn cài
cake dàn gāo; cake shop/bakery gāobǐng diàn
calculate; figure out jìsuàn
calculator jìsuànjī
callous; unfeeling lěngkù
calm, be; composed zhènjìng
camera zhàoxiàng jī; camera lens jìngtóu
camping lùyíng
can; can of guàntou; can opener kāiguàn qì; canned goods; tin can guàntóu
Canada jiā ná dà; Canadian person jiā ná dà rén
canal yùnhé
cancel qǔxiāo
cancer áizhèng
candle làzhú
cane (for walking) shǒuzhàng
canoe dúmùzhōu
cap màozi
capable of, to be nénggòu; capable/able nénggàn de
capital (of a country) shǒudū
captain (boat) chuánzhǎng; captain (plane) jīzhǎng
car; automobile qìchē
car body; chassis chēshēn
cards zhǐpái; poker pūkè pái
careful, be xiǎoxīn
careless bù xiǎoxīn
carp, black qīngyú
carrot hóngluóbo
carry/take away, to názǒu; carry on the back bēi
case; example; instance lìzi
casino dǔchǎng
cassette lùyīn dài; cídài
castle chéngbǎo
cat māo(r)
catalog mùlù

catch a ride with s.o.; hitchhike, to
dā biànchē
catch cold; cold gǎnmào
catch, to; grab; scratch zhuā
Catholic (faith) tiānzhǔ jiào
cattle; cow niú
cause yuányīn
Caution! Zhùyì!
cautious, to be; careful xiǎoxīn
cave; hole dòng
CD/compact disc xīdī
ceiling tiānhuābǎn
celebration, national qìngdiǎn
celery qíncài
cemetery mùdì
center; heart; hub zhōngxīn
central; central authorities
zhōngyāng
century shìjì
ceramic(s) táoqì
certain ... yídìng de ...
certainly; surely; definitely yídìng
certificate of vaccination yùfáng
zhèngmíng shū
chain liànzi
chair yǐzi
changeable duō biàn de
change (buses, etc.) huànchē;
change clothes huàn yīfu
change, give/make zhǎo língqián;
change; coins língqián; change
foreign currency duìhuàn wàibì
change; alteration biànhuà
change; exchange huàn
change; transform; alter gǎibiàn;
change to; revise; correct gǎi
chapel xiǎo jiàotáng
character (Chinese) zì
characteristic; feature tèzhēng
charming; enchanting mírén de
chat; converse tánhuà
cheap; inexpensive piányi
cheat, to; deceive qīpiàn
check (baggage) room xínglǐ jìcún
chù
check (bank) zhīpiào
check in; register dēngjì
check, to; inspect; examine jiǎnchá
check; leave with; deposit jìcún
cheerful; happy gāoxìng
cheese nǎilào
chemistry huàxué
cherries yīngtáo
chest; box; luggage xiāngzi
chest; thorax xiōngbù
chestnut lìzi
chew; bite yǎo

chewing gum kǒuxiāngtáng
child háizi
child's ticket értóng piào
China zhōngguó; Chinese zhōngguó
de; Chinese person zhōngguó rén
chocolate qiǎokèlì
cholera huòluàn
choose; select; choice xuǎnzé
chorus héchàng
Christian jiàotú; Christianity jīdūjiào
church jiàotáng
cigar xuějiā; cigarillo (small cigar)
xiǎo xuějiā
cigarette xiāngyān
circle; ring quān(r)
circulation, blood xuèyì xúnhuán
circus mǎxìtuán
city chéngshì; dūshì; city proper;
urban district shìqū; city wall
chéngqiáng
city government shì zhèngfǔ
claim damages, to suǒpéi
class origin; family origin chūshēn
class, grade děngjí
clean; neat and tidy gānjìng
clear-cut; explicit míngquè de; clear;
distinct; understand clearly
qīngchu
clergyman/woman mùshī
clerk (in store) shòuhuò yuán
climate qìhòu
climax; high tide/water gāocháo
climb; crawl pá
clinic zhěnsuǒ
cloakroom yīmào jiān
clock zhōng
close, shut guān; close a door;
closed (for business) guānmén
cloth bùliào; clothing fúzhuāng;
clothing store fúzhuāngdiàn
cloud yún; cloudy weather yīntiān
clutch; coupling líhé qì
coal méi
coast hǎi àn
coat hanger yījià
cockroach zhāngláng
coconut yézi
coffee kāfēi; coffeehouse kāfēi guǎn
coins yìngbì
cold lěng
cold drink shop lěngyǐn diàn
cold water lěng shuǐ
cold; catch cold gǎnmào
collar lǐngzi
colleague; fellow worker tóngshì
collect, to; gather shōují
college student dà xuéshēng

collide; run into each other xiāngzhuàng

cologne gǔlóng shuǐ

color yánsè; cǎisè

colored yǒu yánsè de; **colored pencil** cǎisè bǐ

column; pillar zhùzi

coma; stupor hūnmí

comb shūzi; **comb hair** shū tóufà

come, to lái; **come in** jìnlái; **come here** lái zhèlǐ; **come again (for a visit)** zài lái

comedy (play) xǐjù

comfortable; well shūfu

commemorate; mark jìniàn; **commemorative stamp** jìniàn yóupiào; **commemorative site** jìniàndì

commercial city shāngyè chéngshì

commercial college; trade school shāngyè xuéxiào

commission; middleman's fee yōngjīn

common; ordinary; average pǔtōng; **common; joint** gòngtóng de

commonly used chángyòng de...

communications; traffic jiāotōng

community college dàzhuān

comparatively bǐjiào

compare; contrast bǐ

compass luópán

compatriots; fellow countrymen guórén

compensate; make up for bǔcháng

complete; finish wánchéng

composer zuòqǔ jiā

comprehend; understand liǎojiě

computer science jìsuànjī kēxué

concerned about, be guānxīn

concert (music) yīnyuè huì

conclude; end; close jiéshù

conditions; situation qíngkuàng

condom bǎoxiǎntào

conduct; hold; run jǔbàn; **conduct a sight-seeing tour; guide** dǎoyóu

conference; meeting huìyì

confirm; verify zhèngshí

confiscate mòshōu

congratulate, to zhùhè

connect; join liánjiē

conquer; surmount kèfú

consent; approve of tóngyì

considerate; attentive; thorough zhōudào

constitution (of a state) xiànfǎ

consulate lǐngshì guǎn

contact; connection liánxì; guānxi

contact; get in touch with jiēchù; **contact; keep contact with** liánxì

container róngqì

contents; substance nèiróng

contest; competition jìngsài

continue; persist chíxù; **continue to** jìxù

contraceptive bǎoxiǎntào; **contraceptive; the pill** bìyùnwán

contract; agreement héyuē; **contract terms** qiānyuē tiáojiàn

convenient; handy fāngbiàn

conversation tánhuà

convert (numerically) zhésuàn

convulsion; spasm jìngluàn

cook; boil zhǔ

cook; chef chúshī

cook/recipe book shípǔ

cooked zhǔguò de; **cooked; well-done** shú de

cookie; biscuit; cracker bǐnggān

cooking; kitchen work chuíshí; **cooking; cook (dishes)** pēngtiáo

cool; cold liáng; **cool and damp** shīlěng

cooperation hézuò

copper tóng

copy; xerox fùyìn

coral shānhú

cordial; genial; warm qīnqiè

corn yùmǐ

corner; nook jiǎoluò

correct, to be; right duì, zhèngquè

correct, to; revise gēngzhèng

corrupt; rotten fǔbài

costs; expenses fèiyòng

costume; dress tàozhuāng

cotton; cotton padded mián

cough késòu; **cough syrup** zhǐkéjì

count on; trust; have faith in xìnlài

count, to; figure; calculate shǔ

counter (in store, etc.) guìtái; chuāngkǒu

country (nation) guójiā; **countryside** xiāngxià

county xiàn

courage yǒngqì

course (in school) kèchéng

courses (of a meal) dào

court (law) fǎtíng

courtesy lǐmào

cousin biǎomèi

cover; conceal gài

cover; lid; top gàizi

cow mǔniú

cozy; comfortable shūfu

crabs; crawfish xiā

cream (dairy) nǎiyóu
cream; ointment rǔyì; rǔgāo
create, to; creation chuàngzuò;
  create; make into zàochéng
creative yǒu chuàngjiàn de
crime/offense, commit a crime
  fànzuì
cross over/cross dùguò; cross the
  border rùjìng
crossing; intersection shízì lùkǒu
crown huángguàn
cry; weep; sob kū; cry out; shout;
  order; name; call jiào
crystal shuǐjīng
cucumber huángguā
culture wénhuà
cupboard; cabinet guìzi
curious hàoqí
curler fàjuǎn
currency; money huòbì
current, be; in general use tōngxíng
curriculum; course kèchéng
customer gùkè
customs (of a people) fēngsú xíguàn
cut (wound) gēshāng
cut, to; slice qiē
cylinder yuántǒng
cypress bóshù

D

daily newspaper rìbào
damage; harm; injure sǔnhài;
  damages; compensation péicháng
damp; moist cháoshī
dance party; ball wǔhuì
dance, to tiàowǔ; dancer wǔdào jiā
Danger! wēixiǎn!
dangerous wēixiǎn
dare to gǎn
dark hēi àn
darling qīn'ài de
data/material zīliào
date (on calendar) rìqī
date; appointment yuēhuì
dates; date palm hǎizǎo
daughter nǚ'ér
day trip yìtiān de lǚxíng
daytime báitiān
dead sǐ de
dear; beloved kě'ài de
debt; liabilities zhàiwù
deceive; cheat qīpiàn
decide; decision juédìng
deck (of ship) jiǎbǎn

decorate; fix up; arrange bùzhì
deed; act xíngwéi
deep (water, etc.); profound shēn
deep sea fishing yuǎnyáng hǎidiào
defecate dàbiàn
definite; regular yídìng de
definitely; surely yídìng
dejected; depressed xiāochén
delay; postpone; put off yánqī
delicate; tender xì nèn
delicious; tasty; delightful
  shìwéi(r)
deliver goods sònghuò
delivery time sònghuò shíjiān
demand, to; request; a demand; a
  request yāoqiú
Denmark dānmài; Danish person
  dānmài rén
dense; thick mì
dentist yáyī
deny, to fǒurèn
department store bǎihuò gōngsī
departure time chūfā shíjiān
deposit (money) yājīn
depth shēndù
descend/go down a mountain
  xiàshān
describe miáoshù
desert shāmò
design; to design shèjì
despite; although suīrán
dessert tiándiǎn
destination mùdìdì
destroy; wreck; smash pòhuài
detailed, be xiángxì; xì; detailed...
  xiángxì de...
details; particulars xìjié
detain; arrest jūliú
detergent xǐdí jì
detour, make a ràolù
diabetes tángniào bìng
diagnose zhěnduàn
diarrhea fùxiè; lā dùzi
diary rìjì
dice shǎizi
die, to qùshì; sǐqù
diet; to diet jiéshí
differ; be different; different;
  difference bùtóng
differentiate; set apart qūfēn
difficult bù róngyì; nán; difficulty;
  trouble kùnnan
digestion xiāohuà
diligent; hard-working nǔlì
dim; dusky; gloomy hūn'àn de
dining car cānchē
dining room cāntīng

dinner wǎncān; **dinner clothes** wǎn lǐfu

diphtheria báihóu

direct; command zhǐhuī

direct; immediate zhíjiē

direct dialing zhíjiē bōhào

direction fāngxiàng

directly zhíjiē

director (film) dǎoyǎn; **director; head; chair** zhǔrèn; **director; manager** zhǔrèn

dirty; soiled zāng; **dirty clothes** zāng yīfu

disadvantage; bad feature huàichù

disappeared bújiàn le

disappointed shīwàng

disaster; calamity zāihuò

disco dísīkē

discount zhékòu; **give a discount** dǎ zhé

discover; find; discovery fāxiàn

disease; illness bìng

disgraceful; shameful chǒu

dish wǎn; pénzi

disinfect xiāodú; **disinfectant** xiāodú shuǐ

disk(ette) cípiàn

dislike bù xǐhuān

disorderly; pell-mell záluàn

dissatisfied bù mǎnyì

dissolute; debauched làngmàn

distance between jùlí

distinct; clear qīngchǔ

distinguishing/special feature tèsè

distribute; hand out fēnfā

distrust, to bù xiāngxìn

disturb, to; bother dǎrǎo; **disturb; interfere with; interference (elec.)** gānrǎo

dive, to (into water) qiánshuǐ

divert oneself; while away time xiāoqiǎn

divide, to fēn; **divide into** fēnchéng

diving board tiàobǎn

division (of a business, organization) bùmén

divorce; get a divorce líhūn

dizzy tóuyūn

do, to zuò

doctor (Ph.D.) bóshì

doctor's certificate jiànkāng bǎoxiǎn dān

document wénjiàn

dog gǒu

doll yáng wáwa

dome yuándǐng

domestic animal jiāchù

domestic flight guónèi hángxiàn

donkey; ass lǘ

door; gate mén; **door of a house; front door** jiāmén

doorman ménfáng

dormitory for students xuéshēng sùshè

double; redouble; twofold jiābèi

doubt; suspicion huáiyí

doubt, to; be suspicious huáiyí

draft (wind) chuāntáng fēng(r)

drama; play xìjù

draw; paint huà; **drawing; painting** huà(r)

dream, to zuò mèng; **dream** mèng

dress; put on clothes chuān yīfu

dressing room gēngyī shì

drill; practice liànxí

drink, to hē

drinkable kěyǐ hē de

drinks; beverages yǐnliào; **drinking water (boiled)** kāishuǐ

drip; dribble shuǐdī

drive, to kāichē; **drive back** kāihuí

driver sījī; **driver's license** jiàshǐ zhízhào

driving teacher jiàshǐ jiàoliàn

drop diào xià

drug store yàodiàn

drum gǔ

drunk; intoxicated hē zuì le

dry gān; **dry, to** nòng gān; **dry cleaning** gānxǐ

duck (fowl) yāzi

due to; because yīnwèi

duplicate chóngfù

durable nàijiǔ de

dusk huánghūn

dust chéntǔ; **dust pan** běnjī

duty; responsibility yìwù

duty; tax shuì

E

each/every one měi yīge

ear ěrduō

ear drops ěrduō yàoshuǐ

early zǎo; **earlier than zǎo** yìdiǎn

earn; make profit zhuàn, zhèng

earphones ěrjī

earrings ěrhuán

earth dìqiú

East, the dōngbù, dōngfāng

easy róngyì

eat chī; **eat a meal** chīfàn; **eat breakfast, to** chī zǎocān
ebb tide tuìcháo
economy; economical jīngjì; **economy class** jīngjì cāng
edible kě chī de
editor biānjí
education jiàoyù
effect, have an qǐ zuòyòng
effect; function; use zuòyòng
effective yǒuxiào
eggplant qiézi
either ... or ... búshì...jiùshì...
elated; exultant táozuì
electric diàn de
electric appliance store diànqì háng
electric generator fādiànjī
electrical machinery diànjī
electrical wire/cable diànxiàn
electricity diàn
elementary school xiǎoxué
elevator diàntī
emancipate; release; free jiěfàng
embroidery cìxiù
emergency jǐnjí qíngkuàng
emergency brake jǐnjí shāchē
emergency exit jǐnjí chūkǒu
emperor huángdì
emphasize; stress zhùzhòng
empire dìguó
employ; use shǐyòng
empty kōng de
end; conclude; close jiéshù
endorse zàntóng; **endorse; approve** zànchéng
engaged, get; engagement dìnghūn
engine (locomotive) huǒchētóu
engineer gōngchéngshī
English yīngwén
enjoy, to; enjoyment xiǎngshòu
enlarge fàngdà
enough gòu le
enter a meeting place rùchǎng
enterprise; company qǐyè
entrance ménkǒu; **entrance; "in" door** rùkǒu
entrust to; trust to wěituō
envelope xìnfēng
environment huánjìng
epilepsy yáng diānfēng
epoch; era shídài; **era; period** qījiān
equal value, of děngzhí de
equipment shèbèi
eraser xiàngpí chā
error; blunder cuòwù
escort, to sòng
esophagus shídào

especially ... tèbié shì ...
essential; indispensable bìxū
establish; set up shùlì
estimate (of cost) gūjià
estimate; appraise gūjì
eternally; always yǒngyuǎn
ethnic zhǒngzú de; **ethnic/national clothing** mínzú fúzhuāng
Europe ōuzhōu; **European** ōuzhōu de; **European person** ōuzhōu rén
even to the point of; so much so that shènzhì
evening wǎnshàng
event; incident shìjiàn
ever since cóng...qǐ
ever; once zéngjīng
every měi(ge); **every time** měi cì
everyday-use articles rìcháng yòngpǐn
everyone suǒyǒu de rén dōu
everywhere dàochù dou
evidence; eyewitness zhèngjiàn
evil; vicious xié'è
examination; test kǎoshì
examine jiǎnchá; kǎochá
example; case instance lìzi
excavate ancient artifacts fājué gǔwù
exceed; go over chāoguò
exception lìwài
excessive; excessively guòfèn
exchange; swap diàohuàn; **exchange letters** tōngxìn
exchange rate duìhuàn lǜ
excuse, an; pretext jièkǒu
exercise; athletics; sports yùndòng
exhibit item zhǎnpǐn; **exhibition** zhǎnlǎn; **exhibitor** zhǎnchūzhě
exist; be cúnzài
expect; hope xīwàng
expenses fèiyòng
expensive guì
experience, to jīnglì
experienced yǒu jīngyàn de
experiment; test shìyàn
explain; explanation jiěshì
export chūkǒu; **exporter** chūkǒu shāng
express (meaning, etc.) biǎodá
expressway gāosù gōnglù
exquisite; graceful yōuměi
extend; prolong yáncháng
exterior; outward appearance wàibiǎo
extra; added; additional éwài de
extremely fēicháng
eye yǎnjīng

eye shadow yǎnliǎn
eyebrow méimáo
eyedrops yǎnyào shuǐ

F

facilitate; effect cùchéng
fact shìshí
factory gōngchǎng
fair; equitable gōngpíng
fall over; topple dǎo
false teeth jiǎyá
false; phony jiǎ de
fame míngshēng; **famous ...** yǒumíng de...
family jiātíng; **family name; last name** xìng
fan (ventilator) diànfēngshàn
far yuǎn
fare chēfèi
farewell dinner, give a jiànxíng
farewell, bid gàobié
farmer nóngfū; **farming/peasant family** nóngjiā
far-off yuǎn de
fashion show fúzhuāng biǎoyǎn
fashion, in; fashionable liúxíng; fēngqì
fast; quick; soon kuài
fast food kuàicān
fat; stout pàng; **fat (on meat, etc.)** zhīfáng
father fùqīn
faucet shuǐlóngtóu
fault; slip; error guòshī
fax chuánzhēn
fear; be afraid of hàipà
fearful; terrible kěpà
feather yǔmáo
feel; sense; think gǎnjué; **feeling** gǎnjué
female nǚxìng de
fetch; get ná
fever; have a fever fāshāo
few; little shǎo; **few, a; some** jǐ ge
fiance wèihūn fu
fiancee wèihūn qī
fields; farmland nóngtián
figure out; calculate jìsuàn
figured out wrongly suàn cuò le
fill in; stuff tián
fill out (a form, etc.) tiánxiě
film (for camera) jiāojuǎn
film; movie diànyǐng
filter guòlǜqì

filthy; dirty āngzāng
final; in the end zuì hòu
final stop (on trip) zhōngzhàn
finally; at long last zhōngyú
finance cáizhèng
fine (money penalty) fákuǎn
fine; delicate xì
finger shǒuzhǐ
fingernail zhǐjia
fire huǒ
fire alarm bào huǒjǐng
fire department xiāofángduì
fire extinguisher mièhuǒ qì
fireworks, set off fàng yānhuǒ
firm (solid) gùdìng de; jiāngù de
firm; company gōngsī
firm; tough; obstinate yìng
first (one); first dì yī
first aid; emergency treatment jíjiù; **first aid kit** jíjiùxiāng
first class; top grade yì liú de
first, at shǒuxiān
first; beforehand xiān
fish yú
fish, to diào yú
fish store yúdiàn
fishing port yúgǎng
flame huǒyàn
flashlight shǒudiàntǒng
flat; level; even píng
flat footed píngdǐjiǎo
flavor; smell qìwèi
flea market jiùhuò shìchǎng
flimsy; weak; light báo
flinch; recoil wèisuō
flirt with tiáoqíng
flood shuǐzāi
floor; story lóu
florist huādiàn
flow, to liú
flow into liúrù
flower huā
flower bouquet huāshù
flower vase huāpíng(r)
flu; heavy cold zhòng gǎnmào
flute dízi
fly (insect) cāngyíng
fly, to fēi
flying; flight fēixíng
fog wù; **foggy** yǒu wù de
folk music mínjiān chuántǒng gēqǔ; mín gē
folkways; folk customs mínsú
follow (along a road, etc.) yánzhe
follow; comply with zūncóng
food; dish cài; shíwù
food; provisions huǒshí

food poisoning shíwù zhòngdú
food store shípǐn diàn
foolish; stupid; clumsy bèn
foot jiǎo
foot brake jiǎo shàchē
for (the benefit of) gei…; **for (the purpose of)** wèile…
forbidden jìnzhǐ
force; compel qiángpò
foreign … wàiguó de…
foreign country wàiguó
foreign exchange wàihuì
foreigner wàiguó rén
foresee; predict yùjiàn
foresight; vision yǎnguāng
forest shùlín
forgive yuánliàng
forgot wàngjì
fork chāzi
form (printed) biǎogé
form; make up/compose zǔchéng
form; shape xíngshì
formerly; in the past yǐqián
fortress yàosài
fortuitous; by chance ǒurán
fortune; luck yùnqi
forty sìshí
forward/go ahead xiàng qián
forward, to; relay zhuǎndì
foundation (funded) jījīnhuì
fountain pen zìláishuǐ bǐ
four sì
four-cornered; square sìjiǎoxíng de
fourteen shísì
fracture (of a bone) gǔzhé
France fǎguó
free (of charge) miǎnfèi
free; unrestrained zìyóu de
free time; break (for rest) xiūxi shíjiān
freedom; liberty zìyóu
freeze, to lěngdòng
freeze; ice up jiébīng
French fǎguó de; **French language** fǎyǔ; **Frenchman** fǎguó rén
french fries shǔtiáo
frequently; often chángcháng
fresh (food, etc.) xīnxiān
Friday xīngqī wǔ
fried meat chǎoròu
friend péngyou; **friendship** yǒuyí
friendly yǒuhǎo de; **friendly; kind** héqì
frightened, be xiàle yí tiào
from (a place/time) cóng
front qiántou; **front of, in** zài…qiántou

front; preceding; ahead; before qián
frost shuāngdòng
fruit shuǐguǒ; **fruits (in general)** guǒshí
fruit stand shuǐguǒ tān
fry; stir-fry; saute chǎo
full (after eating) chībǎo le
fully mǎnman de
fun; interest; delight qùwèi
funds; outlay; expenses jīngfèi
fur; hide; leather pízi; **fur coat** pí dàyī
furnished dài jiājù
furniture jiājù
futile effort túláo de
future; in the future jiānglái; **future events** jiānglái de shìqing

G

gain; achieve huòdé
gains; results; harvest shōuhuò
gallbladder dǎnnáng
gamble dǎdǔ
game (for child, etc.); play a game yóuxì
garage chēkù
garbage; trash lājī
garbage bag lājīdài
garbage can/bin lājītǒng
garden huāyuán
gardener yuándīng
garlic dàsuàn, suàn
gas(oline) qìyóu; **get gas, to** jiāyóu
gas pedal yóumén
gas station jiāyóu zhàn
gear (on car, etc.) dǎng; **gearshift** huàndǎng
general agency zǒng dàilǐ
general agent zǒng dàilǐ shāng
general manager zǒng jīnglǐ
general store záhuòdiàn
generous; liberal; unselfish kāngkǎi
gentle and soft wēnróu
gentleman; Mr. xiānsheng
geography dìlǐ
geology dìzhì
get; obtain; fetch qǔ
get in touch with; contact; connection liánxì
get married; marriage jiéhūn
get out of car/off a train xiàchē
get used to; suit; adapt shìyìng
girl nǚ háizi

give gěi; **give back; return** huán; **give a gift, to** sòng lǐwù
give up; abandon fàngqì
give/have an injection dǎzhēn
glass (the substance) bōli
glass; cup bēizi
gloves shǒutào
glue jiànghú; jiāoshuǐ
gnat wénzi
go for a walk sànbù
go over; pass by guòqù
go there dào nàli qu
go through/experience jīngyàn
go up shàngqu
go up/ascend a mountain shàngshān
go, to; go to qù; go in; enter jìnqù; go out; exit chūqù
go/walk down zǒu xiàqù
goal; purpose mùdì
God shén
gold jīnzi; **gold and silver jewelry** jīnyín shǒushì
golden jīn de
golden yellow jīnhuáng sè de
gold-plated; get gilded dùjīn
golf; golf ball gāoérfū qiú; **golf course** gāoérfū qiúchǎng
Good evening! Good night! wǎn'ān
good; fine; OK hǎo
good idea hǎo zhǔyì
good intentioned hǎoyì de
good time, had a wánde yúkuài
good-bye zàijiàn
goods; merchandise huòwù
gorge; ravine xiágǔ
government zhèngfǔ
grab hold of zhuāzhù
grade; rank; class děngjí
grandchild sūnzi
grandfather zǔfù
grandmother zǔmǔ
grape sugar/candy pútáotáng
grapes pútáo
graphic arts, graphics bǎnhuà yìshù
grass cǎo; **grassland; meadow; lawn** cǎodì
grave fénmù
gravel xiǎo shízi
grease/oil, to shàng yóu
greasy, oily yóunì de
great; mighty wěidà
great! jíhǎo de
Great Wall of China chángchéng
Greece xīlà
green lǜsè
greet, to dǎ zhāohū
grey huīsè

grief; trouble yōushāng
grill/roast meat kǎoròu
grocery stand/stall shūcài tān
group; school; faction pàibié; **group; team; organization** tuántǐ
grove; thicket shùcóng
grow up zhǎngdà
guarantee bǎozhèng
guard; watch kānshǒu
guess; make a guess cāi yì cāi
guest kèrén
guidebook; guide zhǐnán; lǚyóu zhǐnán
guitar jítā
gymnastics tǐcāo; **gymnastics, to do** tǐcāo

H

habit xíguàn
hail bīngbáo
hair (on animal); feather máo
hair (on human) tóufà
hair dryer chuīfēng jī
hair spray pēnfā jì
haircut, get a; do one's hair, to lǐfà; **hairstyle** fāxíng
hairstyle; top (of sth.); chief tóu(r)
half; one half yī bàn
hall, main; parlor dà tīng
halt; stop tíng
ham huǒtuǐ
hammer chuízi
hamper zǔráo
hand shǒu
hand, to; give (to someone) dìgěi
hand brake shǒu shàchē
hand-carried luggage shǒutí xínglǐ
hand over; surrender jiāochū
handbag shǒutíbāo
handball shǒuqiú
handicraft; handwork shǒugōng
handkerchief shǒujuànr
handle; deal with; dispose of chǔlǐ
handle; grip bǎshǒu
handmade shǒugōng de
handsome; attractive piàoliang
hang up; suspend guà
hanging guàzhe
happen; occur fāshēng
happiness yúkuài
happy; delighted gāoxìng
hard; stiff yìng; **hardness** yìngdù
hardly jīhū bù
harm, to sǔnhài

harmful yǒuhài
hastily; in a hurry cōngmáng
hat màozi
have; own; possess yǒu
have an allergy to... duì...guòmǐn
have confidence in; trust xìnrèn
have/catch a cold shāngfēng
hay fever huāfěn rè
head tóu
headache tóutòng
headache tablets tóuténg yào
heal; cure zhìliáo
health jiànkāng; shēntǐ; **healthy** jiànkāng de
health insurance company jiànkāng bǎoxiǎn gōngsi
hear; hearing (sense of) tīng; tīngjué
heart xīnzàng
heart attack xīnzàng bìng
heart trouble n xīnzàng bìng
heart; inner being nèixīn
heat, supply gōng nuǎnqì; **heating** nuǎnqì
heat; warm jiārè
heaven tiān
heavy; weighty zhòng
height gāodù
helicopter zhíshēngjī
hello hālóu
help, to; assistance bāngzhù
herb zhíwù; zácǎo; **herbs (for medicine)** cǎoyào
here zhèlǐ
herring qīngdāo yú
hesitant yóuyù bùjué
hesitate chíyí
hide; conceal yǐncáng
high; tall gāo
high pressure (weather) gāo qìyā
high speed kuài sùdù
highway; road gōnglù
hill; mountain shān
him; her tā
hip túnbù
his; her tā de
historic site gǔjī
history lìshǐ
hit song liúxíng gēqǔ
hoarse shāyǎ
hobby yèyú àihào
hockey qǔgùn qiú
hold (a meeting, etc.) jǔxíng
hole dòng
holiday jiérì
holy shénshèng de
home owner fángzhǔ

homeland; native land zǔguó
hometown; native place jiāxiāng
honey fēngmì
honor; glory róngyào
hook gōuzi
hope; expect xīwàng
hope; expectation xīwàng
hopeless juéwàng
horse mǎ; **horsepower** mǎlì; **horse race; horse racing** sàimǎ
hose; tube xiàngpí guǎn
hospital yīyuàn
hospitality hàokè
host; hostess zhǔrén
hostile chóushì de
hot rè
hotel bīnguǎn
hour xiǎoshí; zhōngtóu
house; small building fángzi; **house number** ménhào; ménpái
housewife jiātíng zhǔfù
how to zěnme
however; but dànshì
huge; enormous; powerful jù dà de
human nature rénxìng
humanity; humankind rénlèi
hundred bǎi
hunger jī è; **hungry** è
husband and wife fūqī
hut máowū

I

I; me wǒ
I'm delighted to learn that ... xīnwén ...
ice bīng
ice cream bīngqílín
ice cube bīngkuài
ice skate liūbīng
iced bīnglěng de
iced coffee bīng kāfēi
ID card shēnfènzhèng
idea; plan zhǔyì
idea; thought xiǎngfǎ
identify; make out rènchū
identity; status shēnfen
idiom; set phrase chéngyǔ
if; in case rúguǒ
illuminate zhàomíng
Illustrated magazine huàkān
illustration tújiě
imagine xiǎngxiàng
immediately mǎshàng
impolite bú kèqì

import jìnkǒu; **importer** jìnkǒu shāng
important zhòngyào
impose a fine; fine; penalty fákuǎn
impossible bù kěnéng; **impossible to comprehend** bù kě lǐjiě de
impractical bù shíjì
impression yìnxiàng
improper; dishonorable bú zhèngjīng
improve; strengthen tígāo
improve (by changing) gǎishàn
in; on; at zài; **in(side)** zài...lǐ; **in all; altogether** zǒnggòng; **in charge of; responsible for** fùzé; **in fact** qíshí; **in general** yìbān; **in the first place; first of all** shǒuxiān; **in the rear; at the back** hòumiàn
incapable; powerless wúlì
incisive; penetrating; sharp jiānruì de
inclination piānhào
include; consist of bāokuò
income shōurù
incomplete bù wánquán
inconvenient bù fāngbiàn
incorrect; wrong búduì
increase zēngjiā
indefinite bú quèdìng de
indigestion xiāohuà bùliáng
indispensable bìyào
industrial fair hángyè shāngzhǎn
industry gōngyè
ineffective wúxiào
inexperienced méi jīngyàn de
infantile paralysis xiǎoér mábì
infect gǎnrǎn
infectious chuánrǎn de
inflammable yìrán de
inflammmation fāyán
inflate; pump up gěi...dǎqì
influence; effect yǐngxiǎng
inform; notice tōngzhī
inform; relate; tell gàosù
information xìnxī
infuriate; flare up fānù
inhabitants (of a city, etc.) jūmín
inhalation xī zhēngqì zhìliáo fǎ
inland; interior nèilù
inn lǚshè
innocent; innocent person wúgū de
inoculate, to dǎ yùfángzhēn
inquire; find out about dǎtīng; **inquiry** xúnwèn
insane; mad fēng le
insect kūnchóng
inside; within lǐmiàn, lǐbiān

insist on; persist in jiānchí
insomnia shīmián
inspect; examine jiǎnchá
install ānzhuāng
institute of learning xuéyuàn
insufficient búgòu
insulin yídǎo sù
insult; humiliate wǔrù
insure; insurance bǎoxiǎn
intact; complete wánzhěng
intelligent; smart; clever cōngmíng
intentional(ly) gùyì de
intercourse; contact wǎnglai
interested in duì ... gǎn xìngqù
interesting yǒu yìsi
interests xìngqu
intermediary (person) zhōngjiè shāng
international guójì de
international call guójì diànhuà
intersection; crossing shízì lùkǒu
intestines chángzi
intravenous, on an dǎ diàndī
introduce; recommend jièshào;
invade; transgress qīnfàn
invent; invention fāmíng
investigate, to diàochá
invite yuē, qǐng; **invite guests** qǐng kèren
iodine diǎn
iron (the metal) tiě
iron; press yùndǒu; **iron clothes** yùn yīfu
iron wire tiěsī
irregular breathing hūxī búshùn
Islam huíjiào
island dǎo
item; thing dōngxi
itinerary lǚxíng lùxiàn

J

jacket jiákè
jade yù
jam; marmalade guǒjiàng
Japan rìběn; **Japanese person** rìběn rén
jazz juéshì
jealous; jealousy jìdù
jeans niúzǎi kù
jellyfish shuǐmǔ
jet plane pēnqìshì fēijī
jeweler zhūbǎo shāng; **jewelry** shǒushi
Jewish person yóutài rén

job gōngzuò
jog pǎobù; mànpǎo
join; link liánjiē
joint (i.e., knee, elbow, etc.) guānjié
joint-venture enterprise hézī qǐyè
joke xiàohuà
journalist jìzhě
joy; happiness yúkuài
judge (court) fǎguān
judge; determine; judgment pànduàn, pànjué
judo róudào
juice (fruit) guǒzhī
juicy duōzhī de
jump, to tiào
just now gānggāng
justice zhèngyì

K

karate kōngshǒudào
keep (somebody) company péibàn
keep; maintain; preserve bǎochí; **keep (food) fresh** bǎoxiān
kerosene méiyóu
key (to a lock) yàoshi
kick up a row; din; noise chǎonào
kidney shènzàng
kidney stone shènjiéshí
kilogram gōngjīn
kilometer gōngchǐ; mǐ
kindergarten; nursery school yòuéryuán
kindly; affable hé'ǎi
king guówáng
kiss; to kiss wěn
kitchen chúfáng
knapsack bèibāo
knee xīgài
knife; sword; blade dāozi
knight wǔshì
knock, to qiāo
knot jié
know; realize zhīdào
know, to (a person) rènde
knowledge zhīshi
knuckle jiégǔ
Korea; South nán cháoxiān; **North** běi cháoxiān; **Korean person** cháoxiān rén

L

laboratory shíyànshì
lack; short of quēfá

ladder tīzi
lady; woman; Mrs. tàitai
lake hú
lamp; light dēng
land, to (airplane) jiàngluò
land; territory tǔdì
language yǔyán
last zuì hòu
last one, the; final zuì hòu de
late wǎn; **come late** chídào
laugh, to xiào
laurel yuèguàn
lava huǒshān róngyán
law fǎlǜ
lawn cǎopíng
lawyer; attorney lǜshī
lay down; recline tǎngxià
lazy lǎn
lead, to lǐngdǎo
leadership; leaders lǐngdǎo
learn, to; study xuéxí
leasing fēnqī fùkuǎn
leather jacket pí jiákè
leather store píhuò diàn
leather; skin; hide pí
leave behind; leave liúxià
leave the country chūjìng
leave; depart from líkāi; **leave on a journey; leave** dòngshēn
lecture; talk yǎnjiǎng
left (side) zuǒbiān
leftover(s) shèngxià
lemon níngméng
lend, to; borrow from, to jiè
length chángdù
let; allow ràng
letter; mail xìn
letter paper; stationery xìnzhǐ
library túshūguǎn
license zhízhào
license plate number chēhào
lid; cover gàizi
lie (untruth) huǎngyán
lie down, to tǎngxià
life; livelihood; to live shēnghuó; **life (living conditions)** shēnghuó; **life span** shēngmìng
lifeboat jiùshēng tǐng
lift; raise tí qǐlái
light; pale (color) qiǎn
light a fire diǎn huǒ
light bulb dēngpào
light switch kāiguān
lighter dǎhuǒ jī
light-house dēngtǎ
lightning; flash of lightning shǎndiàn

like; love; be fond of xǐ'ài
like this; this way zhèyàng
like, to (prefer) xǐhuān
likeable; popular shòu huānyíng de
likely; probably dàyuē
lilac (color) zǐ sè
limited company yǒuxiàn gōngsī
line is busy zhànxiàn
line up, to páiduì
linen má de
lining chènlǐ
lips zuǐchún
lipstick kǒuhóng
list; bill; form dānzi; list of names
  míngdān
listen; hear, to tīng
listener(s); audience tīngzhòng
little bit, a yìdiǎn
live; reside; spend the night zhù
live music xiànchǎng yǎnzòu
lively shēngdòng
liver gānzàng
living huó de
loan; credit; grant a loan dàikuǎn
lobster lóngxiā
local běndì de; local specialty tèchǎn
lock (on door, etc.) suǒ
lock up suǒshàng
locker; changing room gēngyī shì
lodgings zhùsù; lodgings with three
  meals bāo sāncān de zhùsù
lonely; lonesome jímò
long; lengthy cháng
long-distance call chángtú diànhuà
look, to; see; watch kàn
look after; care for; attend to
  zhàogù
look at kànkan; look into; examine
  chákàn
look for; search zhǎo
look forward to, to; be happy
  (about) wèi...gāoxìng
lookout point (to view scenery)
  guānjǐng tái
looks like; appear to be kàn qǐlái
loose sōng le
loose coat; outer garment wàitào
lose; misplace diū
lose one's job; be out of work shīyè
lost; lose one's way mílù le
lost and found shīwù zhāolǐng chù
loud and clear liàng
loud voice dàshēng
loudspeaker lǎbā
lounge jacket xīfú shàngzhuāng
lovable; likeable kě'ài
love (btw. people) àiqíng

love, to ài
low (in height) dī
low (in status, etc.) dīxià
low pressure (weather) dī qìyā
lower; reduce; cut down jiàngdī
loyal zhōngshí
luggage; baggage xíngli
lumbago yāobù fēngshī bìng
lunch wǔfàn
lung fèizàng
luxury, luxurious háohuá

M

machine jīqì
magazine zázhì
magnolia; cotton rose mùlián
mail (send by) jì
mailbox xìnxiāng
mailman yóudìyuán
main dish zhǔcān
main entrance, main door dàmén
main post office yóuzhèng zǒngjú
main station zǒngzhàn
main street dà jiē
mainland; continent dàlù
mainly zhǔyào
make change zhǎo qian
make friends jiāo péngyou
make up for, to bǔhuí
make/become cool liàng
malaria nüèjí
male nán de; nánxìng
man nánrén
manage guǎnlǐ
management guǎnlǐ
mandarin oranges júzi
mango mángguǒ
manual shuōmíngshū
many; a lot of xǔduō
map dìtú
marble dàlǐshí
margarine zhíwù yóu
marital status hūnyīn
  zhuàngkuàng
mark; sign jìhào
market; sell jīngxiāo; marketing
  shìchǎng jīngxiāo; marketplace
  shìchǎng
marriage; wedding jiéhūn
marry; get married jiéhūn;
  matrimony hūnyīn
massage ànmó
Master (form of address for skilled
  worker) shīfu

match (for lighting) huǒcái;
  matchbox huǒcái hé
match; competition; compete bǐsài
material (clothing) bùliào; **raw**
  material zhíliào
material (for a report, etc.) cáiliào
mathematics shùxué
matter; affair shìqing
mattress chuángdiàn
may; be permissable kěyǐ
maybe kěnéng
mayor shìzhǎng
me too; each other bǐcǐ
me; I wǒ
mealtime chīfàn shíjiān
mean; signify; imply yìwèizhe
meaning; significance yìyì
meanwhile zài cǐ qíjiān
measles mázhěn
measure, to liáng
measurement; dimension chǐcùn
meat ròu
mechanic jīxiè shīfu
medal xūnzhāng
medicine (the science) yīxué;
  Chinese medicine zhōngyī
medicine; drugs yào
Mediterranean dìzhōnghǎi
meet; encounter; run into pèngjiàn,
  yùjiàn
meeting; conference huìyì; **meeting**
  center huìhé zhōngxīn
melon guā
member huìyuán
mend; patch; repair bǔ
menstruation yuèjīng
merit; strong point yōudiǎn
mess, What a zāogāo!
method; means; way fāngfǎ
miasma zhàngqì
microphone màikèfēng
middle; center zhōngjiān
Middle Ages zhōnggǔ shìjì
middleman zhōngjiè rén
midnight; middle of the night bànyè
midwife zhùchǎnshì
migraine zhōuqíxìng tóutòng
mild; temperate; gentle wēnhé
military affairs jūnshì
military control jūnshì guǎnzhì
milk niúnǎi
mineral kuàngwù; **mineral water**
  kuàngquán shuǐ
minibus xiǎoba
ministry (government) xíngzhèng
  bùmén
minute (of time) fēn

mirage (fig./lit.) hǎi shì shèn lóu
mirror jìngzi
miscarriage liúchǎn
mishap; accident shìgù
miss; let slip cuòguò
Miss; Ms. nǚshì; **Miss; unmarried**
  woman xiǎojiě
mistake cuòwù
mistake, made a nòng cuò le
Mister; teacher; gentleman
  xiānsheng
mistreat; abuse nüèdài
misunderstand wùjiě
misunderstanding wùhuì
mixed hùnhé de
model (for fashion, etc.) mótèér
model; example diǎnfàn
model; pattern móxíng
modern xiàndài
moment; little while yìhuǐr
monastery xiūdàoyuàn
Monday xīngqī yī
money qián
monk héshàng
monopoly; monopolize zhuānmài;
  lǒngduàn
monosyllabic dānyīn de
month yuè; **monthly** měi yuè
moon yuèliàng
more; many duō
moreover érqiě
morning zǎoshàng
mortgage; pawn diǎnyā
mother mǔqīn
motor mótuō; mǎdá
mountain shān; **mountains** shānmài
mouth (of a person) zuǐ
mouth (river) hékǒu
move; shift dòng
moved, be (emotionally) gǎndòng
movie actor/actress diànyǐng
  yǎnyuán
movie theater diànyǐng yuàn
mud; clay ní
muddleheaded; absentminded
  hūntóu hūnnǎo
muscle jīròu
museum bówùguǎn
mushrooms mógū
music yīnyuè
musical (play) gēwǔ jù
must; have to xūyào
mustard jièmò
mutton yángròu
mutually; mutual hùxiāng
my; mine wǒ de
myth shénhuà

N

nail polish zhǐjia yóu
nail polish remover qù zhǐjia yóu
nail scissors zhǐjiadāo
naked luǒtǐ
name; title míngzi
named, be; name/call, to jiào
napkin cānjīn
narcotic; drug dúpǐn
narrow zhǎi
nation; country guójiā; national…
  guójiā…
national park guójiā gōngyuán
nationality (national origin) guójí
naturally; of course zìrán
nature zìrán
nausea ě xīn
navel dùjǐ
near; close by jìn
nearby; close fùjìn
nearsighted jìnshì
necessary bìxū
necessity bìyàoxìng
neck bózi
necktie lǐngdài
need; require; demand xūyào
needle zhēn
negative side fǎnmiàn de
negligent; careless mǎmahūhu
negotiations; discussions tánpàn
neighbor línjū
neither…nor búshì…yě búshì…
nephew zhízi
nerve shénjīng
nervous jǐnzhāng
net wǎng
neutrality zhōnglì
never … cónglaibù…
never mind; it doesn't matter méi
  shénme
nevertheless; although suīrán
new; fresh xīn; new and original;
  novel xīnyǐng
news (in a newspaper) xīnwén
news (tidings) xiāoxí;
newspaper bào, bàozhǐ
newstand shūbào tān
next one, the xià yí ge; next time xià
  yí cì
next to; beside zài… pángbiān
niece zhínǚ
night; at night; evening wǎnshàng
night club yèzǒnghuì
nine jiǔ
ninety jiǔshí
nipple (for baby bottle) nǎizuǐ

no; not bù
no matter what you use bùguǎn
  yòng shénme
no way; under no circumstances
  juéduì bù
nobility; gentry guìzú
noble; high; elitist; privileged
  gāoguì
nonsmoker bù xīyān de
noodles miàntiáo
noon zhōngwǔ
normal zhèngcháng, píngcháng
normally speaking yìbān de shuo
North, the běibù
northern … běibù de…
Norway nuówēi
Norwegian person nuówēi rén
nose bízi
nosebleed liú bíxuě
not bù; méiyǒu; not at all gēnběn bu;
  not only búdan
not have; be without; there is not
  méiyǒu
not until; only when … cái
note/jot down, to jì xiàlái
notebook; booklet běnzi
notes; jottings bǐjì
nothing at all yìdiǎn yě méiyǒu
notice; circular tōngzhī
notice, to zhùyì
notify; inform tōngzhī
novel (book) xiǎoshuō
now; at present xiànzài
nowhere méiyǒu yí ge dìfang
number; figure (1, 2, 3, etc.) shùzì
number; serial number biānhào
numerous; many; much duō
nun nígū
nurse hùshì
nut (screw) luómǔ
nutrition; nourishment yíngyǎng
nutritious yǒu yíngyǎng de

O

oar huájiǎng
oatmeal màipiàn
object (thing) dōngxī; goal; objective
  duìxiàng
objective; unbiased kěguān de
obligated, to be; have the duty to
  yǒu yìwù
obligation; duty yìwù
observatory tiānwén tái

observe; abide by zūnshǒu
observe; survey; inspect guānchá
obstacle zhàngài
obstruct; stop zǔdǎng
obvious míngxiǎn
occasionally ǒuér
occupation zhíyè
ocean hǎiyáng
office worker; staff zhíyuán
office; place of business bàn gōng
shì
official (person) guānyuán,
gōngwùyuán
official... guānfāng...
official business gōngwù
often chángcháng
oil; fat; grease yóu
oil change huàn rùnhuáyóu
oil painting yóuhuà
ointment yàogāo
okay; permissible kěyǐ de
old lǎo
on zài...shàng; on an empty stomach
kōngfù; on board a plane zài fēijī
shàng; on the floor/ground
dìshàng; on the left zài zuǒbiān; on
the way; en route túzhōng; on top
of ... zài...shàngmiàn
once; one time yí cì; once more zài
yí cì
one yī
one and a half yí ge bàn; one-day
ticket yìtiān yǒuxiào de piào; one
fourth sì fēn zhī yī; one half; half yī
bàn; one person; alone yí ge rén;
one third sānfēn zhī yī; one; one of
yí ge
one's own zìjǐ de
oneself zìjǐ
onion yángcōng
only zhǐ; only one; sole one wéiyī de
open; open up kāi, dǎkāi
open-air stage lùtiān jùchǎng
opera gējù
operation (surgical) shǒushù;
kāidāo; operation, have an dòng
shǒushù; kāidāo
opinion; view jiànyì
opportunity; chance jīhuì
oppose fǎnduì
opposite (contrary) xiāngfǎn
opposite (side) duìmiàn
optometrist's (store) yǎnjìng háng
or; perhaps; maybe huòzhě
orangeade; lemonade júzi shuǐ
orchestra yuètuán
order; subscribe to; book dìng

orderly; tidy zhěngjié
ordinary; common; average pǔtōng
organ (musical instrument)
guǎnfēngqín
organization; system zǔzhī
organize, to zǔzhī
Orient, the dōngfāng
original article yuánjiàn
other; another; different one bié de
otherwise bùrán
ours wǒmen de
out, go; exit chūmén
outdoor bathing place yùchǎng
outlook; view yìjiàn; kànfǎ
outside; surface wàimiàn, wàibiān
outside of cǐwài
outside world wàijiè
outstanding; remarkable jiéchū
outward appearance; exterior
wàibiǎo
oven; furnace; stove lúzi
over there nàbiān
overcharge; fleece s.o. qiāo
overcoat; coat dàyī
overdo (sth.); go beyond guòdù
overdue, be; exceed time limit guòqī
overseas hǎiwài
owe, to (money, etc.) qiàn
oyster mǔlì

P

pack; package bāozhuāng
pack in; load on zhuāng zài; packed
too full zhuāng le tài mǎn le
pack up dǎbāo
package bāoguǒ; mail yóubāo
packet xiǎo bāo
page yè; zhāng
pain; suffering; painful tòngkǔ, tòng
painkiller zhǐtòng yào
paint; draw huìhuà
painter huàjiā
pair of... yìshuāng...
pajamas shuìyī
palace huánggōng
pale; pallid cāngbái
panorama; scenery fēngjǐng
pants; trousers kùzi
paper zhǐ
paper bag zhǐdài
paper clip huíxíngzhēn
paprika qīngjiāo
parade; march; demonstrate
yóuxíng

paralysis mábì
parasol; sunshade yángsǎn
parcel (mail) yóujì
parents fùmǔ
park (public) gōngyuán
park, to (vehicle) tíngchē; **parking lot** tíngchē chǎng
part; portion bùfèn
participate in; join cānguān
party, have a; invite guests qǐngkè
pass by (while walking, etc.) zǒuguò
pass by/through a place lùguò
pass on; transfer; convey to zhuǎn
passageway tōngdào
passenger chéngkè
passport hùzhào
passport check jiǎnchá hùzhào
past, the; in the past guòqù
pastries served with tea chádiǎn
path xiǎolù
patience; patient nàixīn
patient, be yǒu nàixīn
pattern; fashion fāngshì
pavilion tínggé
pay (money) fù; **pay a bill** fùzhàng; **pay a sum of money** fùkuǎn; **pay attention to; notice** zhùyì; **pay cash** fù xiànjīn; **pay out money; expenditure** zhīchū; **pay taxes** jiǎoshuì
payment terms/conditions fùkuǎn tiáojiàn
peace; peaceful hépíng
peaches táozi
peak; height; summit gāofēng
peak season wàngjì
pear lízi
pearl zhēnzhū
peas wāndòu
peasant; peasantry nóngmín
pedal tàbǎn
pedestrian xíngrén
pedestrian zone xíngrén qū
pencil qiānbǐ
people rénmen; **people, the** rénmín
pepper hújiāo
percent bǎifēnbǐ
percentage bǎifēnlǜ
perfect wánměi
perform; act biǎoyǎn
performance yǎnchū
perfume xiāngshuǐ
perhaps; maybe yěxǔ
period of time, a yíduàn shíqī
perk up; refresh oneself tíshén
perm, get a tàngfà
permanent; lasting yǒngjiǔ de

permit; allow xǔkě
permit; permission zhǔnxǔ
Persian bōsī rén
person; people rén
personal gèrén de
personal computer gèrén diànnǎo
personnel zhígōng
pharmaceutical studies yàojì xué
philosophy zhéxué
photoflash; flash lamp shǎn guāng dēng
photograph zhàopiàn
photograph, to zhàoxiàng
photostat yǐngyìn jī
physics wùlǐ
physiology shēnglǐ xué
pick; pluck zhāi
pickpocket páshǒu
picture postcard fēngjǐng míngxìn piàn
picturesque yōuměi de
pie (dessert) pái
piece of ... ...kuài; ...ge
pier; wharf mǎtóu
pig; hog zhū
pill (medicine) yàopiàn, yàowán
pillow zhěntóu
pilot jiàshǐ yuán
pin dàtóuzhēn
pine tree sōngshù
pineapple fènglí
pink fěnhóng sè
pinyin (system of spelling) pīnyīn
pipe (for smoking) yāndǒu
piston; valve huósāi
place; location dìfāng
place; put fàng
place into fàngjìn
place of birth chūshēngdì
place of worship zōngjiào shèngdì
plains (geog.) píngyuán
plan; project; program jìhuà
plan to dǎsuàn
plant; flora zhíwù
plaster shígāo
plaster (medical) yàogāo
plastic sùliào
plate; dish; tray pánzi
play, to; have fun wán(r)
playground yóulèchǎng
please; invite qǐng; **Please come in!** qǐngjìn!
pleased mǎnyì
plug (electric) chātóu
plum lǐzi
plunder; pillage qiǎngjié
pneumonia fèiyán

pocket kǒudài
pocketknife xiǎodāo
pointed; sharp jiān de
poison; narcotics dú
poisoned, be zhòngdú
poisonous yǒu dú
police jǐngchá
polite yǒu lǐmào
political party zhèngdǎng
politics zhèngzhì
poor qióng
popular edition pǔjíběn
porcelain cíqì
pork zhūròu
pornographic; sexy sèqíng
port; harbor gǎngkǒu
porter bānyùn de
position; seat wèizhi
position; status dìwei
positive; directly/openly zhèngmiàn de
possess special traits jùyǒu tèxìng
possibility kěnéngxìng
possible; possibly kěnéng
post office yóujú
postage yóuzī
postcard míngxìnpiàn
poster hǎibào
postpone; put off tuīchí
pot guōzi
pot; basin pénzi
potatoes tǔdòu
pottery táoqì
powder fěn
power; authority quánlì
power; force lìliàng
practical; functional shíyòng
practice; drill liànxí
pragmatic xiànshí
praise, to zànměi
pray, prayer qídǎo
pregnant huái yùn
premiere shǒuyǎn
prepare to; preparations zhǔnbèi
prescription yàofāng
present; gift lǐwù
present, the; now xiànzài
preservation of historic sites bǎohù gǔjī
press circles; the press xīnwénjiè
pretty; handsome hǎokàn; piàoliàng
prevent; guard against yùfáng; **stop; prohibit** zǔzhǐ
price jiàqián; **price list** jiàgébiǎo; **price of admission** rùchǎngfèi
priest (Catholic) shénfù
printed matter yìnshuā pǐn

printer (worker) yìnshuā gōng
printing press yìnshuā jī
priority; preference yōuxiānquán
prison jiānyù
private sīrén de
probably; likely dàgài
process; course jīngguò
process; machining jiāgōng
produce; production shēngchǎn
producer chǎnshāng
product chǎnpǐn
professor jiàoshòu
profit; make a profit yínglì
profound; deep shēn
program; item on program jiémù
progress; improvement jìnbù
prohibit; forbid jìnzhǐ
Prohibited! jìnzhǐ…
promise; agree to dāyìng
promote (raise status of) tíshēng
promote sale of; peddle tuīxiāo
pronounce; pronunciation fāyīn
proof; prove zhèngmíng
propaganda xuānchuán
proprietor (of a shop) diànzhǔ
protect; safeguard bǎohù
protest kàngyì
prove; proof zhèngmíng
province shěng
provisional línshí; zànshí
provisions; food shípǐn
psychology xīnlǐ xué
public… gōnggòng de…
public relations gōnggòng guānxì
publish chūbǎn
pull; drag lā
pulse màibó
pumpkin nán guā
punctual zhǔnshí
punishment chǔfá
purchase, to gòumǎi
purple zǐ sè
push, to tuī
pustule nóngbāo
put; place fàng
put on; be dressed in chuān
put s.o. to the trouble of… láo nín…
put up; construct dāqǐ
put up with; bear rěnshòu

Q

quality zhíliàng
quantity; amount shùliàng
quarrel, to chǎojià

queen wánghòu
question wèntí
quickly; hastily gǎnkuài
quiet; peaceful ānjìng
quite/rather good bǐjiào hǎo

R

rabbit tùzi
rabies kuángquán bìng
race (on foot) sàipǎo
radiate; emit fàngshè
radio shōuyīnjī
radioactive fàngshèxìng de
rail(s) tiěguǐ
railing; bar zhàlán
railroad tiělù; **railroad car** chēxiāng
railroad accident tiělù shìgù
rain yǔ; **rainy season** yǔjì
rain, to xià yǔ
rain boots/galoshes yǔxié
raincoat yǔyī
raise; heighten; improve tígāo
raisins pútáo gān
rank; class děngjí
rape qiángjiān
rapid; speedy xùnsù
rarely; not often bù cháng
rather; prefer to nìngkě
rational; reasonable hélǐ
raw shēng de
ray (of light) guāngxiàn
reach; arrive at dǐdá
read aloud; study niàn
real zhēnshí de
realize; put into effect shíxiàn
really; truly zhēn de
rear wheel hòulún
rearview mirror hòushìjìng
reason; cause yuányīn
rebuild, to chóngjiàn
receipt shōujù
receive shōudào
**receive (guests, etc.); treat
　(customers, etc.)** zhāodài
received (a letter, etc.) shōudào le
recently zuìjìn
reception (for guests, etc.) jiēdài huì
reception room jiēdàitīng
recipe shípǔ
reckon; make a guess gūjì
recognize; know; meet rènshi
recommend tuījiàn
record player chàngjī
record store chàngpiàn háng

recording (music) chàngpiàn
recuperate; convalesce liáoyǎng
red hóng sè
red traffic light hónglǜdēng
reduce; lower; cut jiǎndī
reef jiāoshí
refreshments; snacks xiǎochī
refrigerator bīngxiāng
refuse jùjué
region; area dìqū
register; check in dēngjì;
　registration; check-in desk dēngjì
　chù
registered letter guàhào xìn
registered mail guàhào yóujiàn
regular pattern guīlǜ
regulate, to; adjust tiáozhěng
regulation; rule guīdìng
rehearse (theater) páiyǎn
relationship; bearing guānxi
relatives; kin; kinship qīnshǔ
relevant yǒu guānxi
reliable kěkào
religion zōngjiào
religious zōngjiào de
religious service lǐbài
remember; think of xiǎngqǐ
remind; warn; alert tíxǐng
remit money; remittance huìkuǎn
remote; out of the way piānpì de
rent; hire zū
rent money zūjīn
rent out chūzū
repair, to; fix xiūlǐ
repay bàodá
replace tìdài
reply; answer huídá
report; make known bàogào
report; term paper bàogào
report card chéngjī dān
represent; representative dàibiǎo
request; ask qǐngqiú
require; requirement yāoqiú
requirements; conditions; terms
　tiáojiàn
resemble; be similar xiāngsì
reserve; book; order dìng
reserve, to yùdìng
residence zhùzhǎi
residents shìmín
responsible for; in charge of
　zhǔguǎn
rest; take a break xiūxi
rest/remaining, the shèngxià
rest stop xiūxi zhàn
restaurant cāntīng
restrict; confine xiànzhì

result; as a result jiéguǒ
resume; personal data lǚlì
retailer língshòu shāng
retire; retirement tuìxiū
retreat; draw back hòutuì
return (for exchange) tuìhuàn;
  return/give back money huán qián;
  return; refund tuìhuí
return (here) huílái
return home huí jiā
return trip huíchéng
revert to; return guīhuán
reward; remuneration; pay
  bàochou
rheumatism fēngshī
rice (raw) dàomǐ; **cooked** báifàn
rice paddies; paddy rice shuǐdào
rich; wealthy yǒu qián
riches cáifù
ride a horse, to qímǎ
ridiculous; laughable kě xiào de
right, on the; right side yòubiān
right, to be; correct duì le
right away mǎshàng
ring (for finger) jièzhǐ
ring a bell ànlíng
ripe; mature chéngshú
risk; hazard fēngxiǎn
river hé, héliú
road dàolù
road map gōnglù dìtú
roadside línjiē de yímiàn
roadwork (construction) xiūlù
rock; stone yánshí
rod; pole; stick gùnzi
role/part (in a play, etc.) juésè
roller skates liūbīng xié
Rome luómǎ
roof wūdǐng
room (in a hotel, etc.) fángjiān
rooster gōngjī
rope; string shéngzi
rose (flower) méiguì huā
rotten; corrupt fǔlàn
rouge kǒuhóng
round; circular yuán de
round-trip ticket huíchéng piào
route; line lùxiàn
row; column háng
row a boat; boating huá chuán
rubber xiàngpí
rubbish lājī
rug; carpet dìtǎn
ruined; gone bad huài le
ruins fèixū
rule; regulation fǎtiáo; guīdìng
run; run away pǎo

Russia è guó; **Russian** è guó de;
  Russian language è yǔ; **Russian
  person** è guó
rust tiěxiù

S

sack; bag dàizi
sad nánguò
saddle mǎ'ān
safe; safety ānquán
safe; security box bǎoxiǎn xiāng
safety belt ānquán dài
safety pin biézhēn
safety/security check ānquán
  jiǎnchá
sail, to; navigate hángxíng
sailing boat; junk fānchuán
sailor hǎiyuán
salad shālā
salami (Italian) yìdàlì xiāngcháng
salary; wages xīnshuǐ
sales xiāoshòu
sales contract mǎimài héyuē
sales network jīngxiāo wǎng
salmonella shāshì xìjùn
saloon píjiǔ guǎn
salt yán
same; identical yíyàng
same; similar; equal tóngyàng
sample; specimen yàngběn
sand shā; **sandy** duō shā de
sandals liángxié
sandwich sānmíngzhì
sardine shādīng yú
satire/satirical play fěngcì jù
satisfy; satisfied mǎnyì
Saturday xīngqī liù
sauce (from meat) ròujiàng
sauna sānwēnnuǎn
sausage xiāngcháng
save, to (rescue) jiù
save, to; economize jiéshěng
save/keep (for use) liú xiàlai
say, to shuō; **tell** gàosu
say good-bye/farewell gàobié
say hello to; greet dǎ zhāohū
scale (for weighing) chèngzi
scar shāngbā
scarf wéijīn
scarlet xīnghóng rè
scenery fēngjǐng
schedule, flight bānjī
schedule; be scheduled to yùdìng
school xuéxiào

science kēxué
scissors jiǎndāo
scold, to; rebuke; talk badly of mà
scorpion xiēzi
scratch, to; itch yǎng
scream, to jīngjiào
screw luósī; screwdriver luósī qǐzi
scrub; brush, to shuā
sculpture diāosù
sea hǎi
sea urchin hǎidǎn
seagull hǎiōu
seal; stamp gàizhāng
sealed; closed fēngbì de
seas and oceans; ocean hǎiyáng
seasick yūnchuán de
seaside hǎibīn; seaside resort hǎibīn
   yùchǎng
season (of the year) jìjié
seasoning tiáowèipǐn
seat; place zuòwèi
second (1/60 of a minute) miǎo
second from last zuì hóu dì èr ge
second one dì èr ge
second point/item dì èr diǎn
secret mìmì de
secretary mìshū
secretary's office mìshū chù
section of highway lùduàn
security; safe ānquán
security police gōng'ān jǐngchá
sedative; tranquilizer zhènjìng jì
see; look at; watch kàn
seek advice of; consult, to qǐngjiào
seldom xīshǎo
self-made zìjǐ zuò de
self-service zìzhù shì
sell mài
send (dispatch) pài; send on errand
   dǎfā; send out (in the mail) jìchū
senior high school gāozhōng
sentence jùzi
separate, to fēnkāi
separated fēnkāi de
serial number hàomǎ
serious; earnest; conscientious;
   solemn rènzhēn, yánsù
sermon, give a jiǎngdào
serve; service fúwù
service hours fúwù shíjiān
service person (waiter, etc.)
   fúwùyuán
set out; start off chūfā
several yìxiē
sew, to féng
sex xìngbié
sexual disease xìngbìng

sexual organs xìng qìguān
shadow yǐngzi
shame, it's a kěxí
shameless; brazen wú chǐ de
shampoo xǐfǎjì
shave, to guā húzi
she; he tā
sheep yáng
shellfish bèiké
shine; glitter fāliàng
shining fāliàng de
ship; boat chuán
shirt; blouse chènshān
shoe xiézi
shoe store xiédiàn
shoelaces xiédài
shoot, to fāshè
shop, to; shopping mǎi dōngxī
shop assistant huǒji
short duǎn
short circuit duǎnlù
short of; lack quēshǎo
shortcut jiéjìng
should; ought to yīnggāi
shoulder jiānbǎng
shout, to hǎnjiào
shower bath chōngzǎo; línyù
shrimp xiǎo xiā
shrink; reduce in size suōxiǎo
shut; closed guānshàng
side; margin; edge; rim biān(r)
side effects fù zuòyòng
sidewalk rénxíngdào
sight; range of vision shìyě
sign; mark; symbol biāozhì
sign; plaque páizi
signal xìnhào
signature; sign one's name qiānzì,
   qiānmíng
significance; meaning yìyì
silk sī; silk stockings; socks sīwà
silver yín; silver-plate dùyín
simple jiǎndān
simply don't gēnběn bù
simultaneous tóngshí
since (the time of) cóng…yǐlái
sincere rèxīn
sincerity rèqíng
sing, to chànggē
singer gēshǒu
singing gēchàng
single, unmarried dānshēn
single room dānrén fáng
sister (older) jiějie; sister (younger)
   mèimei; sister-in-law sǎozi
sit; take a seat zuò; sit down zuòxià
situation; conditions qíngkuàng

six liù
sixfold liùbèi
sixth, the dì liù
size dàxiǎo
ski huáxuě
skillful; dexterous; nimble língqiǎo
skin pífu
skin disease pífu bìng
skinny; slender shòu
skirt qúnzi
skull tóulú
skyscraper mótiān dàlóu
sled xuěqiāo
sleep shuì, shuìjiào
sleeping bag shuìdài
sleeping car ticket wòpù chēpiào
sleeping pills ānmián yào
sleeve xiùzi
slides huàndēng piàn
slippers tuōxié
slope xiépō
slow màn
sly; cunning jiǎohuá
small; tiny xiǎo
smallpox tiānhuā
smell, to wén qǐlái
smoke yān
smoke, to xīyān
smoker xīyān de
smooth píngtǎn de
smuggle, to zǒusī
snack xiǎochī
snake shé
sneeze, to pēntì
snore, to dǎhān
snow xuě; **snowstorm** fēngxuě
snow, to xià xuě
soap féizào
soap powder xǐyī fěn
soccer zúqiú
soccer field zúqiú chǎng
soccer team zúqiú duì
social worker shèhuì gōngzuò rényuán
society shèhuì
sociology shèhuì xué
socks wàzi
sofa shāfā
soft; gentle wēnróu
soft to the touch ruǎn
softly; in a low tone xiǎoshēng
sold out màiwán le
sole of shoe xiédǐ
soloist dúzòu
solve, to jiějué
some yǒude; **someone** mǒu ge rén
son érzi

song gēqǔ
soon; soon after bù jiǔ
sophisticated; most advanced jiānduān
sore throat hóulóng tòng
sorrow dānyōu
sorry, be bàoqiàn
sort; kind; type zhǒnglèi
soul línghún
sound shēngyīn
soup tāng
sour suān
south nánbiān
southern nánbiān de
souvenir jìniàn pǐn
soy beans huángdòu
soy milk dòujiāng
soy sauce jiàngyóu
spare parts bèijiàn
spare ribs páigǔ
spare tire bèitāi
spark huǒhuā
speak; talk; say shuōhuà
special; particular tèbié
special... tèbié de...
special delivery letter kuàixìn
special/favorable treatment yōudài
specialist (medical) zhuānkē yīshēng
spectators; audience guānzhòng
speed sùdù
speed up; accelerate jiākuài
speedometer jìsùbiǎo
spend; expend huāqián; **spend the night** guòyè
spicy hot là
spirit; energy jīngshen
sponge hǎimián
spoon tāngchí
sport(s) yùndòng
sports equipment yùndòng yòngpǐn
spot; stain wūdiǎn
spotlight yuǎnguāng dēng
spray pēnzuǐ
spring (season) chūntiān
spring water quánshuǐ
square; squared fāngkuài(r) de
stage wǔtái
stage play; drama huàjù
stairs lóutī
stamps yóupiào
stamps, to paste on tiē yóupiàn
stand; be on one's feet zhàn
stand s.o., can't shòubùliǎo
stand still, to; to stop zhànzhù
standard; criterion biāozhǔn
star xīngxīng

start, to kāishǐ; **start off/proceed from** chūfā
station (bus, etc.) chēzhàn
stationery store wénjù diàn
steal, to tōu
steamboat/ship lúnchuán
steep; precipitous dǒu
steering wheel fāngxiàngpán
step; pace bùfá
steward hángkōng fúwù yuán
stick; rod gùn(r)
still; yet hái
sting, to; to prick cìrù
stink, to fāchòu
stipulate; provide guīdìng
stipulations; requirements tiáojiàn
stir-fry; saute chǎo
stockings; socks wàzi
stockpile; lay up chúcún
stomach wèi
stomachache wèitòng
stone shítou
stony, rocky duō shítou
stop tíngzhǐ
stop/park a car tíngchē
stopover tíngliú
store, shop diàn
store window chúchuāng
storm fēngbào
story; floor lóu
stove; oven lúzi
straight; continuously yìzhí
straight across héng chuān
straight ahead yìzhí
strange; unfamiliar mòshēng de
stranger bú rènshì de ren
strawberries cǎoméi
stream; river; current shuǐliú
street jiēdào
street corner jiēkǒu
street crossing bānmǎlù
street name lùmíng
street peddler tānfàn
street sign lùbiāi
street traffic jiāotōng
street vendor jiētou tānfàn
streetlight jiēdēng
strength lìqì
strengthen jiāndìng
strict; rigorous yángé
strike, to; beat; hit dǎ
strike up a conversation, to dāshàn
string; rope shéngzi
striped tiáowén de
stroke, have a zhòngfēng
stroll; take a walk zǒu yì zǒu
strong; powerful qiáng

strong drink; spirits lièjiǔ
student xuéshēng
studio gōngzuò shì; **film studio** shèyǐng chǎng
study, to xuéxí
stunt pilot tèjì fēixíng yuán
sturdy; strong qiángzhuàng
style fēnggé
subscribe; book; place an order yùdìng
subsidiary company zǐ gōngsī
substitute for... tì...
subtract; reduce jiǎn
suburbs; outskirts jiāoqū
subway dìxià tiělù; dìtiě
success; be successful chénggōng
sudden túrán de; **suddenly** hūrán
suffer; be in difficulty xīnkǔ; **suffer an accident** yùnàn
sugar táng
suggest; suggestion tíyì
suitable; fitting shìhé
suitable; proper shìdàng de
summer xiàtiān
sun tàiyang
Sunday xīngqī rì
sunglasses tàiyang yǎnjìng
sunlight rìguāng
sunny yǒu yángguāng de
sunrise; at sunrise rìchū
sunset; at sunset rìluò
superficial; shallow qiǎn
supermarket chāojí shìchǎng
supplier gōngyìng shāng
supply gōngyìng
support; uphold zhīchí
surf, to; surfing chōnglàng
surface wàimiàn
surgeon wàikē shǒushù yīshēng
surmise; guess cāicè
surplus; leftovers duōyú
surprised, be xià le yí tiào
surprising; strange; find strange guài
surrounding; vicinity zhōuwéi
suspend; break off zhōngduàn
suspicion; doubt huáiyí
swallow; gulp down tūn xià
swamp zhǎozé
swap; exchange jiāohuàn
sweat hàn
sweat, to chūhàn
sweater máoyī
Swede ruìdiǎn rén; **Sweden** ruìdiǎn; **Swedish** ruìdiǎn de
sweep; clean, to dǎsǎo
sweet tián

sweets tángguǒ
swelling zhǒngdà
swim, to yóuyǒng
swimming pool yóuyǒng chí
swimsuit yóuyǒngyī
swindle; cheat piàn rén
swindler; cheater piànzi
Swiss ruìshì de; **Swiss francs** ruìshì fǎláng; **Swiss person** ruìshì rén
switch on, to àn kāiguān
switchboard; telephone exchange zǒngjī
Switzerland ruìshì
swollen zhǒng le
sympathize with tóngqíng
sympathy tóngqíng
synthetic fiber rénzào xiānwéi

T

table zhuōzi
table tennis zhuōqiú
tablecloth zhuōbù
tailor cáiféng shī
take; bring ná; **take a look** kànkan; **take a photograph** shèyǐng; **take a rest/break** xiūxi; **take along, to** dài; **take away** názǒu; **take back; call in; recall** shōuhuí; **take care of children** zhàogù xiǎohái; **take care of; certainly; surely** bǎoguǎn; **take into account; attend to** gùjí; **take notes; keep minutes; record** jìlù; **take off (plane)** qǐfēi; **take off on time** zhǔnshí qǐfēi; **take shape; form** xíngchéng; **take the place of** dài; **substitute for** dàitì
Taoism dàojiā
tape recorder lùyīnjī
tariff guānshuì
taste; flavor wèidào
tasteless; pale dàn
tasty hǎochī
tax shuì
taxi chūzūchē; **taxi driver** chūzūchē sījī; **taxi meter** jìchéngbiǎo
tea chá
tea leaves cháyè
teach; lecture jiǎngkè
teach (a class); teaching jiāo kè
teach, to jiāo
teacher lǎoshī; **instructor** jiàoshī
team tuánduì
teapot cháhú
tear open sīkāi

teaspoon cháshí
technical college jìshù xuéyuàn
technical draftsman huìtúyuán
technical science jìshù
technician jìshù rényuán
teeth yáchǐ
telegram diànbào
telephone diànhuà
telephone, to; make a phone call dǎ diànhuà
telephone book diànhuà bù
telephone booth diànhuà tíng
telephone calling card diànhuà kǎ
telephone number diànhuà hàomǎ
telescope wàngyuǎn jìng
tell; inform gàosù
temper; mood píqì
temperature wēndù
temple miàoyú
temporarily zànshí
ten shí
tennis wǎngqiú
tent zhàngpéng
terminal point; finish line zhōngdiǎn
terms of delivery gōnghuò tiáojiàn
thank, to gǎnxiè
thanks; thank (you) xièxie
that nà ge
that time, at nà shí
theater jùchǎng
theft tōuqiè
theme, main zhèngjuàn
theology shénxué
there; in that place nàli
there is; there are yǒu
therefore suǒyǐ
thermometer tǐwēn jì
they tāmen
thick hòu
thief xiǎotōu
thin; flimsy báo
thin; slender shòu
thing; article dōngxī
think; feel gǎnjué; **think of; recall** xiǎngdào
think about, to; consider kǎolù; **think of a way to** shèfǎ
third one, the dì sān ge
thirsty kǒukě
this; this one zhè ge; **this kind of** zhèyàng de
thousand, one yì qiān
thread; wire xiàn
throat hóulóng
throat lozenges hóupiàn
throw; fling tóurù

thumbtack túdīng
thunder, to dǎ léi
thunderstorm bào fēngyǔ
Thursday xīngqī sì
ticket piào
ticket office shòupiào chù
ticket-taker jiǎnpiào yuán
tidy; straighten up; pack up
  shōushi
time (period) shíjiān
time; occasion cì
timely; promptly jíshí
timetable; schedule (for buses, etc.)
  xíngchē shíkè biǎo
tip; gratuity xiǎofèi
tire (on car, etc.) lúntāi
tired, extremely lèisǐ le
to (a place) dào...
toast tǔsī
tobacco yāncǎo
tobacco shop yānjiǔ diàn
today jīntiān
toe jiǎozhǐ
together yìqǐ
toil; pains xīnláo
toilet cèsuǒ, xǐshǒujiān
toilet paper wèishēngzhǐ
tomatoes xīhóngshì
tombstone mùbēi
tongue shétou
tonsil biǎntáoxiàn
tonsilitis biǎntáoxiàn yán
too; very tài; too many tài duō
tool gōngjù
toothbrush yáshuā
toothpaste yágāo
toothpick yáqiān
torn sīpò le
total (amount) zǒngjì
total it up yìqǐ suàn
touching; moving gǎnrén
tough; firm; hard yìng
tour lǚyóu
tour group lǚxíng tuán
tour guide/leader dǎoyóu
tourist guān guāng kè
tourist spots/sights fēngjǐng
  míngshèng gǔjī
tow a car; towing tuōchē
toward; in the direction of wǎng,
  xiàng
towel máojīn
tower jiāntǎ
townspeople shìmín
toy, child's wánjù
trace; vestige hénjì
track (railroad) guǐdào

track and field meet tiánjìng sài
trade; line of business hángyè
trade fair jiāoyì huì; shāngzhǎn
trademark pǐnpái
traditional dress chuántǒng
  fúzhuāng
traffic control center jiāotōng guǎnlǐ
  chù
traffic jam sāichē
tragedy (play) bēijù
train huǒchē; train station
  huǒchēzhàn
transfer an account zhuǎnzhàng
transform; change gǎibiàn
translation; translate fānyì
transport, to yùnshū
trash/garbage can lājītǒng
travel, to lǚxíng
travel agency lǚxíng shè
traveler lǚkè
traveler's check lǚxíng zhīpiào
treat; approach; handle duìdài
tree shù
trip; journey lǚxíng
tripod sānjiǎo jià
triumph over an opponent
  déshèng
trouble; troublesome máfán
truck kǎchē
true; real; authentic zhēn de
trunk; chest; box xiāngzi
trustworthy shífēn xìnrèn de
try, to; test, to shì yí shì
T-shirt T-xùshān
tubing (flexible) ruǎnguǎn
Tuesday xīngqī èr
tuna jīnchāngyú
tunnel suìdào
turn, a; curve wān(r); turn a
  corner; make a turn zhuǎnwān;
  turn right/left xiàng yòu/zuǒ
  zhuǎn
turn over; fānzhuǎn; turn over to
  jiāogěi
turn the head huítóu
turn on; open dǎkāi
turret; corner tower jiǎolóu
tweezers; pliers qiánzi
twelve shíèr
twenty èrshí
twice; two times liǎngbèi
two èr
tympanitis zhōngér yán
typhus shānghán
typical diǎnxíng de

U

ugly nánkān
umbrella sǎn
unanimous; identical yízhì
unavoidable bù kě bìmiǎn de
unbelievable bù kě xìn de
uncle shūshu; jiùjiu
unclear bù qīngchǔ
uncomfortable bù shūfu
uncommon; not in fashion bù liúxíng
unconsciousness; faint hūndǎo
under... zài...xià
undergo; pass through jīngguò
underground street crossing dìxiàdào
underneath xiàmiàn
undoubtedly; beyond doubt wúyí de
undress tuō yīfu
uneasy bù ān
unemployed shīyè
unexpected méi xiǎngdào
unfair bù gōngpíng
unforeseen; unexpected yìwài
unfortunately kěxí, búxìng
unfriendly bù yǒushàn
unhappy bù yúkuài
unhealthy bú jiànkāng
unilateral; one-sided piànmiàn de
unimportant bú zhòngyào
united liánhé, tǒngyī
university; college dàxué
unlawful bù guīlǜ de
unlike bùtóng
unlined... dānyī de...
unlined garment dānyī
unload cargo xièhuò
unnecessary méi bìyào
unpack dǎkāi xínglǐ
unsafe bù ānquán
unstable bù wěndìng
unsuitable bù héshì
unwelcome búshòu huānyíng de
up-to-date; new xīn
urgent; critical jǐnjí de
urinate xiǎobiàn
use rouge, to; makeup huàzhuāng
use; employ yòng
used... yòngguò de...
useful yǒuyòng
useless méiyòng de
usually píngcháng
utilize cǎiyòng

V

vacancy; opening; be short of quē
vacation, take a dùjià
vacation; holidays jiàqī
valid yǒuxiào; **validity, have** yǒu xiàolì
valley shān gǔ
valuable thing, a guìzhòng de dōngxī
value-added tax huòwù zēngzhí shuì
VCR/video camera lùxiàng jī
vegetable shūcài
vegetarian diet sùshí
vegetation; plant cover fùgài
vehicles chēliàng
vent one's grievances sùkǔ
verify, to héduì
very hěn
vest bèixīn
veterinarian shòuyī
vexed; irritated; annoyed fán
vicinity fùjìn
victory shènglì
video; videorecord; videotape lùxiàng
view (opinion) yìjiàn
vigor; energy jīnglì
vile; nasty; mean èliè
village cūnzi
vinegar cù
virus bìngdú
visa qiānzhèng
visible kě jiàn de
visit; call on bàifǎng
voice; noise shēngyīn
volcanic mountain huǒshāoshān
volcano huǒshān
volt fútè
vomit ǒutù

W

wages gōngzī
wait děng
waiter pǎotáng; fúwùyuán
waiting room hòuchē shì
wake up; awaken jiàoxǐng, xǐnglái
walk; stroll sànbù; **walk to; walk by** zǒu guòqù; **walk into/near** zǒujìn
Walkman suíshēntīng
wall qiáng
wall socket chāzuò
wallet píjiāzi
walnut hétáo

war zhànzhēng
warm wēnnuǎn; **warm and damp** shīrè
warn; **caution** jǐnggào
wash xǐ
washing machine xǐyī jī
wasp mǎfēng
watch (clock) biǎo
watch; **guard** kānshǒu
watch; **view** guānkàn; **watch carefully/attentively** zhùshì; **watch television, to** kàn diànshì
water shuǐ
water and electricity charges shuǐdiànfèi
water pipe shuǐguǎn
waterfall pùbù
watermelon xīguā
watt (elec.) wǎtè
wave (on the water) hǎilàng
wave/beckon with hand zhāoshǒu
we wǒmen
weak; **inferior** ruò
weakness ruòdiǎn
wear; **put on** chuān
weather tiānqì; qìhòu
weather forecast tiānqì yùbào
wedding hūnlǐ
Wednesday xīngqī sān
week xīngqī; **every week** měi xīngqī
weekend zhōumò
weigh chèng
weight fènliàng
welcome huānyíng
well (for water) jǐng
well-known; **famous** chūmíng
western (part) xībù
western (style, manner, etc.) xīfāng de; **Western-styled clothes** yángzhuāng
wet shī
what shénme
wheat flour miànfěn
wheel chēlún
when; **at the … time** dāng…de shíhou
whether or not shìfǒu
while away time; **divert oneself** xiāoqiǎn
whisk/small broom xiǎo sàobǎ
whiskey wēishìjì
white one, a bái de
whole; **complete; all; the whole thing** quánbù
wide; **expansive** kuān
wife; **Mrs.** tàitai
wig jiǎfǎ

wild yě
wild animal yěshòu
willing to; **want to** yuànyì
win, to yíng
window chuānghu
window seat chuāngwèi
windpipe qìguǎn
windshield wiper yǔshuā
windy yǒu fēng de
wine jiǔ
wing (of a plane) jīyì
winter dōngtiān
wipe off; **erase** mǒ
wipe out; **exterminate** pūmiè
wire; **thread** xiàn
wish happiness to zhùfú
with gēn
without, be méiyǒu
witness zhèngrén
woolen; **sheep's wool** yángmáo; **woolen blanket** máotǎn
woman nǚshì
wood mùtou
wood carving mùdiāo
wood engraving mùkè
wooden shoes; **clogs** mùjī
word zì; cí; **words; language; speech** huà
word order cìxù
word processing system wénshū chǔlǐ xìtǒng
work; **job** gōngzuò
work (of art) zuòpǐn
work, to gōngzuò; **work hard; industrious** nǔlì; **work on (construction)** shīgōng
workday gōngzuò tiān
worker; **employee** gōngrén
world shìjiè
worm; **insect** chóngzi
worry; **feel anxious; to worry about** dānxīn; **have worth/value** yǒu jiàzhí de
worth; **value** jiàzhí
worthless méi jiàzhí de
would rather; **better had** níngyuàn
wound shāngkǒu
wounded; **hurt** shòushāng
wrap up; **wrap** bāo qǐlái
wrapping paper bāozhuāng zhǐ
wrestling match shuāijiāo
wristwatch shǒubiǎo
write, to xiě
writer zuòjiā
writing; **script; characters** wénzì; **in writing** shūmiàn de
wrong cuòle

X

X ray, to get an zhào X-guāng

Y

yacht yóutǐng
yard; courtyard yuànzi
yawn, to dǎ hāqiàn
year nián

yield; concede; step aside ràngbù
you nǐ; **you** nín *(polite);* **you** *(pl)* nǐmen
young niánqīng; **youth; young person** niánqīng rén
yours nǐ de; **yours** *(pl)* nǐmen de

Z

zipper lāliàn

Chinese–English Dictionary

Please note that when a Chinese entry consists of two words, such as *àn kāiguān*, alphabetical order is determined by the first word, such as *àn*.

A

ài to love
àiqíng love (btw. people)
áizhèng cancer
àizībìng AIDS
àn kāiguān to switch on
āngzāng filthy; dirty
ānjìng quiet; peaceful
ànlíng ring a bell
ānmián yào sleeping pills
ànmó massage
ānquán safe; secure
ānquán dài safety belt
ānquán jiǎnchá safety/security check
ànzhào according to
ānzhuāng install
āyí; bómǔ aunt

B

bǎi hundred
bái de a white one
bǎifēnbǐ percent
bǎifēnlǜ percentage
bǎihuò gōngsī department store
bàifǎng visit; call on
báifàn cooked rice
báihóu diphtheria
báitiān daytime
bāléiwǔ ballet
bàn gōng shì office; place of business
bāngzhù to help; assist
bǎnhuà yìshù graphic arts; graphics
bānjí schedule; flight
bānmǎlù street crossing
bànyè midnight; middle of the night
bānyùn de porter
báo flimsy; weak; light
bào; bàozhǐ newspaper
bào fēngyǔ thunderstorm
bào huǒjǐng fire alarm
bāo qǐlái wrap up; wrap
bāo sāncān de zhùsù lodgings with three meals
bǎochí keep; maintain; preserve
bàochou reward; remuneration; pay
bàodá repay
bàogào report; make known; term paper

bǎoguǎn take care of; certainly; surely
bāoguǒ package
bǎohù protect; safeguard
bǎohù gǔjī preservation of historic sites
bāokuò include; consist of
bǎolíng qiú bowling
bàoqiàn to be sorry
bǎoxiān keep (food) fresh
bǎoxiǎn insure; insurance
bǎoxiǎn xiāng safe; security box
bǎoxiǎntào condom; contraceptive
bǎozhèng guarantee
bāozhuāng pack; package
bāozhuāng zhǐ wrapping paper
bǎshǒu handle; grip
bēi carry on the back
bèi back (spine)
běi cháoxiān North Korea
bèibāo knapsack
běibù the North
běibù de ... northern ...
bèijiàn spare parts
bēijù tragedy (play)
bèiké shellfish
bèitāi spare tire
bèixīn vest
bēizi glass; cup
bèn foolish; stupid; clumsy
běndì de local
bēngdài bandage
běnjī dust pan
běnzi notebook; booklet
bǐ compare; contrast
biān(r) side; margin; edge; rim
biānhào number; serial number
biànhuà change; alteration
biānjí editor
biānjiè boundary; border
biānjiè jiǎnchá zhàn border checkpoint/crossing
biǎntáoxiàn tonsil
biǎntáoxiàn yán tonsilitis
biànyā qì; liánjiē chātóu adapter (electrical)
biǎo watch (clock)
biǎodá express (meaning, etc.)
biǎogé form (printed)
biǎomèi cousin
biǎoyǎn perform; act

biāozhì sign; mark; symbol
biāozhǔn standard; criterion
bǐcǐ me too; each other
bié de other; another; different one
bié de dìfang another/different place
biézhēn safety pin
bǐjì notes; jottings
bǐjiào comparatively
bǐjiào hǎo quite/rather good
bìmiǎn avoid
bìng disease; illness
bīng ice
bīng kāfēi iced coffee
bīngbáo hail
bìngdú virus
bǐnggān cookie; biscuit; cracker
bīngkuài ice cube
bīnglěng de iced
bīngqílín ice cream
bīngguǎn hotel
bīngxiāng refrigerator
bǐsài match; competition; compete
bìxū essential; indispensable
bìxū necessary
bìyào indispensable
bìyàoxìng necessity
bìyùnwán contraceptive; the pill
bízi nose
bōli glass (the substance)
bóshì doctor (Ph.D.)
bóshù Cypress
bōsī rén Persian
bówùguǎn museum
bózi neck
bù no; not
bǔ mend; patch; repair
bù; méiyǒu not
bù ān uneasy
bù ānquán unsafe
bù cháng rarely; not often
bù fāngbiàn inconvenient
bù gōngpíng unfair
bù guīlǜ de unlawful
bù héshì unsuitable
bú jiànkāng unhealthy
bù jiǔ soon; soon after
bù kě bìmiǎn de unavoidable
bù kě lǐjiě de impossible to comprehend
bù kě xìn de unbelievable
bù kěnéng impossible
bú kèqi impolite
bù liúxíng uncommon; not in fashion
bù mǎnyì dissatisfied
bù qīngchǔ unclear
bú quèdìng de indefinite
bú rènshì de ren stranger

bù róngyì; nán difficult
bù shíjì impractical
bù shūfu uncomfortable
bù wánquán incomplete
bù wěndìng unstable
bù xīyān de nonsmoker
bù xǐhuān dislike
bù xiāngxìn to distrust
bù xiǎoxīn careless
bù yǒushàn unfriendly
bù yúkuài unhappy
bú zhèngjīng improper; dishonorable
bú zhòngyào unimportant
bǔcháng compensate; make up for
bùdan not only
búduì incorrect; wrong
bùfá step; pace
bùfèn part; portion
búgòu insufficient
bùguǎn qù nǎli anywhere you go
bùguǎn yòng shénme no matter what you use
bùguǎn zài nǎli anywhere
bùhǎo de bad one
bǔhuí to make up for
bújiàn le disappeared
bùliào cloth; material (clothing)
bùmén division (of a business, organization)
bùrán otherwise
búshì … jiùshì … either … or …
búshì … yě búshì … neither … nor …
búshòu huānyíng de unwelcome
bùtóng differ; be different; different; difference; unlike
bùzhì decorate; fix up; arrange

C

cái not until; only when …
cāi yì cāi guess; make a guess
cài; shíwù food; dish
cāicè surmise; guess
cáiféng shī tailor
cáifù riches
cáiliào material (for a report, etc.)
cǎisè bǐ colored pencil
cǎiyòng utilize
cáizhèng finance
cānchē dining car
cāngbái pale; pallid
cānguān participate in; join
cāngyíng fly (insect)

cānjīn napkin
cāntīng dining room; restaurant
cǎo grass
cǎodì grassland; meadow; lawn
cǎoméi strawberries
cǎopíng lawn
cǎoyào herbs (for medicine)
cèsuǒ; xǐshǒujiān toilet
chá tea
chàbùduō almost
chádiǎn pastries served with tea
cháhú teapot
chákàn look into; examine
cháng long; lengthy
chángcháng frequently; often
chángchéng Great Wall of China
chángdù length
chànggē to sing
chàngjī record player
chàngpiàn recording (music)
chàngpiàn háng record store
chángshì attempt; try
chángtú diànhuà long distance call
chángyòng de … commonly used
chángzi intestines
chǎnpǐn product
chǎnshāng producer
chǎo fry; stir-fry; saute
chāoguò exceed; go over
chāojí shìchǎng supermarket
chǎojià argue; to quarrel
chǎonào kick up a row; din; noise
chāopiào bank note; bill; paper money
chǎoròu fried meat
cháoshī damp; moist
cháoxiān rén Korean person
cháshí teaspoon
chātóu plug (electric)
chāzi fork
chāzuò wall socket
cháyè tea leaves
chēfèi fare
chēhào license plate number
chēkù garage
chēliàng vehicles
chēlíng bell (on a bike, etc.)
chēlún wheel
chèng weigh
chéngbǎo castle
chénggōng success; be successful
chéngguǒ achievement; gain
chéngjī dān report card
chéngkè passenger
chéngqiáng city wall
chéngrén adult; grown up
chéngshì; dūshì city

chéngshú ripe; mature
chéngwéi become; turn into
chéngyǔ idiom; set phrase
chèngzi scale (for weighing)
chènlǐ lining
chènshān shirt; blouse
chéntǔ dust
chēshēn car body; chassis
chēxiāng railroad car
chēzhàn bus stop; station (bus, etc.)
chī eat
chī zǎocān to eat breakfast
chībǎo le full (after eating)
chǐcùn measurement; dimension
chídào come late
chīfàn eat a meal
chīfàn shíjiān mealtime
chíxù continue; persist
chíyí hesitate
chóngfù duplicate
chóngjiàn to rebuild
chōnglàng to surf; surfing
chóngx īn again; anew; afresh
chōngzǎo; línyù shower; bath
chóngzi worm; insect
chǒu disgraceful; shameful
chóushì de hostile
chuān put on; be dressed in; wear
chuán boat; ship
chuān yīfu dress; put on clothes
chuáng bed
chuángdiàn mattress
chuānghu window
chuāngwèi window seat
chuàngzuò to create; creation
chuánrǎn de infectious
chuāntáng fēng(r) draft (wind)
chuántǒng fúzhuāng traditional dress
chuánzhǎng captain (boat)
chuánzhēn fax
chūbǎn publish
chúcún stockpile; lay up
chúchuāng store window
chūfā set out; start off; proceed from
chǔfá punishment
chūfā shíjiān departure time
chúfáng kitchen
chuī tóufa to blow-dry hair
chuīfēng jī hair dryer
chuīshì cooking; kitchen work
chuízi hammer
chǔlǐ handle; deal with; dispose of
chúshī cook; chef
chūhàn to sweat
chūjìng leave the country
chūkǒu export

chūkǒu shāng exporter
chūmén go out; exit
chūmíng well-known; famous
chūntiān spring (season)
chūqù go out; exit
chūshēn class origin; family origin
chūshēng birth; to be born
chūshēng niányuèrì birth date
chūshēngdì place of birth
chūshì to have an accident
chūxí attend; be present
chūxiàn appear
chūzū rent out
chūzūchē taxi
chūzūchē sījī taxi driver
cì time; occasion
cípiàn disk(ette)
cíqì porcelain
cìrù to sting; to prick
cìxiù embroidery
cìxù word order
cóng from (a place/time)
cóng … qǐ ever since
cóng … yǐlái since (the time of)
cónglaibù … never …
cōngmáng hastily; in a hurry
cōngmíng intelligent; smart; clever
cù vinegar
cùchéng facilitate; effect
cúnzài exist; be
cūnzi village
cuòguò miss; let slip
cuòle wrong
cuòwù error; blunder
cuòwù mistake

D

dǎ to strike; beat; hit
dà big; large; grand
dā biànchē catch a ride with s.o.; to hitchhike
dǎ diàndī to be on an intravenous
dǎ diànhuà to telephone; make a phone call
dǎ hāqiàn to yawn
dà jiē main street
dǎ léi to thunder
dà tīng main hall; parlor
dà xuéshēng college student
dǎ yùfángzhēn to inoculate
dǎ zhāohū to greet; say hello to
dǎ zhé give a discount
dǎbāo pack up
dàbiàn defecate

dádào achieve
dǎdǔ bet; make a bet; gamble
dǎfā send on errand
dáfù an answer; a reply
dàgài probably; likely
dài to bring along; to take along; take the place of
dài jiājù furnished
dàibiǎo represent; representative
dàikuǎn loan; credit; grant a loan
dǎhān to snore
dǎhuǒ jī lighter
dàilǐ act as agent; proxy; acting …
dàitì substitute for
dàizi bag (for holding things); sack
dàlshí marble
dàlù mainland; continent
dǎkāi turn on; open
dǎkāi xínglǐ unpack
dàn tasteless; pale
dàn gāo cake
dǎng gear (on car, etc.)
dāng … de shíhou when; at the … time
dānmài Denmark
dānmài rén Danish person
dǎnnáng gallbladder
dānrén fáng single room
dānshēn bachelor; single; unmarried
dàmén main entrance; main door
dànshì however; but
dānxīn worry; feel anxious; to worry about
dānyī unlined garment
dānyī de … unlined …
dānyīn de monosyllabic
dānyōu to be apprehensive; sorrow
dānzi list; bill; form
dǎo fall over; topple; island
dào courses (of a meal)
dào … to (a place)
dào nàli qu go there
dàochù dou everywhere
dàodá arrive; reach
dàodá shíjiān arrival time
dàodá shírì arrival date
dàojiā Taoism
dàolù road
dàomǐ rice (raw)
dàoqiàn apologize
dǎoyǎn director (film)
dǎoyóu conduct a sight-seeing tour; tour guide/leader
dāozi knife; sword; blade
dǎpò break; smash
dāqǐ put up; construct
dǎrǎo to disturb; bother

A/Z

dǎsǎo sweep; to clean
dāshàn to strike up a conversation
dàshǐ ambassador
dàshēng loud voice
dàsuàn; suàn garlic
dǎsuàn plan to
dǎtīng inquire; find out about
dàtóuzhēn pin
dāying promise; agree to
dǎzhēn give/have an injection
dàxiǎo size
dàxué university; college
dàyī overcoat; coat
dàyuē approximately; likely; probably
dàzhuān community college
dédào attain; reach
dēng lamp; light
děng wait
děngjí class; grade; rank
dēngjì check in; register
dēngjì chù registration; check-in desk
dēngpào lightbulb
dēngtǎ lighthouse
děngzhí de of equal value
déshèng triumph over an opponent
dī low (in height)
dī qìyā low pressure (weather)
dì èr diǎn second point/item
dì èr ge second one
dì liù the sixth
dì sān ge the third one
dì yī first (one); first
diǎn iodine
diàn electricity; store/shop
diàn de electric
diǎn huǒ light a fire
diǎnfàn model; example
diànbào telegram
diànchí battery
diànfēngshàn fan (ventilator)
diànhuà telephone
diànhuà bù telephone book
diànhuà hàomǎ telephone number
diànhuà kǎ telephone calling card
diànhuà tíng telephone booth
diànjī electrical machinery
diànqì háng electric appliance store
diàntī elevator
diànxiàn electrical wire/cable
diànxíng de typical
diànyā mortgage; pawn
diànyǐng film; movie
diànyǐng yǎnyuán movie actor/actress
diànyǐng yuàn movie theater

diànzhǔ proprietor (of a shop)
diào xià drop
diào yú to fish
diàochá to investigate
diàohuàn exchange; swap
diāosù sculpture
dídá reach; arrive at
dìdi brother (younger)
dìfāng place; location
dìgěi to hand; give (to someone)
dìguó empire
dìlǐ geography
dìng order; subscribe to; book; reserve
dìnghūn to get engaged; engagement
dìqiú earth
dìqū region; area
dísīkē disco
dìshàng on the floor/ground
dìtǎn rug; carpet
dìtú map
diū lose; misplace
dìwei position; status
dīxià low (in status, etc.)
dìxià tiělù; dìtiě subway
dìxiàdào underground street crossing
dìzhǐ address (of a house, etc.)
dìzhí geology
dìzhōnghǎi Mediterranean
dízi flute
dòng cave; hole; move; shift
dòng shǒushù; kāidāo have an operation
dòngshēn leave on a journey; leave
dōngbù; dōngfāng the East
dōngfāng the Orient
dōngtiān winter
dòngwù animal
dōngxi article; thing; object; item
dōu all
dǒu steep; precipitous
dòujiāng soy milk
dòuzi beans
dú poison; narcotics
duǎn short
duàn le broken; split
duǎnlù short circuit
dǔchǎng casino
dùguò cross over; cross
duì le to be right; correct
duì … guòmǐn have an allergy to …
duì; zhèngquè to be correct; right
duìdài treat; approach; handle
duìhuàn lǜ exchange rate
duìhuàn wàibì change foreign currency
duìlì de antagonistic

duìmiàn opposite (side)
duìxiàng goal; objective
dùjī navel
dùjià take a vacation
dùjīn gold-plated; get gilded
dúmùzhōu canoe
duō numerous; many; much; more
duō biàn de changeable
duō shā de sandy
duō shítou stony; rocky
duōyú surplus; leftovers
duōzhī de juicy
dúpǐn narcotic; drug
dùyín silver-plate
dùzi belly
dúzòu soloist

E

è hungry
è guó Russia
è guó de Russian
è guó rén Russian person
é wài de additional; extra
è yǔ Russian language
ě xīn nausea
èiyán pneumonia
èliè vile; nasty; mean
èr two
ěrduō ear
ěrduō yàoshuǐ ear drops
ěrhuán earrings
ěrjī earphones
èrqiě moreover
èrshí twenty
értóng piào child's ticket
érzi son
éwài de extra; added; additional

F

fāchòu to stink
fādiànqì electric generator
fǎguān judge (court)
fǎguó France
fǎguó de French
fǎguó rén Frenchman
fàjuǎn curler
fājué gǔwù excavate ancient artifacts
fákuǎn fine (money penalty); impose a fine; penalty
fāliàng shine; glitter
fāliàng de shining

fǎlǜ law
fāmíng invent; invention
fán vexed; irritated; annoyed
fánchuán sailing boat; junk
fǎnduì oppose; to be against
fàng place; put
fàng yānhuǒ set off fireworks
fāngbiàn convenient; handy
fāngfǎ method; means; way
fàngdà enlarge
fángjiān room (in a hotel, etc.)
fàngjìn place into
fāngkuài(r) de square; squared
fàngqì give up; abandon
fàngshè radiate; emit
fàngshèxìng de radioactive
fāngshì pattern; fashion
fángzhǔ home owner
fángzi house; small building
fànhòu after eating
fànzuì crime/offense; commit a crime
fāngxiàng direction
fāngxiàngpán steering wheel
fǎnmiàn de negative side
fānù infuriate; flare up
fānyì translation; translate
fānzhuǎn turn over
fāshāo fever; have a fever
fāshè to shoot
fāshēng happen; occur
fǎtiáo; guīdìng rule; regulation
fǎtíng court (law)
fàxíng hairstyle
fāxiàn discover; find; discovery
fāyán inflammmation
fāyīn pronounce; pronunciation
fǎyǔ French language
fēi to fly
fēicháng extremely
fēijī airplane
fēixíng flying; flight
fèixū ruins
fèiyòng costs; expenses
fèizàng lung
féizào soap
fēn to divide; minute (of time)
fěn powder
fēnchéng divide into
fēndiàn branch/affiliate store
fēnfā distribute; hand out
fēng le insane; mad
fēngbào storm
fēngbì de sealed; closed
fěngcì jù satire/satirical play
fēnggé style
fěnhóng sè pink

fēngjǐng panorama; scenery
fēngjǐng míngshèng gǔjī tourist
  spots/sights
fēngjǐng míngxìn piàn picture
  postcard
fēngmì honey
fēngshī rheumatism
fēngsú xíguàn customs (of a
  people)
fēngsuǒ blockade; block; seal off
fēngxiǎn risk; hazard
fēngxuě snowstorm
fēnkāi to separate
fēnkāi de separated
fēnpèi allocate; allot
fēnqī fùkuǎn leasing
fēnxi analyze
féng to sew
fènglí pineapple
fènliàng weight
fénmù grave
fó Buddha
fójiào tú Buddhist
fójiào Buddhism
fǒurèn to deny
fóxiàng Buddhist statue
fù pay (money)
fù xiànjīn pay cash
fù zuòyòng side effects
fǔbài corrupt; rotten
fùdān burden; load; bear
fùgài vegetation; plant cover
fùjìn nearby; close
fùjìn vicinity
fùkuǎn pay a sum of money
fùkuǎn tiáojiàn payment
  terms/conditions
fǔlàn rotten; corrupt
fùmǔ parents
fūqī husband and wife
fùqīn father
fútè volt
fúwù serve; service
fúwù shíjiān service hours
fúwùyuán service person (waiter,
  etc.)
fùxiè; lā dùzi diarrhea
fùyìn copy; xerox
fùzé in charge of; responsible for
fùzhàng pay a bill
fúzhuāng clothing
fúzhuāng biǎoyǎn fashion show
fúzhuāngdiàn clothing store

G

gǎi change to; revise; correct
gài build; construct; cover; conceal
gǎibiàn change; transform; alter
gǎishàn improve (by changing)
gàizhāng seal; stamp
gàizi cover; lid; top
gān dry
gǎn dare to
gǎndòng be moved (emotionally)
gānggāng a moment ago; just now
gǎngkǒu port; harbor
gānjìng clean; neat and tidy
gǎnjué feel; sense; think; feeling
gǎnkuài quickly; hastily
gǎnmào cold; catch cold
gǎnrǎn infect
gānrǎo disturb; interfere with;
  interference (elec.)
gǎnrén touching; moving
gǎnxiè to thank
gānxǐ dry cleaning
gānzàng liver
gāo high; tall
gāo qìyā high pressure (weather)
gāo/dī xuěyā high/low blood
  pressure
gàobié to bid farewell; say good-bye
gāobǐng diàn cake shop/bakery
gāocháo climax; high tide/water
gāodù height
gāoěrfū qiú golf; golf ball
gāoěrfū qiúchǎng golf course
gāofēng peak; height; summit
gāoguì noble; high; elitist;
  privileged
gāojí bān advanced class
gàosù inform; relate; tell
gāosù gōnglù expressway
gāoxìng cheerful; happy; delighted
gāozhōng senior high school
gēchàng singing
gēge brother (older)
gěi give
gěi ... dǎqì inflate; pump up
gei ... for (the benefit of)
gējù opera
gēn with
gēnběn bu not at all
gēnběn bù simply don't
gēnggǎi alter; change
gēngyī shì dressing room; locker;
  changing room
gēngzhèng to correct; revise
gēqǔ song
gèrén de personal

gèrén diànnǎo personal computer
gēshāng cut (wound)
gēshǒu singer
gēwǔ jù musical (play)
gōng nuǎnqì heat; supply
gōng'ān jǐngchá security police
gōngchǎng factory
gōngchǐ; mǐ kilometer
gōngchéngshī engineer
gōnggòng de ... public ...
gōnggòng guānxì public relations
gōnggòng qìchē bus
gōnghuò tiáojiàn terms of delivery
gōngjī rooster
gōngjīn kilogram
gōngjù tool
gōnglù highway; road
gōnglù dìtú road map
gōngpíng fair; equitable
gōngrén worker; employee
gōngshì bāo briefcase
gōngsī firm; company
gòngtóng de common; joint
gōngwù official business
gōngyè industry
gōngyìng supply
gōngyìng shāng supplier
gōngyù apartment
gōngyuán park (public)
gōngzhèngrén notary
gōngzī wages
gōngzuò job; work; to work
gōngzuò shì studio
gōngzuò tiān workday
gǒu dog
gōuzi hook
gòu le enough
gòumǎi to purchase
gǔ drum
guà hang up; suspend
guā melon
guā húzi to shave
guàhào xìn registered letter
guàhào yóujiàn registered mail
guài surprising; strange; find
  strange
guān close; shut
guān guāng kè tourist
guānchá observe; survey; inspect
guānfāng ... official ...
guāngxiàn ray (of light)
guānjǐng tái lookout point (to view
  scenery)
guānjié joint (i.e., knee, elbow,
  etc.)
guānkàn watch; view
guānliáo bureaucrats; bureaucratic

guānmén close a door; closed (for
  business)
guānshàng shut; closed
guānshuì tariff
guàntou can; can of; canned goods;
  tin can
guānxīn to be concerned about
guānxi backdoor connections; pull
guānxi relationship; bearing
guānyuán; gōngwùyuán official
  (person)
guānzhòng audience; spectator(s)
guǎnfēngqín organ (musical
  instrument)
guǎngbō broadcast; air
guǎnggào advertisement
guǎnlǐ manage; management
guàzhe hanging
gǔdài ancient times
gùdìng de; jiāngù de firm (solid)
gǔdǒng antiques
guì expensive
guǐdào track (railroad)
guīdìng regulation; rule; stipulate;
  provide
guīhuán revert to; return
guīlǜ regular pattern
guìtái; chuāngkǒu counter (in store,
  etc.)
guìzhòng de dōngxī a valuable thing
guìzi cupboard; cabinet
guìzú nobility; gentry
gùjí take into account; attend to
gūjì estimate; appraise; reckon; make
  a guess
gūjià estimate (of cost)
gǔjī historic site
gùkè customer
gǔlóng shui cologne
gùn(r) stick; rod
gùnzi rod; pole; stick
guòdù overdo (sth.); go beyond
guòfèn excessive; excessively
guójí nationality (national origin)
guójì de international
guójì diànhuà international call
guójiā nation; country
guójiā gōngyuán national park
guójiā ... national ...
guǒjiàng jam; marmalade
guòlǜqì filter
guòmǐn allergy
guónèi hángxiàn domestic flight
guòqī to be overdue; exceed time
  limit
guòqù go over; pass by; the past; in
  the past

guórén compatriots; fellow
  countrymen
guòshī fault; slip; error
guòshí fruits (in general)
guówáng king
guòyè spend the night
guǒzhī juice (fruit)
guōzi pot
gǔtóu bone
gǔzhǎng applaud
gǔzhé fracture (of a bone)
gùyì de intentional(ly)
gùzhàng breakdown; stoppage

H

hǎi sea
hái still; yet
hǎi àn coast
hǎi shì shèn lóu mirage (fig./lit.)
hǎibào poster
hǎibīn seaside
hǎibīn yùchǎng bathing beach;
  seaside resort
hǎidǎn sea urchin
hǎilàng wave (on the water)
hǎimián sponge
hǎiōu seagull
hàipà fear; be afraid of
hǎitān beach
hǎiwān bay
hǎiwài overseas
hǎiyáng ocean(s); sea(s)
hǎiyuán sailor
hǎizǎo dates; date palm
háizi child
hālóu hello
hǎnjiào to shout
hǎo good; fine; OK
hǎo zhǔyì good idea
hǎochī tasty
hǎochù advantage; good point
hǎokàn; piàoliàng pretty;
  handsome
hǎoxiàng appears to be
hǎoyì de good intentioned
hàn sweat
háng row; column
hángkōng fúwù yuán steward
hángkōng gōngsī airline company
hángkōng xìn air mail
hángxiàn airline flight
hángxíng to sail; navigate
hángyè trade; line of business
hángyè shāngzhǎn industrial fair

hánhú ambiguous; vague
háohuá luxury/luxurious
hàokè hospitality
hàomǎ serial number; number
hàoqí curious
hē to drink
hē zuì le drunk; intoxicated
hé; héliú river
hé'ǎi kindly; affable
héchàng chorus
héduì to verify
hēi àn dark
hēi sè black
hēibái black and white
hékǒu mouth (river)
hélǐ rational; reasonable
hěn very
héng chuān straight across
hénjī trace; vestige
hépíng peace; peaceful
héqì friendly; kind
héshàng monk
hétáo walnut
héyuē contract; agreement
hézī qǐyè joint-venture enterprise
hézi box
hézuò cooperation
hóng sè red
hóngluóbo carrot
hónglǜdēng red traffic light
hòu thick
hòuchē shì waiting room
hòulái afterwards
hóulóng throat
hóulóng tòng sore throat
hòulún rear wheel
hòumiàn in the rear; at the back
hòumiàn/tou behind
hóupiàn throat lozenges
hòushìjìng rearview mirror
hòutuì retreat; draw back
hú lake
huā flower
huà words; language; speech; draw;
  paint
huà(r) drawing; painting
huá chuán row a boat; boating
huādiàn florist
huāfěn rè hay fever
huài le broken; gone bad; ruined
huái yùn pregnant
huài; bùhǎo bad
huàichù disadvantage; bad feature
huáiyí to doubt; be suspicious;
  suspicion
huàjiā painter
huájiǎng oar

huàjù stage play; drama
huàkān illustrated magazine
huàláng art gallery
huán give back; return
huàn change; exchange
huán qián return/give back money
huàn rùnhuáyóu oil change
huàn yīfu change clothes
huànchē change (buses, etc.)
huàndǎng gearshift/gearchange
huàndēng piàn slides
huángdì emperor
huángdòu soy beans
huánggōng palace
huángguā cucumber
huángguàn crown
huánghūn dusk
huángyán lie (untruth)
huángyóu butter
huánjìng environment
huānyíng welcome
huāpíng(r) flower vase
huāqián spend; expend
huāshù flower bouquet
huàxué chemistry
huáxuě ski
huāyuán garden
huàzhuāng to use rouge; makeup
huí jiā return home
huíchéng return trip
huíchéng piào round-trip ticket
huídá to reply; to answer
huìhé zhōngxīn meeting center
huìhuà paint; draw
huíjiào Islam
huìkuǎn remit money; remittance
huílái return (here)
huīsè grey
huítóu turn the head
huìtúyuán technical draftsman
huíxíngzhēn paper clip
huìyì conference; meeting
huìyuán member
hújiāo pepper
hūn'àn de dim; dusky; gloomy
hūndǎo unconsciousness; faint
hùnhé de mixed
hūnlǐ wedding
hūnmí coma; stupor
hūntóu hūnnǎo muddleheaded;
  absentminded
hūnyīn matrimony
hūnyīn zhuàngkuàng marital status
huǒ fire
huó de living
huòbì currency; money
huǒchái match (for lighting)

huǒchái hé matchbox
huǒchē train
huǒchētóu engine (locomotive)
huǒchēzhàn train station
huòdé gain; achieve
huódòng activity; maneuver
huǒhuā spark
huǒjì shop assistant
huósāi piston; valve
huǒshān volcano
huǒshān róngyán lava
huǒshāoshān volcanic mountain
huǒshí food; provisions
huǒtuǐ ham
huǒyàn flame
huòluàn cholera
huòwù goods; merchandise
huòwù zēngzhí shuì value-added
  tax
huòzhě or; perhaps; maybe
hūrán suddenly
hùshì nurse
hūxī breathe; breathing
hūxī búshùn irregular breathing
hùxiāng mutually; mutual
hùzhào passport
húzi beard; moustache

J

jì mail (send by)
jì xiàlái to note/jot down
jiā add; increase
jiǎ de false; phony
jiā ná dà Canada
jiā ná dà rén Canadian person
jiā shang add to
jiǎbǎn deck (of ship)
jiābèi double; redouble; twofold
jiāchù domestic animal
jiǎfā wig
jiàgébiǎo price list
jiāgōng process; machining
jiājù furniture
jiákè jacket
jiākuài speed up; accelerate
jiāmén door of a house; front door
jiǎn subtract; reduce
jiān de pointed; sharp
jiānbǎng shoulder
jiǎnchá; kǎochá to check; inspect;
  examine
jiǎnchá hùzhào passport check
jiānchí insist on; persist in
jiǎndī reduce; lower; cut

jiǎndān simple
jiǎndāo scissors
jiǎngdào to give a sermon
jiàngdī lower; reduce; cut down
jiāndìng strengthen
jiānduān sophisticated; most
advanced
jiànghú; jiāoshuǐ glue
jiǎngjià bargain over price
jiǎngkè teach; lecture
jiānglái future; in the future
jiānglái de shìqing future events
jiàngluò to land (airplane)
jiàngyóu soy sauce
jiànkāng bǎoxiǎn dān doctor's
certificate
jiànkāng bǎoxiǎn gōngsi health
insurance company
jiànkāng de healthy
jiànkāng; shēntǐ health
jiānpiào yuán ticket-taker
jiānruì de incisive; penetrating;
sharp
jiāntǎ tower
jiànxíng to give a farewell dinner
jiànyì opinion; view
jiānyù prison
jiànzhú architecture
jiànzhù building; construct; build
jiǎo foot
jiāo to teach
jiào cry; weep; cry out; shout; order;
name; call; to be named
jiāo kè teach (a class); teaching
jiāo péngyou make friends
jiǎo shāchē foot brake
jiāochū hand over; surrender
jiǎodù angle
jiāogěi turn over to
jiǎohuá sly; cunning
jiāohuàn swap; exchange
jiāojuǎn film (for camera)
jiǎolam turret; corner tower
jiǎoluò corner; nook
jiāoqū suburbs; outskirts
jiāoshí reef
jiàoshī instructor
jiàoshòu professor
jiǎoshuì pay taxes
jiàotáng church
jiāotōng communications; street
traffic
jiāotōng guǎnlǐ chù traffic control
center
jiàotú Christian
jiāoxīn tòng angina
jiàoxǐng; xǐnglái wake up; awaken

jiāoyì huì; shāngzhǎn trade fair
jiàoyù education
jiǎozhǐ toe
jiàqī vacation; holidays
jiàqián price
jiārè heat; warm
jiàshǐ jiàoliàn driving teacher
jiàshǐ yuán pilot
jiàshǐ zhízhào driver's license
jiātíng family
jiātíng zhǔfù housewife
jiāxiāng hometown; native place
jiǎyá false teeth
jiāyóu to get gas
jiāyóu zhàn gas station
jiàzhí worth; value
jīchǎng airport
jīchǎngfèi airport tax
jìchéngbiǎo taxi meter
jìchū send out (in the mail)
jīchǔ base; foundation
jìcún check; leave with; deposit
jìdù jealous; jealousy
jīdūjiào Christianity
jiě hunger
jié knot
jiè to lend; to borrow from
jiē diànhuà answer the phone
jiébīng freeze; ice up
jiēchù contact; get in touch with
jiéchū outstanding; remarkable
jiēdài huì reception (for guests, etc.)
jiēdàitīng reception room
jiēdào street
jiēdēng street light
jiědú yào antidote; remedy
jiěfàng emancipate; release; free
jiěfū brother-in-law (of older
sister)
jiégǔ knuckle
jiéguǒ result; as a result
jiéhūn get married; marriage;
wedding; marry
jiějie sister (older)
jiéjìng shortcut
jiějué to solve
jiēkǒu street corner
jièkǒu an excuse; pretext
jièmò mustard
jiémù program; item on program
jiérì holiday
jièshào introduce; recommend
jiéshěng to save; economize
jiěshì explain; explanation
jiéshí diet; to diet
jiēshōu accept; receive
jiéshù conclude; end; close

jiētou tānfàn street vendor
jièzhǐ ring (for finger)
jǐge a few; some
jǐhǎo de great!
jìhào mark; sign
jǐhu bù hardly
jìhuà plan; project; program
jīhuì opportunity; chance
jìjié season (of the year)
jíjiù first aid; emergency treatment
jíjiùxiāng first aid kit
jījīnhuì foundation (funded)
jìlù take notes; keep minutes; record
jímò lonely; lonesome
jìn near; close by
jīn de golden
jìnbù progress; improvement
jīnchāngyú tuna
jǐng well (for water)
jǐngchá police
jīngfèi funds; outlay; expenses
jǐnggào warn; caution
jīngguò process; course; undergo; pass through
jīngjì economy; economical
jīngjì cāng economy class
jīngjiào to scream
jīnglǐ business manager
jīnglì to experience; vigor; energy
jīngluàn convulsion; spasm
jīngqí amazed at; surprised at
jìngsài contest; competition
jīngshen spirit; energy
jìngtóu camera lens
jīngxiāo market; sell
jīngxiāo wǎng sales network
jīngyàn go through/experience
jìngzi mirror
jīnhuáng sè de golden yellow
jìniàn commemorate; mark
jìniàn pǐn souvenir
jìniàn yóupiào commemorative stamp
jìniàndì commemorative site
jǐnjí chūkǒu emergency exit
jǐnjí de urgent; critical
jǐnjí qíngkuàng emergency
jǐnjí shāchē emergency brake
jìnkǒu import
jìnkǒu shāng importer
jìnlái come in
jìnqù go in; enter
jìnshì nearsighted
jìnzhǐ forbidden
jìnzhǐ prohibit; forbid
jìnzhǐ ... Prohibited!
jīntiān today

jīnyín shǒushì gold and silver jewelry
jǐnzhāng nervous
jīnzi gold
jīqì machine
jīròu muscle
jíshí timely; promptly
jìshù technical science
jìshù rényuán technician
jìshù xuéyuàn technical college
jìsuàn calculate; figure out
jìsuànjī calculator
jìsuànjī kēxué computer science
jìsùbiǎo speedometer
jítā guitar
jiù to save (rescue)
jiǔ nine; wine
jiǔba bar; tavern
jiùhù chē ambulance
jiùhuò shìchǎng flea market
jiǔjīng alcohol
jiǔshí ninety
jiùshēng tǐng life boat
jīxiè shīfu mechanic
jīyì wing (of a plane)
jízhuī gǔ backbone; vertebra
jìxù continue to
jīzhǎng captain (plane)
jìzhě journalist
jù dà de huge; enormous; powerful
juǎnxīn cài cabbage
jǔbàn conduct; hold; run
jùchǎng theater
jué bù kěnéng de absolutely impossible
juédìng decide; decision
juéduì bù no way; under no circumstances
juésè role/part (in a play, etc.)
juéshì jazz
juéwàng hopeless
jùjué refuse
jùlí away from; be apart; distance between
jūliú detain; arrest
jūmín inhabitants (of a city, etc.)
jūnshì military affairs
jūnshì guǎnzhì military control
jǔxíng hold (a meeting, etc.)
jùyǒu tèxìng possess special traits
júzi mandarin oranges
jùzi sentence
júzi shuǐ orangeade; lemonade

A/Z

K

kǎchē truck
kāfēi coffee
kāfēi guǎn coffeehouse
kāi; dǎkāi open; open up
kāichē to drive
kāiguān light switch
kāiguàn qì can opener
kāihuā blossom; bloom; flower; feel elated
kāihuí drive back
kāishǐ begin; start; beginning; to start
kāishuǐ drinking water (boiled)
kàn to look; see; watch; look at
kàn diànshì to watch television
kàn qǐlái apparently; seemingly
kàn qǐlái looks like; appear to be
kāngkǎi generous; liberal; unselfish
kàngyì protest
kànkan look at; take a look
kānshǒu guard; watch
kǎogǔ archeology
kàojìn to approach
kǎolǜ to think about; consider
kǎoròu grill/roast meat
kǎoshì examination; test
kě chī de edible
kě jiàn de visible
kě xiào de ridiculous; laughable
kě'ài lovable; likeable
kě'ài de dear; beloved
kèchéng course (in school); curriculum
kèfú conquer; surmount
kèguān de objective; unbiased
kèhù business partner
kěkào reliable
kěnéng maybe; possible; possibly
kěnéngxìng possibility
kěpà fearful; terrible
kèrén guest
késòu cough
kěxí it's a shame
kěxí; búxìng unfortunately
kēxué science
kěyǐ may; be permissible
kěyǐ de okay; permissible
kěyǐ hē de drinkable
kōng de empty
kōngfù on an empty stomach
kōngqì air
kōngshǒudào karate
kǒudài pocket
kǒuhóng lipstick; rouge
kǒukě thirsty
kǒuxiāngtáng chewing gum

kū sob
kǔ bitter; hard to endure
kuài fast; quick; soon
kuài sùdù high speed
kuàicān fast food
kuàijì accountant
kuàixìn special delivery letter
kuān wide; expansive
kuángquán bìng rabies
kuàngquán shuǐ mineral water
kuàngwù mineral
kūnchóng insect
kùnnan difficulty; trouble
kùzi pants; trousers

L

là spicy hot
lā pull; drag
lābā loudspeaker
lái to come
lái zhèlǐ come here
lājī garbage; trash; rubbish
lājīdài garbage bag
lājītǒng trash/garbage can/bin
lāliàn zipper
lǎn lazy
làngmàn dissolute; debauched
lánqiú basketball
lánsè blue
lànyòng abuse; misuse
lǎo old
láo nín ... put s.o. to the trouble of ...
lǎobǎn boss
lǎoshī teacher
làzhú candle
lèisǐ le extremely tired
lěng cold
lěng shuǐ cold water
lěngdòng to freeze
lěngkù callous; unfeeling
lěngqì air conditioner
lěngyǐn diàn cold drink shop
liǎngbèi twice; two times
liáng cool; cold; to measure
liàng bright; brilliant; loud and clear; make/become cool
liángxié sandals
liánhé; tǒngyī united
liánjiē connect; join; link
liánxì; guānxi contact; keep contact with; get in touch with; connection
liànxí drill; practice
liànzi chain
liǎojiě comprehend; understand

liáoyǎng recuperate; convalesce
lǐbài religious service
lièjiǔ strong drink; spirits
lǐfà get a haircut; to do one's hair
lǐfà shī barber
líhé qì clutch; coupling
líhūn divorce; get a divorce
líkāi leave; depart from
líkāi le away; gone; left
lìliàng power; force
lǐmào courtesy
lǐmiàn; lǐbiān inside; within
lǐngdài necktie
lǐngdǎo to lead; leadership; leaders
línghún soul
língqiǎo skillful; dexterous; nimble
língqián change; coins
lǐngshì guǎn consulate
língshòu shāng retailer
língxià below zero
lǐngzi collar
línjiē de yímiàn roadside
línjū neighbor
línshí; zànshí provisional
lìqì strength
lìshǐ history
liú to flow
liù six
liú bíxuě noseblled
liú xiàlai save/keep (for use)
liùbèi sixfold
liūbīng ice skate
liūbīng xié roller skates
liúchǎn miscarriage
liúrù flow into
liúxià leave behind; leave
liúxíng gēqǔ hit song
liúxíng; fēngqì in fashion; fashionable
liúxuě bleed
lìwài exception
lǐwù present; gift
lízi pear
lìzi case; example; instance; chestnut
lǐzi plum
lóngxiā lobster
lóu floor; story
lóutī stairs
lǘ donkey; ass
lùduàn section of highway
lùguò pass by/through a place
lǚkè traveler
lǚlì resume; personal data
lùmíng street name
lúnchuán steamboat/ship
lúntāi tire (on car, etc.)
luómǎ Rome

luómǔ nut (screw)
luópán compass
luósī screw
luósī qǐzi screwdriver
luǒtǐ naked
lùpái street sign
lǜsè green
lǚshè inn
lǜshī lawyer; attorney
lúsǔn asparagus
lùtiān jùchǎng open-air stage
lùxiàn route; line
lùxiàng video; video recorder; videotape
lùxiàng jī VCR/video camera
lǚxíng to travel; trip; journey
lǚxíng lùxiàn itinerary
lǚxíng shè travel agency
lǚxíng tuán tour group
lǚxíng zhīpiào traveler's check
lùyīn dài; cídài cassette
lùyíng camping
lùyīnjī tape recorder
lǚyóu tour
lúzi oven; furnace; stove

M

mǎ horse
mà to scold; rebuke; speak badly of
má de linen
mábì paralysis
mǎ'ān saddle
máfán trouble; troublesome
máfán de burdensome; troublesome
mǎfēng wasp
mǎi to buy; purchase
mài sell
mǎi chēpiào buy a ticket
mǎi dōngxi to shop; shopping
màibó pulse
mǎifāng buyer
màikèfēng microphone
mǎimài héyuē sales contract
màipiàn oatmeal
màiwán le sold out
mǎlì horsepower
mǎmahūhū negligent; careless
màn slow
mángcháng yán appendicitis
mángcháng appendix
mángguǒ mango
mànman de fully
mǎnyì pleased; satisfy; satisfied
máo hair (on animal); feather

māo(r) cat
máojīn towel
máotǎn woolen blanket
máowū hut
máoyī sweater
màozi cap; hat
mǎshàng immediately; right away
mǎtam pier; wharf
mǎxìtuán circus
mázhěn measles
mázuì anesthesia
méi coal
méi bìyào unnecessary
měi cì every time
méi jiàzhí de worthless
méi jīngyàn de inexperienced
měi nián annually
méi shénme never mind; it doesn't matter
méi wèikǒu to have no appetite
méi xiǎngdào unexpected
měi xīngqī every week
měi yíge each/every one
měi yuè monthly
měi(ge) every
mèifū brother-in-law (of younger sister)
méiguì huā rose (flower)
měiguó rén American
měiguó America; United States
měilì beauty; beautiful
méimáo eyebrow
mèimei sister (younger)
měiróng yuàn beauty parlor
méiyòng de useless
méiyes kerosene
méiyǒu not have; be without; there is not
méiyǒu yí ge dìfang nowhere
mén door; gate
ménfáng doorman
mèng dream
ménhào; ménpái house number
ménkǒu entrance
ménpiào admission ticket
mì dense; thick
mián cotton; cotton padded
miànbāo bread
miànbāo diàn bakery
miǎnfèi free (of charge)
miànfěn wheat flour
miàntiáo noodles
miǎo second (1/60 of minute)
miáoshù describe
miàoyú temple
mièhuǒ qì fire extinguisher
mìfēng bee

mílù le lost; lose one's way
mìmì de secret
míngdān list of names
míngpiàn business card
míngquè de clear-cut; explicit
míngshēng fame
míngxiǎn obvious
míngxìnpiàn postcard
míngzi name; title
mínjiān chuántǒng gēqǔ; mín gē folk music
mínsú folkways; folk customs
mínzú fúzhuāng ethnic/national clothing
mírén de charming; enchanting
mǐsè beige; cream color
mìshū secretary
mìshū chù secretary's office
mǒ wipe off; erase
momē mushrooms
mòshēng de strange; unfamiliar
mòshōu confiscate
mótèér model (for fashion, etc.)
mótiān dàlóu skyscraper
mótuō; mǎdá motor
motor model; pattern
mǒu ge rén someone
mù act (section of a play)
mùbēi tombstone
mùdì cemetery; goal; purpose
mùdiāo wood carving
mùdìdì destination
mùjī wooden shoes; clogs
mùkē wood engraving
mǔlì oyster
mùlián magnolia; cotton rose
mùlù catalog
mǔniú cow
mǔqīn mother
mùshī clergyman/woman
mùtou wood

N

ná fetch; get; take; bring
nà ge that
nà shí at that time
nàbiān over there
nǎilào cheese
nàijiǔ de durable
nǎipíng baby bottle
nàixīn patience; patient
nǎiyóu cream (dairy)
nǎizhào bra
nǎizuǐ nipple (for baby bottle)

nàli there; in that place
nán cháoxiān South Korea
nán de; nánxìng male
nán guā pumpkin
nánguò sad
nánbiān south
nánbiān de southern
nánhái boy
nánkān ugly
nánrén man
nǎo zhèndàng brain concussion
nǎolì brains; mental power
nàozhōng alarm clock
názǒu to carry/take away
nèilù inland; interior
nèiróng contents; substance
nèixīn heart; inner being
néng; nénggòu; kěyǐ able to
nénggàn able; skilled
nénggàn de capable; able
nénggòu to be capable of
nǐ you
ní mud; clay
nǐ de yours
nián year
niàn read aloud; study
niánhuì annual meeting
niánjì age (of a person)
niánqīng young
niánqīng rén youth; young person
niǎo(r) bird
nígū nun
nǐmen you *(pl)*
nǐmen de yours *(pl)*
nín *(polite)* you
níngkě rather; prefer to
níngméng lemon
níngyuàn would rather; better had
niú cattle; cow
niǔkòu button
niúnǎi milk
niúròu beef
niúzǎi kù jeans
nòng cuò le made a mistake
nòng gān to dry
nóngbāo pustule
nóngfū farmer
nóngjiā farming/peasant family
nóngmín peasant; peasantry
nóngtián fields; farmland
nuǎnqì heating
nüèdài mistreat; abuse
nüèjí malaria
nǚér daughter
nǚháizi girl
nǚlì diligent; hard-working;
  industrious

nǚshì woman; Miss; Ms.
nuówēi Norway
nuówēi rén Norwegian person
nǚxìng de female

O

ǒuér occasionally
ǒurán fortuitous; by chance
ǒurán de accidentally; by chance
ǒutù vomit
ōuzhōu Europe
ōuzhōu de European
ōuzhōu rén European person

P

pá climb; crawl
pái pie (dessert)
pài send (dispatch)
pàibié group; school; faction
páiduì to line up
páigǔ spare ribs
páiyǎn rehearse (theater)
páizi sign; plaque
pànduàn; pànjué judge; determine;
  judgment
pàng fat; stout
pánzi plate; dish; tray
pǎo run; run away
pǎobù; mànpǎo jog
pǎotáng; fúwùyuán waiter
páshǒu pickpocket
péibàn keep (somebody) company
péicháng damages; compensation
pēnfà jì hairspray
pèngjiàn; yùjiàn meet; encounter;
  run into
pēngtiáo cooking; cook (dishes)
péngyou friend
pèngzhuàng to bump into
pēnqìshì fēijī jet plane
pēntì to sneeze
pénzi pot; basin
pēnzuǐ spray
pí leather; skin; hide
pí dàizi belt; strap
pí dàyī fur coat
pí jiákè leather jacket
piàn rén swindle; cheat
piānhào inclination
piànmiàn de unilateral; one-sided
piānpì de remote; out of the way

piányi cheap; inexpensive
piànzi swindler; cheater
piào ticket
piàoliang handsome; attractive
pídài leather belt
pífu skin
pífu bìng skin disease
píhuò diàn leather store
píjiāzi wallet
píjiǔ beer
píjiǔ guǎn saloon
píng flat; level; even
píngcháng usually
píngdǐjiǎo flat-footed
píngduàn arbitrate
píngguǒ apple
píngjūn average; equally
píngmiàn tú blueprint; plan
píngtǎn de smooth
píngyuán plains (geog.)
píngzi bottle
pīnpái trademark
pīnyīn pinyin (system of spelling)
píqi temper; mood
pízi fur; hide; leather
pò le broken; damaged; torn
pòhuài destroy; wreck; smash
pōlà bad tempered; aggressive
pòliè to burst; split
pùbù waterfall
pǔjíběn popular edition
pūkè pái poker
pūmiè wipe out; exterminate
pǔtōng common; ordinary; average
pútáo grapes
pútáo gān raisins
pútáotáng grape sugar/candy

Q

qì anger
qí zìxíngchē to ride a bicycle
qǐ zuòyòng have an effect
qiǎn light; pale (color); superficial; shallow
qián front; preceding; ahead; before; money
qiàn to owe (money, etc.)
qiānbǐ pencil
qiáncān appetizer; hors d'oeuvre (on a menu)
qiáng strong; powerful; wall
qiángjiān rape
qiǎngjié plunder; pillage
qiángpò force; compel

qiángzhuàng sturdy; strong
qiánshuǐ to dive (into water)
qiántou front
qiánzi tweezers; pliers
qiānyuē tiáojiàn contract terms
qiānzhèng visa
qiānzì; qiānmíng signature; sign one's name
qiāo overcharge; fleece s.o.; to knock
qiáo bridge
qiǎokèlì chocolate
qìchē car; automobile
qìchuǎn asthma
qǐchuáng arise; get up from bed
qídǎo pray; prayer
qiē to cut; slice
qiézi eggplant
qǐfēi take off (plane)
qìguǎn windpipe
qìhòu climate
qījiān era; period
qímǎ to ride a horse
qīn'ài de darling
qíncài celery
qīnfàn invade; transgress
qǐng please; invite
qǐng kèrén invite guests
qīngchu clear; distinct; understand clearly
qìngdiǎn national celebration
qīngdǎo yú herring
qīngjiào seek advice of; to consult
qīngjiāo paprika
qǐngjìn! Please come in!
qǐngkè have a party; invite guests
qíngkuàng conditions; situation
qǐngqiú request; ask
qīngyú black carp
qīngzhǒng bruise
qīnqiè cordial; genial; warm
qīnshǔ relatives; kin; kinship
qióng poor
qīpiàn to cheat; deceive
qíshí in fact
qiú ball (for playing)
qiūtiān autumn
qìwèi flavor; smell
qìyā air pressure
qǐyè business; enterprise
qìyóu gas(oline)
qù to go; go to
qǔ get; obtain; fetch
qù zhǐjia yóu nail polish remover
quān(r) circle; ring
quánbù whole; complete; all; the whole thing
quàngào to advise; counsel

quánlì power; authority
quánshuǐ spring water
quē vacancy; opening
quēfá lack; short of; fault
quēshǎo to be missing
qūfēn differentiate; set apart
qǔgùn qiú hockey
qúnzi skirt
qùshì; sǐqù to die
qùwèi fun; interest; delight
qǔxiāo cancel

ruǎnguǎn tubing (flexible)
rùchǎng enter a meeting place
rùchǎngfèi price of admission
rúguǒ if; in case
ruìdiǎn Sweden
ruìshì Switzerland
rùjìng cross the border
rùkǒu entrance; "in" door
ruò weak; inferior
ruòdiǎn weakness
rǔyì; rǔgāo cream; ointment

R

ràng let; allow
ràngbù yield; concede; step aside
ránhòu after that; and then
ràolù make a detour
rè hot
rén person; people
rén gōng xīnzàng artificial heart
rènchū identify; make out
rènde to know (a person)
réngōng de artificial
rénlèi humanity; humankind
rénmen people
rénmín the people
rènshi recognize; know; meet
rěnshòu bear; endure; put up with
rénxìng human nature
rénxíngdào sidewalk
rénzào pí artificial leather
rénzào xiānwéi synthetic fiber
rènzhēn, yánsù serious; earnest; conscientious, solemn
rèqíng sincerity
rèxīn sincere
rìbào daily newspaper
rìběn Japan
rìběn rén Japanese person
rìcháng yòngpǐn everyday-use articles
rìchū sunrise; at sunrise
rìguāng sunlight
rìjì diary
rìluò sunset; at sunset
rìqī date (on calendar)
róngqì container
róngyào honor; glory
róngyì easy
ròu meat
róudào judo
ròujiàng sauce (from meat)
ròupù butcher shop
ruǎn soft to the touch

S

sāichē traffic jam
sàimǎ horse race; horse racing
sàipǎo race (on foot)
sāizhù blocked up; stopped
sǎn umbrella
sànbù walk; stroll; go for a walk
sānfēn zhī yī one third
sānjiǎo jià tripod
sānmíngzhì sandwich
sānwēnnuǎn sauna
sǎozi sister-in-law
sàobǎ broom
sèqíng pornographic; sexy
shā sand
shàchē brake a car; brakes
shādīng yú sardine
shāfā sofa
shǎizi dice
shālā salad
shāmò desert
shān mountain; hill
shān gǔ valley
shān guāng dēng photoflash; flash lamp
shǎndiàn lightning; flash of lightning
shàng chuán board a boat
shàng fēijī board a plane
shàng yóu to grease/oil
shāngbā scar
shāngbiāo brand name
shàngchē board a bus/car/train
shāngfēng have/catch a cold
shānghán typhus
shāngkǒu wound
shàngmiàn above
shàngqu go up
shàngshān go up/ascend a mountain
shāngyè cāng business class
shāngyè chéngshì commercial city

A/Z

shāngyè wǎnglái business connections
shāngyè xuéxiào commercial college; trade school
shānhú coral
shānmài mountains
shǎo few; little
shāo burn; heat; roast; stew
shāoshāng ruǎngāo burn medicine/cream/ointment
shāshì xìjùn salmonella
shāyǎ hoarse
shé snake
shèbèi equipment
shèfǎ think of a way to
shèhuì society
shèhuì gōngzuò rényuán social worker
shèhuì xué sociology
shèjì design; to design
shēn deep (water, etc.); profound
shén God
shēndù depth
shēnfen identity; status
shēnfènzhèng ID card
shénfù priest (Catholic)
shěng province
shēng de raw
shēngchǎn produce; production
shēngdòng lively
shēnghuó life; livelihood; to live
shènglì victory
shēnglǐ xué physiology
shēngmìng life span
shēngqì be angry; get mad
shēngrì birthday
shēngwù biology
shēngyīn sound; voice; noise
shēngyì business; trade
shèngxià the rest; remaining; leftover(s)
shéngzi rope; string
shénhuà myth
shénjīng nerve
shènjiéshí kidney stone
shénme what
shénshèng de holy
shēntǐ body
shénwèi altar
shénxué theology
shènzàng kidney
shènzhì even to the point of; so much so that
shétou tongue
shèyǐng take a photograph
shèyǐng chǎng film studio
shī wet

shí ten
shì be; is
shì yí shì to try; to test
shì zhèngfǔ city government
shìchǎng marketplace
shìchǎng jīngxiāo marketing
shídài epoch; era
shìdàng de suitable; proper
shídào esophagus
shíèr twelve
shífēn xìnrèn de trustworthy
shìfǒu whether or not
shīfu Master (form of address for skilled worker)
shígāo plaster
shīgōng work on (construction)
shìgù mishap; accident
shìhé suitable; fitting
shìjì century
shíjiān time (period)
shìjiàn event; incident
shìjiè world
shīlěng cool and damp
shīmián insomnia
shìmín residents; townspeople
shípǐn provisions; food
shípǐn diàn food store
shípǔ cookbook/recipe book; recipe
shìqíng matter; affair
shìqū city proper; urban district
shīrè warm and damp
shìshí fact
shísì fourteen
shítou stone
shīwàng disappointed
shìwéi(r) delicious; tasty; delightful
shīwù zhāolǐng chù lost and found
shíwù zhòngdú food poisoning
shíxiàn realize; put into effect
shìyàn experiment; test
shìyànshì laboratory
shīyè lose one's job; be out of work; unemployed
shìyě sight; range of vision
shìyìng get used to; suit; adapt
shǐyòng employ; use
shíyòng practical; functional
shìzhǎng mayor
shízì lùkǒu crossing; intersection
shòu skinny; slender; thin
shǒu hand
shòu huānyíng de likeable; popular
shǒu shāchē hand brake
shǒubèi arm
shǒubiǎo wristwatch
shòubùliǎo can't stand
shōudào receive

shōudào le received (a letter, etc.)
shōudiàntōng flashlight
shōudū capital (of a country)
shōugōng handicraft; handwork
shōugōng de handmade
shōuhuí take back; call in; recall
shōuhuò gains; results; harvest
shòuhuò yuán clerk (in store)
shōují to collect; gather
shōujù receipt
shōujuàn handkerchief
shòupiào chù ticket office
shōuqiú handball
shōurù income
shōushi tidy; straighten up; pack up
shōushi jewelry
shōushù; kāidāo operation (surgical)
shōutí xínglǐ hand-carried luggage
shōutào gloves
shōutíbāo handbag
shōuxiān at first; in the first place; first of all
shōuyǎn premiere
shōuyīnjī radio
shōuzhǐ finger
shōuzhàng cane (for walking)
shòushāng wounded; hurt
shòuyī veterinarian
shù tree
shǔ to count; figure; calculate
shū book
shú de cooked; well-done
shū tóufǎ comb hair
shù'é amount
shuā scrub; to brush
shuāijiāo wrestling match
shuāngdòng frost
shuāzi brush; to brush
shūbào tān newstand
shūcài vegetable
shūcài tān grocery stand/stall
shùcóng grove; thicket
shūdiàn bookstore
shūfu comfortable; well; cozy
shuǐ water
shuì duty; tax
shuì; shuìjiào sleep
shuìdài sleeping bag
shuǐdào rice paddies; paddy rice
shuǐdī drip; dribble
shuǐdiànfèi water and electricity charges
shuǐguǎn water pipe
shuǐguǒ fruit
shuǐguǒ tān fruit stand
shuǐjīng crystal
shuǐliú stream; river; current

shuǐlóngtóu faucet
shuǐmǔ jellyfish
shuǐpào blister; bubble
shuìyī pajamas
shuǐzāi flood
shùlì establish; set up
shùliàng quantity; amount
shùlín forest
shūmiàn de in writing
shuō to say
shuōhuà speak; talk; say
shuōmíngshū manual
shúrén acquaintance; friend
shūshu; jiùjiu uncle
shǔtiáo french fries
shūxuě blood transfusion
shùxué mathematics
shǔyú belong to
shūzi comb
shùzì number; figure (1, 2, 3, etc.)
sì four
sī silk
sǐ de dead
sì fēn zhī yī one fourth
sījī driver
sìjiǎoxíng de four-cornered; square
sīkāi tear open
sīpò le torn
sīrén de private
sìshí forty
sīwà silk stockings; socks
sòng to escort
sōng le loose
sòng lǐwù to give a gift
sòngfēngjī air blower
sònghuí accompany back
sònghuò deliver goods
sònghuò shíjiān delivery time
sōngshù pine tree
suān sour
suàn cuò le figured out incorrectly
suànzhàng figure out a bill
sùdù speed
suí nǐde biàn as you wish
suìdào tunnel
suīrán despite; although; nevertheless
suíshēntīng Walkman
suíyì as one pleases
sùkǔ vent one's grievances
sùliào plastic
sǔnhài damage; harm; injure
sūnzi grandchild
suǒ lock (on door, etc.)
suǒpéi to claim damages
suǒshàng lock up
suōxiǎo shrink; reduce in size

suǒyǐ therefore
suǒyǒu de rén dōu everyone
suǒyǒu rén all people/persons
suǒyǒude ... all of the ...
sùshí vegetarian diet

T

T-xùshān T-shirt
tā him; her; she; he
tā de his; her
tàbǎn pedal
tài too; very
tài duō too many
tàitai lady; woman; Mrs.; wife
tàiyang sun
tàiyang yǎnjìng sunglasses
tāmen they
tānfàn street peddler
tāng soup
táng sugar
tāngchí spoon
tàngfà get a perm
tángguǒ sweets
tángniào bìng diabetes
tǎngxia to lie down
tǎngxià lay down; recline
tánhuà chat; converse
tánhuà conversation
tánpàn negotiations; discussions
táoqì ceramic(s); pottery
tàozhuāng costume; dress
táozi peaches
táozuì elated; exultant
tèbié special; particular
tèbié de ... special ...
tèbié shì ... especially ...
tèchǎn local specialty
tèjì fēixíng yuán stunt pilot
téngtòng ache; pain; soreness
tèsè distinguishing/special feature
tèxiàoyào antibiotic
tèzhēng characteristic; feature
tì ... substitute for ...
tí qǐlái lift; raise
tiān heaven
tián fill in; stuff; sweet
tiándiǎn dessert
tiānhuā smallpox
tiānhuābǎn ceiling
tiánjìng sài track and field meet
tiānqì yùbào weather forecast
tiānqì; qìhòu weather
tiānwén tái observatory
tiánxiě fill out (a form, etc.)

tiānzhǔ jiào Catholic (faith)
tiào to jump
tiàobǎn diving board
tiáojiàn requirements; conditions;
    terms; stipulations
tiáoqíng flirt with
tiáowèipǐn seasoning
tiáowén de striped
tiàowǔ to dance
tiáozhěng to regulate; adjust
tiáozi brief note
tǐcāo gymnastics; to do gymnastics
tìdài replace
tiē yóupiàn to paste on stamps
tiě iron (metal)
tiěguǐ rail(s)
tiělù railroad
tiělù shìgù railroad accident
tiěsī iron wire
tiěxiù rust
tígāo raise; heighten; improve;
    strengthen
tíng halt; stop
tīng listen; hear; to hear
tíngchē stop/park a car; to park
    (vehicle)
tíngchē chǎng parking lot
tínggé pavilion
tíngliú stopover
tīngjué hearing (sense of)
tíngzhǐ stop
tīngzhòng listener(s), audience
tíshén perk up; refresh oneself
tíshēng promote (raise status of)
tǐwēn jì thermometer
tíxǐng remind; warn; alert
tíyì suggest; suggestion
tīzi ladder
tóng bronze
tóng copper
tōngdào passageway
tōngfēng to air out
tòngkǔ; tòng pain; suffering; painful
tóngqíng sympathize with; sympathy
tóngshí simultaneous
tóngshì colleague; fellow worker
tōngxìn exchange letters
tōngxíng be current; in general use
tóngyàng same; similar; equal
tóngyì consent; approve of; to agree
tōngzhī notice; circular; inform;
    notify
tōu to steal
tóu head
tóu(r) hair style; top (of s.t.); chief
tóufà hair (on human)
tóulú skull

tóunǎo brain
tóurù throw; fling
tōuqiè theft
tóuténg yào headache tablets
tóutòng headache
tóuyūn dizzy
tuánduì team
tuántǐ group; team; organization
tǔdì land; territory
túdīng thumbtack
tǔdòu potatoes
tuī to push
tuìcháo ebb tide
tuīchí postpone; put off
tuìhuàn return (for exchange)
tuìhuí return; refund
tuījiàn recommend
tuīxiāo promote sale of; peddle
tuìxiū retire; retirement
tújiě illustration
túláo de futile effort
tūn xià swallow; gulp down
túnbù hip
tuō yīfu undress
tuōchē tow a car; towing
tuōxié slippers
tuōyùn xínglǐ chù baggage room
túshūguǎn library
tǔsī toast
túzhōng on the way; en route
tùzi rabbit

W

wàibiǎo exterior; outward appearance
wàiguó foreign country
wàiguó de ... foreign ...
wàiguó rén foreigner
wàihuì foreign exchange
wàijiè outside world
wàikē shǒushù yīshēng surgeon
wàimiàn; wàibiān outside; surface
wàitào loose coat; outer garment
wǎn late
wǎn lǐfu dinner clothes
wǎn; pénzi dish
wān(r) bent; curved; crooked; turn/curve
wán(r) to play; have fun
wǎn'ān! Good evening!; Good night!
wǎncān dinner
wánchéng complete; finish
wāndòu peas
wánde yúkuài had a good time

wǎng; xiàng net; toward; in the direction of
wánghòu queen
wàngjì forgot; peak season
wǎnglai intercourse; contact
wǎngqiú tennis
wàngyuǎn jìng telescope
wánjù child's toy
wánměi perfect
wǎnshàng night; at night; evening
wánzhěng intact; complete
wǎtè watt (elec.)
wàzi stockings; socks
wèi stomach
wèi ... gāoxìng to look forward to; be happy (about)
wěidà great; mighty
wèidào taste; flavor
wèihūn fu fiancé
wèihūn qī fiancée
wéijīn scarf
wèikǒu; shíyù appetite
wèile ... for (the purpose of)
wèishēngzhǐ toilet paper
wēishìjì whiskey
wèisuō flinch; recoil
wèitòng stomachache
wēituō entrust to; trust to
wěixiǎn; wēixiǎn! dangerous; Danger!
wéiyī de only one; sole one
wèizhi position; seat
wěn kiss; to kiss
wèn to ask
wén qǐlái to smell
wēndù temperature
wēnhé mild; temperate; gentle
wénhuà culture
wénjiàn document
wénjù diàn stationery store
wēnnuǎn warm
wēnróu soft; gentle
wénshū chǔlǐ xìtǒng word processing system
wèntí question
wénzi gnat
wénzì writing; script; characters
wǒ I; me
wǒ de my; mine
wǒmen we
wǒmen de ours
wòpù chēpiào sleeping car ticket
wù fog
wú chǐ de shameless; brazen
wǔdào jiā dancer
wūdiǎn spot; stain
wūdǐng roof

wǔfàn lunch
wúgū de innocent; innocent person
wǔhuì dance party; ball
wùhuì misunderstanding
wùjiě misunderstand
wùlǐ physics
wúlì incapable; powerless
wúliáo boring; uninteresting
wǔrǔ insult; humiliate
wǔshì knight
wǔtái stage
wúxiào ineffective
wúyí de undoubtedly; beyond doubt

X

xì fine; delicate
xǐ bathe; to clean; wash
xī zhēngqì zhìliáo fǎ inhalation
xì nèn delicate; tender
xǐ'ài like; love; be fond of
xiā crabs; crawfish
xiā de blind person
xià le yí tiào be surprised
xià xuě to snow
xià yí cì next time
xià yí ge the next one
xià yǔ to rain
xiàchē get out of car/off a train
xiágǔ gorge; ravine
xiàle yí tiào be frightened
xiàmiàn underneath
xiàmiàn/tou below
xiān first; beforehand
xiàn county; thread; wire
xiāngcháng sausage
xiànchǎng yǎnzòu live music
xiàndài modern
xiànfǎ constitution (of a state)
xiàng qián forward/go ahead
xiàng yòu/zuǒ zhuǎn turn right/
  left
xiǎngdào think of; recall
xiǎngfǎ idea; thought
xiāngfǎn opposite (contrary)
xiāngjiāo banana
xiàngpí rubber
xiàngpí chā eraser
xiàngpí guǎn hose; tube
xiǎngqǐ remember; think of
xiǎngshòu to enjoy; enjoyment
xiāngshuǐ perfume
xiāngsì resemble; be similar
xiāngxià countryside
xiāngxiàng be alike; resemble

xiǎngxiàng imagine
xiāngxìn to believe; believe in; trust
  in
xiāngyān cigarette
xiāngzhuàng collide; run into each
  other
xiāngzi chest; box; luggage
xiānsheng gentleman; Mr; teacher
xiàngsheng burlesque (Chinese)
xiángxì de ... detailed ...
xiángxì; xì be detailed
xiàngzi alley
xiànshí pragmatic
xiànzài now; at the present
xiànzhì restrict; confine
xiào to laugh
xiǎo small; tiny
xiǎo bāo packet
xiǎo fángjiān booth; cabin
xiǎo jiàotáng chapel
xiǎo sàobǎ whisk/small broom
xiǎo shízǐ gravel
xiǎo xiā shrimp
xiǎo xuějiā cigarillo (small cigar)
xiǎoba minibus
xiǎobiàn urinate
xiāochén dejected; depressed
xiǎochī snack; refreshment
xiǎodāo pocket knife
xiāodú disinfect
xiāodú shuǐ disinfectant
xiǎoér mábì infantile paralysis
xiāofángduì fire department
xiǎofèi tip; gratuity
xiāohuà digestion
xiāohuà bùliáng indigestion
xiǎojiě Miss; unmarried woman
xiǎolù path
xiāoqiǎn divert oneself; while away
  time
xiǎoshēng softly; in a low tone
xiǎoshí; zhōngtóu hour
xiāoshòu sales
xiǎoshuō novel (book)
xiǎotōu thief
xiāoxi news (tidings)
xiǎoxīn to be cautious; careful
xiǎoxué elementary school
xiàohuà joke
xiàshān descend/go down a
  mountain
xiàtiān summer
xiàwǔ afternoon
xībù western (part)
xīdī CD/compact disc
xǐdí jì detergent
xiě to write

xiě dìzhǐ write an address
xié'è evil; vicious
xiédǐ sole of shoe
xiédài shoelaces
xiédiàn shoe store
xièhuò unload cargo
xiépō slope
xièxie thanks; thank (you)
xiézi shoe
xiēzi scorpion
xǐfàjì shampoo
xīfāng de western (style, manner, etc.)
xīfú shàngzhuāng lounge jacket
xīgài knee
xīguā watermelon
xíguàn accustomed to; used to; habit
xīhóngshì tomatoes
xǐhuān to like (prefer)
xìjié details; particulars
xǐjù comedy (play)
xìjù drama; play
xīlà Greece
xīn new; fresh; up-to-date
xìn letter; mail
xìnfēng envelope
xǐng to be awake; wake up
xìng family name; last name
xìng qìguān sexual organs
xìngbié sex
xìngbìng sexual disease
xíngchē shíkè biǎo timetable; schedule (for buses, etc.)
xíngchéng take shape; form
xíngdòng action; operation; move about
xīnghóng rè scarlet
xínglǐ luggage; baggage
xínglǐ jìcún chù check (baggage) room
xínglǐ tuīchē baggage cart
xīngqī week
xīngqī èr Tuesday
xīngqī liù Saturday
xīngqī rì Sunday
xīngqī sān Wednesday
xīngqī sì Thursday
xīngqī wǔ Friday
xīngqī yī Monday
xìngqu interests
xíngrén pedestrian
xìngrén almond
xíngrén qū pedestrian zone
xíngshì form; shape
xíngwéi behavior; deed; act
xīngxīng star

xíngzhèng bùmén ministry (government)
xíngzhèng dānwèi administrative unit
xíngzhèng jīguān administrative organ
xìngzi apricot
xìnhào signal
xīnkǔ suffer; be in difficulty
xìnlài count on; trust; have faith in
xīnláo toil; pains
xīnlǐ fēnxī jiā analyst (psychology)
xīnlǐ xué psychology
xìnrèn have confidence in; trust
xīnshuǐ salary; wages
xīnwén news (in a newspaper)
xīnwénjiè press circles; the press
xìnxí information
xīnxiān fresh (food, etc.)
xìnxiāng mailbox
xìnyǎng belief; faith
xīnyǐng new and original; novel
xīnzàng heart
xīnzàng bìng heart attack; heart trouble
xìnzhǐ letter paper; stationery
xiōngbù chest; thorax
xiōngzhēn brooch
xīshǎo seldom
xiūdàoyuàn monastery
xiūlǐ to repair; fix
xiūlù roadwork (construction)
xiūxi rest; take a break
xiūxi shíjiān free time; break (for rest)
xiūxi zhàn rest stop
xiūyǎng accomplishment; self cultivation; training
xiùzi sleeve
xīwàng expect; hope; expectation
xìxīn attentive; careful
xīyān to smoke
xīyān de smoker
xǐyī fěn soap powder
xǐyī jī washing machine
xǐzǎojiān bathroom (for bathing)
xuānchuán propaganda
xuǎnzé choose; select; choice
xǔduō many; a lot of
xuě blood; snow
xuějiā cigar
xuékē academic subject
xuěqiāo sled
xuéshēng student
xuéshēng sùshè dormitory for students
xuéxí to learn; study

xuéxiào school
xuěxíng blood type
xuěyā blood pressure
xuěyì xúnhuán blood circulation
xuéyuàn academy; institute (of
  learning)
xuēzi boots
xǔkě permit; allow
xūnzhāng medal
xūyào must; have to
xūyào need; require; demand
xùnsù rapid; speedy
xúnwèn inquiry
xǐzǎo take a bath

Y

yáchǐ teeth
yágāo toothpaste
yājīn deposit (money)
yān smoke
yán salt
yǎn qián at present; before one's eyes
yáncháng extend; prolong
yǎnchū performance
yāncǎo tobacco
yāndǒu pipe (for smoking)
yǎng to scratch; itch
yáng sheep
yáng diānfēng epilepsy
yáng wāwa doll
yàngběn sample; specimen
yángcōng onion
yángé strict; rigorous
yángmáo woolen; sheep's wool
yángròu mutton
yángsǎn parasol; sunshade
yǎnguāng foresight; vision
yángzhuāng Western-style clothes
yàngzi appearance; style; manner
yǎnjīng eye
yǎnjiǎng lecture; talk
yǎnjìng háng optometrist's (store)
yānjiū diàn tobacco shop
yǎnliàn eye shadow
yánqī delay; postpone; put off
yánsè; cǎisè color
yánshí rock; stone
yànxuè blood test; do a blood test
yǎnyào shuǐ eyedrops
yǎnyuán actor/actress
yánzhe follow (along a road, etc.)
yǎo chew; bite
yào medicine; drugs
yāobù fēngshī bìng lumbago

yàodiàn drug store
yàofāng prescription
yàogāo ointment; plaster (medical)
yàojì xué pharmaceutical studies
yàomián absorbent/sterilized cotton
yàopiàn; yàowán pill (medicine)
yāoqiú to demand; request; a
  demand; a request; require;
  requirement
yàosài fortress
yàoshi key (to a lock)
yáqiān toothpick
yáshuā toothbrush
yǎsīpǐlín aspirin
yáyī dentist
yàzhōu de Asiatic
yàzhōu rén Asian person
yàzhōu Asia
yāzi duck (fowl)
yě also; wild
yè; zhāng page
yěshòu wild animal
yěxǔ perhaps; maybe
yèyú àihào hobby
yézi coconut
yèzǒnghuì night club
yī one
yī bàn half; one half
yí cì once; one time
yí ge one; one of
yí ge bàn one and a half
yí ge rén one person; alone
yì liú de first class; top grade
yì qiān one thousand
yìbān in general
yìbān de shuo normally speaking
yìchéng agenda
yídǎo sù insulin
yìdàlì xiāngcháng salami (Italian)
yìdiǎn a little bit
yìdiǎn yě méiyǒu nothing at all
yídìng certainly; surely; definitely
yídìng de definite; regular
yídìng de … certain …
yíduàn shíqí a period of time
yǐhòu … after …
yìhuǐr moment; little while
yìjiàn; kànfǎ outlook; view (opinion)
yǐjīng already
yījià coat hanger
yīmào jiān cloakroom
yǐn addiction
yín silver
yǐncáng hide; conceal
yíng to win
yìng firm; tough; obstinate; hard;
  stiff

A/Z

yīng ér baby; infant
yīng ér shípǐn baby food
yìngbì coins
yìngdù hardness
yīnggāi should; ought to
yínglì profit; make a profit
yīngměi Anglo-American
yīngtáo cherries
yīngwén English
yǐngxiǎng influence; effect
yíngyǎng nutrition; nourishment
yíngyè shíjiān business hours
yìngyìn jī photostat
yǐngzi shadow
yínháng bank
yǐnliào drinks; beverages
yǐnqǐ to arouse
yìnshuā gōng printer (worker)
yìnshuā jī printing press
yìnshuā pǐn printed matter
yīntiān cloudy weather
yīnwèi due to; because
yìnxiàng impression
yīnyuè music
yīnyuè huì concert (music)
yìqǐ together
yìqǐ suàn total it up
yǐqián formerly; in the past
yìrán de inflammable
yìshù art
yìshù jiā artist
yìshù pǐn art object
yìshù shǐ art history
yìshù xuéyuàn art academy
yìshuāng ... pair of ...
yìshùpǐn màoyìshāng art dealer
yìtiān de lǚxíng day trip
yìtiān yǒuxiào de piào one-day ticket
yìwài accident; mishap; unforeseen; unexpected
yìwèizhe mean; signify; imply
yìwù duty; responsibility; obligation
yìxiē several
yīxué medicine (the science)
yìyì meaning; significance
yíyàng same; identical
yīyuàn hospital
yǐzi chair
yìzhī artificial limb
yízhì unanimous; identical
yìzhí straight; continuously; straight ahead
yòng use; employ
yòngguò de ... used ...
yòngjīn commission; middleman's fee

yǒngjiǔ de permanent; lasting
yǒngqì courage
yǒngyuǎn eternally; always
yōudài special/favorable treatment
yōudiǎn merit; strong point
yōuměi exquisite; graceful
yōuměi de picturesque
yōushāng grief; trouble
yōuxiānquán priority; preference
yǒu have; own; possess; there is; there are
yóu oil; fat; grease
yòu; zài again
yǒu chuàngjiàn de creative
yǒu dú poisonous
yǒu fēng de windy
yǒu guānxi relevant
yǒu jīngyàn de experienced
yǒu jiàzhí de have worth/value
yǒu lǐmào polite
yǒu nàixīn be patient
yǒu qián rich; wealthy
yǒu wù de foggy
yǒu xiàolì have validity
yǒu yángguāng de sunny
yǒu yánsè de colored
yǒu yíngyǎng de nutritious
yǒu yìsi interesting
yǒu yìwù to be obligated; have the duty to
yóubāo mail
yòubiān on the right; right side
yǒude some
yóudìyuán mailman
yǒuhǎo de friendly
yǒuhài harmful
yóuhuà oil painting
yóujì parcel (mail)
yóujú post office
yóulèchǎng playground
yóulèyuán amusement park
yǒulì de advantageous
yóumén gas pedal
yǒumíng de ... famous ...
yóunì de greasy, oily
yóupiào stamps
yóutài rén Jewish person
yóutǐng yacht
yóuxì game (for child, etc.); play a game
yǒuxiàn gōngsī limited company
yǒuxiào effective; valid
yóuxíng parade; march; demonstrate
yǒuyí friendship
yǒuyì de beneficial; profitable
yóuyǒng to swim

A/Z

yǒuyòng useful
yóuyǒng chí swimming pool
yóuyǒngyī swimsuit
yóuyù bùjué hesitant
yóuzhèng zǒngjú main post office
yóuzī postage
yú fish
yù jade
yǔ rain
yuǎn far
yuǎn de far-off
yuán de round; circular
yuándīng gardener
yuándǐng dome
yuǎnguāng dēng spotlight
yuánjiàn original article
yuánliàng forgive
yuántǒng cylinder
yuǎnyáng hǎidiào deep-sea fishing
yuányīn reason; cause
yuànyì willing to; want to
yuànzi yard; courtyard
yuánzi bǐ ballpoint pen
yùchǎng outdoor bathing place
yúdiàn fish store
yùdìng to reserve; schedule; be
  scheduled to; subscribe; book; place
  an order
yuè month
yuē; qǐng invite
yuēdìng agree upon
yuèguàn laurel
yuēhuì date; appointment
yuèjīng menstruation
yuèliàng moon
yuètuán orchestra
yùfáng prevent; guard against
yùfáng zhèngmíng shū certificate of
  vaccination
yúgǎng fishing port
yǔjì rainy season
yùjiàn foresee; predict
yúkuài happy; happiness; joy
yúlè amusement; recreation
yǔmáo feather
yùmǐ corn
yún cloud
yùn yīfu to iron clothes
yùnàn suffer an accident
yūnchuán de seasick
yùndǒu to iron; press
yùndòng exercise; athletics; sport(s)
yùndòng chǎng athletic field
yùndòng yòngpǐn sports equipment
yùndòng yuán athlete
yùnhé canal
yùnqi fortune; luck

yùnshū to transport
yǔshuā windshield wiper
yǔxié rain boots/galoshes
yǔyán language
yǔyī rain coat

Z

záhuòdiàn general store
zài in; on; at
zài cǐ qījiān meanwhile
zài fēijī shàng on board a plane
zài jiā at home
zài lái come again (for a visit)
zài yí cì once more
zài zuǒbiān on the left
zài ... lǐ in(side)
zài ... pángbiān next to; beside
zài ... qiántou in front of
zài ... shàng on
zài ... shàngmiàn on top of ...
zài ... xià under ...
zāihuò disaster; calamity
zàijiàn good-bye
záluàn disorderly; pell-mell
zànchéng endorse; approve
zāng dirty; soiled
zāng yīfu dirty clothes
zànměi to praise
zànshǎng appreciate; admire
zànshí temporarily
zàntóng approve of; endorse
zǎo early
zǎo yìdiǎn earlier than
zǎocān breakfast
zàochéng create; make into
zāogāo! What a mess!
zǎopén bathtub
zǎoshàng morning
zázhì magazine
zébèi blame; reprove
zēngjiā increase
zéngjīng ever; once
zěnme how to
zhāi pick; pluck
zhǎi narrow
zhàiwù debt; liabilities
zhàlán railing; bar
zhàn stand; be on one's feet
zhǎnchūzhě exhibitor
zhàngài obstacle
zhǎngdà grow up
zhànghù account (in a bank, etc.)
zhàngpéng tent
zhàngqì miasma

zhānglángé cockroach
zhǎnlǎn exhibition
zhǎnpǐn exhibit item
zhànxiàn line is busy
zhànzhēng war
zhànzhù to stand still; to stop
zhǎo look for; search
zhǎo língqián give/make change
zhǎo qian make change
zhào X-guāng to get an X ray
zhāodài receive (guests, etc.); treat
  (customers, etc.)
zhāoshǒu wave/beckon with hand
zhǎozé swamp
zhàogù look after; care for; attend to
zhàogù xiǎohái take care of children
zhàomíng illuminate
zhàopiàn photograph
zhàoxiàng to photograph
zhàoxiàng jī camera
zhè ge this; this one
zhékòu discount
zhèli here
zhēn needle
zhēn de really; truly
zhēn de true; real; authentic
zhěnduàn diagnose
zhèngcháng; píngcháng normal
zhèngdǎng political party
zhèngfǔ government
zhèngjiàn evidence; eyewitness
zhěngjié orderly; tidy
zhèngjuàn main theme
zhèngmiàn de positive;
  directly/openly
zhèngmíng proof; prove
zhèngquè accurate
zhèngrén witness
zhèngshí confirm; verify
zhèngyì justice
zhèngzhì politics
zhènjìng be calm; composed
zhènjìng jì sedative; tranquilizer
zhēnjiǔ acupuncture
zhēnshí de real
zhěnsuǒ clinic
zhěntóu pillow
zhēnzhū pearl
zhésuàn convert (numerically)
zhéxué philosophy
zhèyàng like this; this way
zhèyàng de this kind of
zhǐ only
zhǐ paper
zhǐ wài beyond; outside of ...
zhǐ yào as long as
zhīchí support; uphold

zhīchū pay out money; expenditure
zhǐdài paper bag
zhīdào know; realize
zhīfáng fat (on meat, etc.)
zhígōng personnel
zhǐhuī direct; command
zhǐjia fingernail
zhǐjia yrn nail polish
zhǐjiadāo nail scissors
zhíjiē direct(ly); immediate
zhíjiē bōhào direct dialing
zhíliàng quality
zhíliào raw material
zhìliáo heal; cure
zhínán; lǚyóu zhǐnán guidebook;
  guide
zhínǚ niece
zhǐpái cards
zhīpiào check (bank)
zhīqìguǎn bronchial tube
zhìshǎo at least
zhíshēngjī helicopter
zhīshi knowledge
zhǐtòng yào painkiller
zhíwù plant; flora
zhíwù yóu margarine
zhíwù; zácǎo herb
zhíwùyuán botanical gardens
zhíyè occupation
zhíyuán office worker; staff
zhízhào license
zhízi nephew
zhōng clock
zhòng heavy; weighty
zhòng gǎnmào flu; heavy cold
zhǒng le swollen
zhǒngdà swelling
zhōngdiǎn terminal point; finish line
zhòngdú be poisoned
zhōngduàn suspend; break off
zhōngér yán tympanitis
zhòngfēng have a stroke
zhōnggǔ shìjì Middle Ages
zhōngguó China
zhōngguó de Chinese
zhōngguó rén Chinese person
zhōngjiān middle; center
zhōngjiè rén middleman
zhōngjiè shāng intermediary
  (person)
zhǒnglèi sort; kind; type
zhōnglì neutrality
zhōngshí loyal
zhōngwǔ noon
zhōngxīn center; heart; hub
zhōngyāng central; central
  authorities

A/Z

zhòngyào important
zhōngyī Chinese medicine
zhōngyú finally; at long last
zhōngzhàn final stop (on trip)
zhǒngzú de ethnic
zhōudào considerate; attentive; thorough
zhōumò weekend
zhōuqīxìng tóutòng migraine
zhōuwéi surrounding; vicinity
zhù live; reside; spend the night
zhū pig; hog
zhǔ cook; boil
zhuā to catch; grab; scratch
zhuǎn pass on; transfer; convey to
zhuàn; zhèng earn; make profit
zhuǎndì to forward; relay
zhuāng le tài mǎn le packed too full
zhuāng zài pack in; load on
zhuānkē yīshēng specialist (medical)
zhuānmài; lǒngduàn monopoly; monopolize
zhuǎnwān turn a corner; make a turn
zhuǎnzhàng transfer an account
zhuāzhù grab hold of
zhūbǎo shāng jeweler
zhǔcān main dish
zhùchǎnshì midwife
zhùfú wish happiness to
zhǔguǎn responsible for; in charge of
zhǔguò de cooked
zhùhè to congratulate
zhúlán basket (bamboo)
zhǔnbèi prepare to; preparations
zhǔnshí punctual
zhǔnshí qǐfēi take off on time
zhǔnxǔ allow; to let
zhǔnxǔ permit; permission
zhuōbù tablecloth
zhuōqiú table tennis
zhuōzi table
zhǔrén host; hostess
zhǔrèn director; head; chair; manager
zhūròu pork
zhùshì watch carefully/attentively
zhùsù lodgings
zhǔyào mainly
zhùyì pay attention to; notice
Zhùyì! Caution!
zhǔyì idea; plan
zhùzhǎi residence
zhùzhòng emphasize; stress
zhùzi column; pillar
zì; cí word; character (Chinese)
zǐ gōngsī subsidiary company
zǐ sè lilac (color); purple

zìdòng automatic
zìdòngtíkuǎn ATM (money machine)
zìjǐ oneself
zìjǐ de one's own
zìjǐ zuò de self-made
zìláishuǐ bǐ fountain pen
zīliào data/material
zìrán naturally; of course; nature
zìxíngchē bicycle
zìxíngchē bǐsài bicycle race
zìyóu freedom; liberty
zìyóude free; unrestrained
zìzhù shì self-service
zǒng dàilǐ general agency
zǒng dàilǐ shāng general agent
zǒng jīnglǐ general manager
zǒnggòng in all; altogether
zǒngjī switchboard; telephone exchange
zǒngjì amount to; add up to; total (amount)
zōngjiào religion
zōngjiào de religious
zōngjiào shèngdì place of worship
zōngsè brown
zǒngshì always
zǒngzhàn main station
zǒu guòqù walk to; walk by
zǒu xiàqù go/walk down
zǒu yì zǒu stroll; take a walk
zǒuguò pass by (while walking, etc.)
zǒujìn walk into/near
zǒusī to smuggle
zū rent; hire
zǔchéng form; make up/compose
zǔdǎng obstruct; stop
zǔfù grandfather
zúgòu abundant; enough
zǔguó homeland; native land
zuǐ mouth (of a person)
zuì duō at the most
zuì hǎo de the best
zuì hòu final; in the end; last
zuì hòu de the last one; final
zuì hòu dì èr ge second from last
zuǐchún lips
zuìjìn recently
zūjīn rent money
zǔmǔ grandmother
zūncóng follow; comply with
zūnshǒu observe; abide by
zúqiú soccer
zúqiú chǎng soccer field
zúqiú duì soccer team
zuò to do; sit; take a seat
zuò mèng to dream

A/Z

zuǒbiān left (side)
zuòjiā writer
zuòpǐn work (of art)
zuòqǔ jiā composer
zuòwèi seat; place
zuòxià sit down

zuòyǐ armchair
zuòyòng effect; function; use
zǔráo hamper
zǔzhī organization; system; to organize
zǔzhǐ prevent; stop; prohibit